The Persuasive Preacher

"There are not enough books like this, calling preachers of the gospel back to the old path of dependence on the power of God. Christensen writes *The Persuasive Preacher* with maturity, insight, and clarity, reminding us that a faithful proclamation of the biblical message will equip us with an ethically sourced concept of what it means to be a soul-winner."

—**Garrett Soucy**, Pastor, Christ the King Church

"For decades David Christensen has not only studied and taught the proper use of persuasion in preaching and ministry, he has also practiced it. His book provides the historical and biblical background for understanding the issues involved. It is filled with practical examples, both positive and negative, which equip the reader to both preach and pastor with greater integrity and effectiveness."

—**David Lambertson**, faculty member, New England Bible College/Grace Evangelical Seminary

"David Christensen's newest book is much-needed. The author, a pastor who not only grew up on the mission field but also served much of his life as a college professor and administrator, calls us to recognize that our preaching and all forms of ministry expression are systemic outworkings of our hearts. That means that our persuasion is influence and our influence must serve its purpose from pure motives. The book is a must-read for all Christian leaders who speak and write for ministry."

—**Dave Deuel**, Academic Dean Emeritus, The Master's Academy International

"*The Persuasive Preacher* calls pastors to present God's word with biblical authority and boldness. Christensen, a seasoned pastor and professor, understands and effectively communicates why and how preachers should use biblical persuasion techniques. He also acknowledges the responsibility of listeners to respond, without any unethical manipulation from the preachers. Numerous illustrations reinforce his pertinent arguments. I consider this book a welcome companion to my own volume, *Persuasive Preaching*."

—**R. Larry Overstreet**, retired Professor, Corban University School of Ministry

"There's no shortage of books on how to preach effective sermons, but rarely can you find a work that digs deep into the inner workings of how persuasion can be done with biblical authority and integrity. Drawing from a well dug deep through years of experience as a pastor and educator, David Christensen unpacks both the historic and popular techniques used by preachers and examines whether they measure up to the biblical standard for conveying doctrine, reproof, correction, and training in righteousness."

—**Rick Francis**, New England Consultant for the Cecil B. Day Foundation

"As the Apostle John warned in his third letter about leaders like Diotrephes, David pierces through poisonous agendas to carefully divide between manipulation and the way of the Spirit of true holiness. This book is a heart check for each spiritual leader's soul and a guide to walking in the wisdom of the responsibility to speak the truth in love, and to rest in the Spirit for the results."

—**Jamie Bickel**, Pastor, South Hope Community Church

# The Persuasive Preacher

*Pastoral Influence in a Marketing World*

David A. Christensen

WIPF & STOCK · Eugene, Oregon

THE PERSUASIVE PREACHER
Pastoral Influence in a Marketing World

Copyright © 2020 David A. Christensen. All rights reserved. Except for brief quotations in critical publications or reviews, no part of this book may be reproduced in any manner without prior written permission from the publisher. Write: Permissions, Wipf and Stock Publishers, 199 W. 8th Ave., Suite 3, Eugene, OR 97401.

Wipf & Stock
An Imprint of Wipf and Stock Publishers
199 W. 8th Ave., Suite 3
Eugene, OR 97401

www.wipfandstock.com

PAPERBACK ISBN: 978-1-7252-6599-8
HARDCOVER ISBN: 978-1-7252-6600-1
EBOOK ISBN: 978-1-7252-6601-8

Manufactured in the U.S.A.                                                    07/07/20

# Contents

*Acknowledgments* | vii
*Other Books by David Christensen* | ix
*Introduction* | xi

1. Pulpit Power | 1
2. For the Love of Rhetoric | 13
3. Sophistry and the Cross | 29
4. Informers or Persuaders? | 42
5. Influence's Arsenal | 63
6. Logos: The Central Route | 82
7. Shortcuts: Peripheral Routes | 98
8. Ethical Controls: Process | 118
9. Ethical Controls: Decision | 134
10. Paul and Philemon: A Case Study in Pastoral Influence | 151

*Appendix: Pastoral Influence Health Index (PIHI)* | 161
*Bibliography* | 167

# Acknowledgments

I AM ACUTELY AWARE, the older I get, that nothing worth doing that I have ever done has been done alone. Writing this book reminds me of the many people who have shaped my thinking through their insights and examples. My heartfelt thanks go to the board members of The Rephidim Project who have supported me in this endeavor. A special thank you goes to Mark Halfacre, my friend and co-worker in the ministry.

To my colleagues at New England Bible College, thank you. There is nothing quite like the faculty room of a small college to stimulate, provoke, modify, and qualify one's thinking. I can still remember discussions thirty years ago with Harlan Shepardson about some of the very topics I cover in this book. Thank you, David Lambertson, for being a wise friend off whom I have bounced so many of my thoughts over the years. To my numerous students whom I had the privilege to teach, thank you. You taught me through your questions and discussions as much as I taught you in my lectures.

How can I thank my church family, Galilee Baptist Church, enough for your love and encouragement? Together we walked through many of the lessons I share in this book. You stood with me when I failed, encouraged me when I struggled, and rejoiced with me when we saw God do some amazing things in our midst. This reluctant pastor learned to love pastoral ministry because of you. Thank you.

I want to thank the four men who read the rough draft of this book and shared their insights and suggestions with me. Thank you, David Deuel, Stephen Witmer, David Lambertson, and Mark Halfacre. You improved this book immeasurably with your critiques, and I much appreciate the time you took to thoughtfully interact with my ideas in ways that helped me express them better.

## ACKNOWLEDGMENTS

Thank you, Matt Wimer and the rest of the editorial team at Wipf & Stock Publishers, for helping me navigate the publishing process from start to finish.

Most of all, I want to thank my wife Janie. Your patience as I closeted myself in my study to write and your encouragement to keep at it made this book possible.

# Other Books by David Christensen

*Transformed by Adoption: The Spiritual Life
of a Normal Christian* (2014)

*Friends with Jesus: Experiencing the Depths
of Spiritual Intimacy* (2017)

*Expository Insights on John 13–17:
A Workbook for Expository Preaching* (2017)

*The Faces of Forgiveness: Healing
for the Hurts We Feel* (2017)

*Expository Insights on 2 Corinthians 2:14—7:4:
A Workbook for Expository Preaching* (2019)

www.rephidimproject.org

# Introduction

"Polished."

That is how Andrew described his church to me. Disappointed more than angry, he explained to me why he was looking for another church. His pastor preached the gospel, and he liked him, but the church had changed since the early days of his involvement. Size was part of it. The church was much bigger now, but it wasn't just size. His church felt more like the large corporation where he worked than a community of faith. Perpetual self-promotion marked the ministry.

"They talk more about what they are doing and the ministries they are promoting than they do about Jesus," Andrew said.

Most churches market themselves, of course. We recently promoted a conference at our church through social media. The promotion stressed that the conference was "75% full so get your registrations in soon. You don't want to miss out on this opportunity." There is nothing inherently wrong with such advertisements unless we become manipulative or deceptive. However, we are using a well-known sales technique, and selling our ministries caters to consumerism. The scarcity principle falls under the broader category of psychological reactance in modern influence peddling. The acronym FOMO—fear of missing out—captures the essence of the scarcity principle. It works! We know it works, so we use it to persuade people.

I have been writing this book for thirty years. Early in my ministry, I began to wrestle with the tension between persuasion and manipulation. As a professor in a Bible college and the pastor of a local church, I had ample opportunity to analyze and apply persuasive methods tempered by the biblical warnings against depending on human abilities to accomplish God's work. The church became an incubator to test the principles I was teaching in the classroom. Teaching pastoral theology and homiletics forced me to analyze the church growth methods I was studying, while pastoring a church allowed me to test some of those methods in ministry.

The church grew. We went to two services and began to build a new worship center. Four years later, we moved into the new worship center. We continued to grow and soon went to two services in the new building. I read much from the church growth movement to help me with the practical issues we faced as a church during these years. However, questions about the ethics of many of the methods being advocated nagged me. What was happening in our ministry that only God could do? How much of what was happening was the result of applying human methods of persuasion?

Our methods, not just our message, must consciously and intentionally depend on the Spirit of God so the faith of our people rests not on the wisdom of men but the power of God. Paul wrote:

> My message and my preaching were not in persuasive words of wisdom, but in demonstration of the Spirit and of power, so that your faith would not rest on the wisdom of men, but on the power of God. (1 Cor 2:4–5)[1]

My dual ministry immersed me in the tension between ethical and effective pastoral influence. I knew the dual pressures of leading a church to grow numerically and the expectations people have for a pastor to lead effectively. The church growth movement provided many helpful tools for my ministry but also created a sense of unease with the methods of pastoral influence. I was also teaching new pastors the skills of expository preaching and wrestling with the questions they posed about the tension between ethical and effective persuasion.

I believe our goal in preaching should be persuasion, but we need a model that balances Paul's spiritual concerns with effective tools the pastor can use in his ministry. We all want to be successful pastors. No one wants to be a failure in ministry. Success by God's standards means we are both effective and ethical in our spiritual leadership. We need to think carefully about the nexus between ethics and influence, especially as it relates to the church growth movement and the modern marketing methods we use in our churches today. We need a grid derived from the New Testament to become preachers like Paul, intentionally persuasive but God-dependent.

Sadly, the field of ethics has fallen on hard times of late. In our consumer-oriented society, if an action is not illegal, it is acceptable if it is

---

1. In this book I will be citing from the New American Standard Bible, updated edition (1995), unless otherwise noted.

effective. Winning and success trump ethics. In some Christian circles, if an action is not immoral, it is acceptable if it is effective. Beyond morality, we are free to do as we please according to many. Ethics covers the territory between moral and immoral, legal and illegal. Ethics argues even if an action is legal, moral, and effective, it still may not be acceptable. God calls us to a higher standard than moral pragmatism.

Pragmatism rules our culture and infects our ministries. Whatever works is good. As Christians, we certainly would add the qualifier that our methods must not be immoral, but beyond the condition of biblical morality we rarely question our methods. We openly market the methods as the means of growing the church. We have made a science of methodology and often place more faith in the methods than the message. The right use of effective means will grow a church, according to the experts. This doctrine of human methods is a modern version of an ancient error—sophistry. The sophists idolized methods, skills, and techniques, turning the art of persuasion into a science of manipulation. Sophistry is pragmatic. The sophist reduces persuasion to a transaction between speaker and listener. The results of that transaction validate the methods. Numerical growth in churches proves methods matter, leading to spiritual sophistry. Whenever a pastor places more faith in the methods than the message, the persuasive preacher is practicing modern sophistry.

The sophistic pastor makes Christianity transactional. The church produces a product listeners purchase with their time and money. What do people want to hear, see, and feel? This was the question of the ancient sophist. Give the people what they want in exchange for their support. If people want a polished worship experience, give them one. If people want excellent programs and high-quality facilities, produce and promote those products. If people want sermons that talk to them about their felt needs, give them sermons on topics they want to hear about. Even the gospel can be reduced to a product, shaped to appeal to a target audience. The listener chooses to buy the product or not, requiring a strong emphasis on marketing. Christianity becomes transactional. Paul warned us about transactional faith in 1 Corinthians 2:1–5. The message of the cross is not transactional but transformative. The cross transforms people not by human methods but by the power of God. When Christianity becomes transactional, the persuasive preacher becomes a sophist, and the gospel loses its transformative power.

## INTRODUCTION

How do we measure success? Consumer Christianity measures success by counting nickels and noses. Other pastors with growing ministries and expanding influence get the accolades, the book contracts, and the speaking engagements, so we want to emulate their methods. Envy grips our hearts. We begin to adopt the marketing methods that will make us successful. As the church grows, pride seeps slowly into our souls. Success is heady stuff. The temptation to manipulate, intimidate, and dominate people to get our way is powerful. Spiritual influence can be an addictive tonic for leaders. Every year we read the news reports of yet another pastor who fell not because of sex or money but because of power and pride. They began to manipulate and control people until their sins caught up with them because of the damage being done to God's church. Self-promotion, manipulation, and coercion are all signs of unbelief. We don't trust God. Bullying people to achieve success rises from a lack of faith in God. We don't start there, but we may end there if we do not heed God's warnings. Like Jesus in the temple, God occasionally cleanses his church of those who merchandise his message.

Dependence! What do we depend on: Our clever methods or God's transforming message? Do we depend on our marketing efforts and persuasive skills to build the church? Does the message become secondary to the method? Do we begin to manipulate, or worse, coerce people to accomplish our goals? Some argue all persuasion is wrong. The preacher must not seek to persuade but rather to proclaim. Our job as preachers is merely to inform people so we protect against human manipulation or coercion. We must not be persuasive preachers at all because the very act of persuasion abrogates our dependence on God.

I disagree.

I believe our goal as preachers is to be persuasive, but our faith is not in our persuasive methods. The biblical message must be central, not peripheral. Paul was persuasive in a God-dependent way. God wants preachers who are dependent on him and his word. God wants preachers who depend on the message of the cross, not the methods of marketing. God wants preachers who promote him and what he is doing rather than promoting themselves and what they are doing. The test of our persuasion is dependence.

How can a preacher be persuasive without huckstering, manipulating, or coercing people?

# 1

# Pulpit Power

QUINTESSENTIAL NEW ENGLAND, THE little white clapboard church stood between the river and the town green. Two front doors under the bell tower faced the street reminiscent of colonial meeting houses where men and women entered through separate doors. The meeting house was dedicated on July 31, 1851, but the church purchased the pews four years earlier on June 2, 1847. An auction to purchase pews was one of the first acts of the newly formed church. Those straight-backed wooden pews still filled the well-kept sanctuary as the new pastor began his ministry. The latest minister in the long history of the church, Pastor George was zealous for the gospel, passionate about the Bible, and ambitious to grow the village church into a beacon for Christ in the area. The congregation of forty on a good Sunday warmly welcomed him and appreciated his biblical sermons each week.

I visited the church on a few occasions and listened to Pastor George preach. He preached with an overly emotional revivalistic zeal but loved the Lord and sought to reach people for Christ. He also pushed the church to update its style to reach a modern audience. The pews simply had to go. He used the pulpit to stress the need to reach non-Christians by eliminating the pews and modernizing the sanctuary. A few in the church became upset. They began a petition in the village to protect the pews. Pastor George called for a congregational business meeting, and the meeting house was packed. Many residents in the village, it turned out, were still members even though they had not attended in years. Family ties with people in the church were strong. The church voted to remove the pews. Pastor George had won his battle. Someone called for a second vote. The congregation voted to remove Pastor George from his position as pastor.

Pastor George left. The pews stayed. A bully pulpit had backfired.

## Shadows Beyond Life

Revolution was in the air as Peter von Muhlenberg stood in the pulpit of his Episcopal church in Woodstock, Virginia, on January 21, 1776. George Washington had sent out a circular letter to Protestant churches asking for pastors to help recruit soldiers for the army. Muhlenberg preached from Ecclesiastes 3:1–8 that day: "There is an appointed time for everything. And there is a time for every event under heaven." Peter's passionate sermon touched the hearts of his people as he concluded with these words. "In the language of Holy Writ, there is a time for all things. There is a time for war and a time for peace; there is a time to pray and a time to fight. And now is the time to fight." He dramatically opened his clerical robes to reveal the uniform of a Colonel in the Continental Army and led 300 men from his church and the surrounding churches to enroll in the 8th Virginia Regiment of the Continental Army. He became known as the "fighting parson of the American Revolution." Today his statue stands in the National Statuary Hall of the United States Capitol.[1]

Pulpit power is real. Preachers have always been persuasive for good or bad down through history. If the intent to persuade is what distinguishes normal communication from persuasive communication, then preaching is almost always persuasive. Persuasive preaching might even be considered a tautology, so rare is it to hear a sermon that is not intended to persuade in some way.[2]

Preachers intend for people to call on the name of the Lord and be saved, making preaching inherently persuasive (Rom 10:13–14). The message may be folly to many, but it is the power of God to those who are being saved (1 Cor 1:18).

God uses preaching to transform lives, even extending through generations of people. On their 25th anniversary, Joe Stowell and his wife Martie stayed in a quaint bed-and-breakfast in England. There were four other couples whom they had never met staying at the inn as well. That evening they compared stories around a fireplace after dinner. One of their new friends asked Joe, "What do you do?"

During those years, Stowell was president of Moody Bible Institute in Chicago. He doubted someone in England would even know about the

---

1. Millard, "Preachers and Pulpits," lines 47–62. Federer, "Fighting Parson," lines 1–13.

2. McLaughlin, *Ethics of Persuasive Preaching*, 14–29.

school much less understand what he did, so he said, "I'm with a group of ministries in Chicago known as Moody Bible Institute."

Two other couples quickly leaned in and asked, "Of Moody—Sankey? That Moody and Sankey?"

He replied, "yes," in surprise.

They responded with excitement, "We have Sankey hymnals that have been passed down through our families for generations."

The old couple voiced the same sentiment. Moody and Sankey had preached in England over 120 years before, yet their impact was still being felt in the lives of people. Stowell writes, "I walked out of that room that night . . . saying to God that I wanted my life to be lived so faithfully that I too would cast long shadows for Him. Shadows far beyond my life."[3] That is the power of persuasive preaching.

I stood behind the pulpit—Billy Graham's traveling pulpit—at "The Cove" in Montreat, North Carolina, and reflected on his life. Here was a man whose gifts God had used to reach 214 million people in 195 cities around the world through 417 crusades. When he stood behind that pulpit on the platforms of this world, God called many to decide for Christ through his persuasive preaching. My father-in-law, John Bond, came to Christ at a Billy Graham crusade at the old Bangor Auditorium in Maine on October 21, 1964. Graham influenced a generation of preachers with his persuasive preaching style. Many attempted to emulate him without success. He became the voice of God to a sinful world in the post-war era of the twentieth century.

The pulpit was carefully designed for the evangelist down to precise details that would help him appeal to the hearts of people. It would travel with him to many crusades around the world, and he practiced many sermons behind that pulpit in preparation for his evangelistic events. Billy Graham was meticulous in his preparations for preaching. He used every innovation available to reach people for Christ. He had begun his ministry with Youth for Christ, and their motto defined his lifelong ministry: "Geared to the Times, Anchored in the Rock." His sermons were intentionally persuasive and gospel centered. The crusades were carefully planned for maximum effect, extensively promoted and organized. William Randolph Hearst instructed his newspapers to puff the young preacher. The altar calls climaxed each event with Billy Graham patiently waiting with bowed head

---

3. Stowell, *Shepherding the Church*, 223–24.

on the platform as the choir sang, "Just as I Am," and the crowds surged forward.[4] Billy Graham was the epitome of the persuasive preacher.

## The Seduction of Power

Influence is power. We live in a culture seduced by power, so people shamelessly pursue influence. Power brokers in our society wield great influence in corporations, politics, and economics. These cultural trappings of power infiltrate the churches, which increasingly structure themselves around a corporate executive model in their leadership. Megachurches run powerful programs in buildings which "often compete with corporate office buildings for the impressive architecture of power."[5] Celebrity pastors lead popular followings through their conferences, book sales, radio, television, and internet markets. Richard Quebedeaux was one of the earliest writers to identify the "rise of personality cults" in evangelicalism at the end of the twentieth century.[6] The marketing power of large churches tempts pastors to seek similar influence in our world.

We need to ask ourselves two important questions as pastors: Should we use any means that work to influence others, and are there ethical limits on our persuasive methods? The biblical answers are clearly no and yes! The power of influence corrupts the persuader even as it abuses the persuaded. The quest for personal power seduces preachers to sell their integrity in the pursuit of influence and is one of the great temptations facing evangelical pastors.[7] For example, Mark Driscoll and Mars Hill Church used a marketing scheme in 2012 to manipulate the bestseller list so his book, *Real Marriage*, would become a *New York Times* No. 1 bestseller. They spent over $200,000 to purchase 6,000 books through a third party. They also purchased 5,000 books and distributed them to ninety different addresses to boost the sales numbers. The marketing scheme, while not illegal, was unethical. The purpose was to puff up his influence as a celebrity pastor for which he has since apologized.[8] Unfortunately, deceptive schemes to manipulate book sales are more common than we realize and should be condemned as unethical.[9]

4. Grossman, "Billy Graham," lines 1–50.
5. MacArthur, *Our Sufficiency in Christ*, 29–34.
6. Quebedeaux, *By What Authority*.
7. Myers, "Better Way," 39.
8. Tracy, "Mars Hill Defends," paras. 3–5; Weber, "Mark Driscoll Retracts," paras. 3, 11.
9. Smith, "Buying a Bestseller," para. 2.

Power pastors are vulnerable to the fatal flaw of ego. The result is the pursuit of power corrupts both church and preacher.

Marketing power is seductive because it is pragmatic. It works! Churches grow numerically using marketing methods. Marketing is not intrinsically wrong, of course. The test is how much faith we put in marketing over message to grow the church. George Barna, an influential proponent of marketing the church, is very popular with evangelical pastors.[10] His research is helpful to preachers if we are careful not to overstate the value of marketing. A simple Google search demonstrates the appeal marketing has among pastors. Entries included "6 Marketing Ideas from Retail Giants You can Use for Your Church; 3 Elements of Effective Church Marketing; and 4 Must-Know Church Marketing Secrets." One advertising agent who works for Christian causes stated:

> Back in Jerusalem where the church started, God performed a miracle there on the day of Pentecost. They didn't have the benefits of buttons and media, so God had to do a little supernatural work there. But today, with our technology, we have available to us the opportunity to create the same kind of interest in a secular society.[11]

Faith in marketing methods can replace faith in God if we are not careful. The seductive power of influence can lead us to depend on our techniques, not unlike the Greco-Roman world of the New Testament.

The emphasis on the power of marketing parallels the rhetorical concepts prevalent in the Hellenistic world. The heart of Greco-Roman rhetoric was "the power of language and ideas to sway men's minds."[12] Rhetoric never entirely separated itself from the almost magical implications of supernatural power associated with the spoken word or the techniques of oratory. Persuasion was magical not in a shamanistic way, but in the faith orators placed in the power of words to move humans to act according to the objectives of the speaker.[13] The danger inherent in the church growth movement is we will place our faith in human methods instead of God's power to achieve results. The annual convention of the American Society for Church Growth, which became the Great Commission Research Network in 2009, invited Duane Litfin to address the issues

---

10. Barna, *Marketing the Church*. See the critique by Webster, *Selling Jesus*.
11. Guinness, *Sounding Out the Idols*, para. 30.
12. Litfin, *St. Paul's Theology of Proclamation*, 245.
13. Litfin, *St Paul's Theology of Proclamation*, 37; Litfin, *Paul's Theology of Preaching*, 75–80.

of rhetoric and marketing. He argued faith in marketing methods is a modern echo of ancient Greek rhetoric. The temptation is we can become dependent on human power to produce human results instead of God's power to transform lives.[14]

As rhetoric solidified its hold on the Greco-Roman world, the result was an educational system known as *paideia*. The term described the primary means of influence in society. Influence came through a system of education that imparted social values and ideals to the citizenry. Such an educational system in turn produced loyal support for the decisions of the leaders.[15] The system, which was fully developed in the fourth century after Christ, focused on specific rules of rhetoric to produce an educated, elite class in society which utilized persuasive techniques to control the uneducated masses.[16] Philo, a contemporary of Paul, criticized the use of the techniques taught in *paideia* because they were intended to "seduce the hearers with sophistic magic" to pad the pockets of the leaders instead of teaching truth and virtue.[17] Early Christian leaders also avoided the rigid reliance on rhetorical techniques. They presented themselves as outside the class of cultured *paideia* to appeal to the poverty-stricken masses of people.[18]

Wrestling with the power of persuasion is nothing new for the church and her leaders. Power struggles have been part of the church since the first century. The danger of oratory, both sacred and secular, is the power seduces the speaker so he loses touch with his moral responsibility for truth. Character for the orator means accepting the moral responsibility which is inherent in ethical persuasion.[19] Abusive church leaders develop over time, not all at once, as the power of influence slowly corrupts their leadership.[20] Some consider all persuasion to be immoral, while others see only persuasion with concealed intentions to be wrong.[21] In the late twentieth century, many sociologists began to see the power of marketing as dangerous for our society. Influence peddling was so pervasive that Vance Packard called for the American Psychological Association to develop a code of ethics

---

14. Litfin, *Paul's Theology of Proclamation*, 358. For his full analysis see 350–59.
15. Brown, *Power and Persuasion in Late Antiquity*, 4.
16. Brown, *Power and Persuasion in Late Antiquity*, 40–60.
17. Winter, *Philo and Paul among the Sophists*, 80–94.
18. Brown, *Power and Persuasion in Late Antiquity*, 71–117.
19. Kennedy, *Art of Persuasion in Greece*, 24.
20. Enroth, *Churches that Abuse*, 216.
21. Perloff, *Dynamics of Persuasion*, 19–20.

for "people-manipulators."[22] Sadly, many increasingly lumped television preachers together with other influencers as hucksters, selling Christianity using the tools of mass marketing.

## The Challenges of the Pastorate

Richard Haass writes about the frustrations of working in the bureaucracy of the federal government, and those same frustrations can be observed in many pastorates.[23] He cites an insightful letter written by President Harry Truman to his sister regarding the problems of political leadership.

> The people can never understand why the President does not use his supposedly great power to make 'em behave. Well, all the President is, is a glorified public relations man who spends his time flattering, kissing and kicking people to get them to do what they are supposed to do anyway.[24]

Many pastors echo Truman's sentiments from time to time! Most pastors function in a context where persuasion is their primary means of ministry. Congregational government ensures the pastor is limited in the decisions he can make, but he may be held accountable for the outcome of those decisions. Often the pastor has no formal authority such as a vote, veto, or hiring/firing power. Power is the primary means of decision-making in the corporate world where authority resides in the power of the leader to hire and fire, to establish salaries, and to veto undesirable choices. The pastor in a congregationally governed church does not exercise that same kind of power. Instead, the pastor exercises the power of influence.

"Leadership is influence," Oswald Sanders wrote in his classic book *Spiritual Leadership*.[25] Hans Finzel asks, "How do you spell leadership? I-n-f-l-u-e-n-c-e." Then he adds, "A leader takes people where they would never go on their own."[26] Preachers are spiritual leaders, meaning they are spiritual persuaders. Perhaps my favorite definition of a spiritual leader comes from Henry and Richard Blackaby. "Spiritual leadership is moving

---

22. Packard, *Hidden Persuaders*, 156.

23. Haass, *Power to Persuade*, 15; see 6–67 for additional anecdotal evidence of leadership frustrations.

24. Truman, in a private letter to his sister in 1947, quoted by Haass, *Power to Persuade*, 17.

25. Sanders, *Spiritual Leadership*, 31.

26. Finzel, *Top Ten Mistakes Leaders Make*, 16.

people on to God's agenda."²⁷ The pulpit is a primary means of moving people on to God's agenda. Joseph Stowell asks what "is God's intended outcome of preaching that measures and defines effectiveness" for pastors? He answers his question by saying "effective preaching is transformational preaching."²⁸ God intends to transform lives through preaching. Lives are supposed to be changed through our spiritual leadership. Transformation is the goal of every preacher.

The congregation expects the pastor to lead them, which is a great responsibility before God. We lead our people by persuading them to act, and all too often it is action they should have already taken. Great responsibility with little authority is a recipe for frustration leading to the temptation for manipulation. The success of a pastor (from a human perspective) rests on his ability to persuade others to act. The action may be adapted as it passes through channels of church government. The pastor shepherds those decisions from start to finish. Many goal-blockers exist along the path, so persuasion becomes a primary skill for any effective pastor. Frustrated pastors sometimes resort to coercion or manipulation to overcome the goal-blockers in the church.

Pastors face this ethical dilemma in their preaching ministries. Raymond McLaughlin's surveys revealed this was one of the top ethical concerns of pastors in 1974.²⁹ H. B. London and Neil Wiseman call the pastoral abuse of power one of the top fifteen "hazards" of the evangelical pastorate in America.

> Regardless of his church's size, every pastor is tempted to use power abusively—often every day. An ego craving to be in control—a problem which nauseates pastors in laypeople—is even more poisonous to a pastor. Embers of spiritual vigor are going out in many congregations because there is civil war for control in progress.³⁰

Ronald Enroth made the abuse of power the central theme of his book as he told the stories of abusive authority in various churches and organizations.³¹ It is always tempting when we read such exposes to see

---

27. Blackaby and Blackaby, *Spiritual Leadership*, 36. For additional definitions of leadership, see 32.

28. Stowell, *Shepherding the Church*, 254–55.

29. McLaughlin, *Ethics of Persuasive Preaching*, 22–26.

30. London and Wiseman, *Pastors at Risk*, 48. See also Shelley, "Surviving the Power Play," 67–80.

31. Enroth, *Churches that Abuse*, 53–90.

these churches as fringe churches, and so minimize the danger to our own ministries. The story of Shiloh, however, is the story of a church much like most evangelical churches despite its history of abusive authority. I live less than an hour from Shiloh and know the current pastor. Shiloh illustrates how a church can emphasize an orthodox theology and slip into an abusive authority structure, yet with the right leadership can return to effective ministry. The pastor today has effectively led his church out of its past abusive history into a biblical understanding of authority and a healthy relationship with area churches. Enroth warns: "Spiritual abuse can take place in the context of doctrinally sound, Bible preaching, fundamental, conservative Christianity. All that is needed is a pastor accountable to no one and therefore beyond confrontation."[32]

Conflict in church stresses a pastor's persuasive skills perhaps more than any other aspect of ministry. No matter what decisions a pastor makes, there is almost always someone who disagrees or criticizes the choice. I led our church through a four-year church-building process culminating in a near-unanimous decision to finance and construct our new worship center only to have one family leave the church because they didn't agree with the roof structure. Their criticism stung because we were good friends with the family, and our children played together regularly. Marshall Shelley writes, "Even in the best of times, pastoral ministry demands a high emotional investment, and sometimes you wonder if there's a return. With the addition of conflict, you're tempted to conclude ministry is a loss."[33] The task of getting everyone in a church to work together as a team is a major feat, and certainly one of the most difficult persuasive tasks a pastor must accomplish.[34]

Most leadership tasks in our world involve persuading people to work with people to produce a product. The pastor of a church must convince people to work with people to produce people. The process is far more unpredictable and riskier. No two people are the same, so no two people react in the same way.[35] The church is a kaleidoscope of opinions and perspectives. Conflict inevitably erupts. Each person is different. Yet, our goal is to produce Christlike people united in Christ to call others to come to Christ. The persuasive preacher is an agent of change in God's hands to unify the

---

32. Enroth, *Churches that Abuse*, 189.
33. Dobson et al., *Mastering Conflict and Controversy*, 173, see also 191.
34. Anthony, *Effective Church Board*, 120, 126.
35. Stowell, *Shepherding the Church*, 85–86.

community of faith in a common cause. We persuade both in the pulpit and in person as we lead the church through conflict.

A conflict developed in our church years ago over whether a divorced man could become a deacon. A faithful husband-and-wife team in our church had served for many years as Sunday school teachers and members of our Board of Christian Education. They taught both of my girls in their classes. Chuck and Arlene were the epitome of mature and godly believers, with a long track record of faithful witness for Christ. However, Chuck was divorced. His wife left him over twenty-five years earlier with two young children to raise. He married Arlene, and together they grew a wonderful family. Someone nominated Chuck to become a deacon, setting off the conflict. I spent a year with our Board of Deacons studying the Scriptures together, teaching them what God's word said about divorce and remarriage as well as the qualifications to be a deacon. I also preached from the pulpit on the subject to help our people understand the issues. We decided together that Chuck had more than demonstrated he was a one-woman man (1 Tim 3:12). The church voted to make Chuck a deacon, and he accepted. One of our deacons disagreed and resigned. I met with him and his wife in their home seeking to persuade them to accept the decision of the church, but they could not. They left our church, although we remained friends and greeted one another warmly whenever we met in later years. Sometimes there are unavoidable casualties in the process of change. We will not persuade everyone, and sometimes we must learn to disagree agreeably.

Unfortunately, conflict can affect and infect the pastor as well. Situations like that provide ample temptation for the pastor to exercise unethical persuasion. We must be willing to step back and respect one another in the conflict to avoid coercive influence. It is all too easy to slip into manipulating others to accomplish our goals during disagreements. If nothing more, conflict will leave its mark on the soul of the pastor and may even cause him to leave a specific ministry. Shelley concludes, "Pastors who survive church wars unscathed are a small minority; those who left a pulpit under less than happy circumstances are a legion."[36]

Leading a church through substantive change is a serious challenge for any pastor. Oswald Sanders enumerates the hazards, problems, and dangers of pastoral influence in his book on leadership.[37] Aubuchon writes,

---

36. Dobson et al., *Mastering Conflict and Controversy*, 79.
37. Sanders, *Spiritual Leadership*, 142–152.

"The presence of a problem is the absence of an idea,"[38] and many times pastors are called upon to provide the idea which leads to change. Kouzes and Posner, in *The Leadership Challenge*, identify five practices necessary for effective leadership through change. The five practices are "challenge the process; inspire a shared vision; enable others to act; model the way; and encourage the heart."[39] All five certainly test the persuasive skills of a spiritual leader too. We depend on the Holy Spirit to accomplish true change, but the Holy Spirit uses us to do his persuasive work. Since change rarely happens by coincidence in any organization, including the church, "when you see an organization in which changes are occurring regularly and without serious disorder, you can bet there are people in that organization who are skilled persuaders."[40] God uses persuasive preachers to bring about effective change in a church.

## Power on a Leash

Tension filled the streets of Boston in the summer of 1765. Hair-trigger emotions led to violent protests as the "Sons of Liberty" attacked the home of Andrew Oliver, the stamp collector. Governor Bernard retreated to his fortress and wrote a letter to General Thomas Gage that the mobs had been unleashed in the city. Pastor Jonathan Mayhew stood in his pulpit less than two weeks later to preach on the text, "I would they were even cut off which trouble you" (Gal 5:12). His full sermon is not extant, but we have a record that what was said inflamed the crowd at church. Members said they were so aroused they could hardly wait to begin the work of cutting off the troublers. The mob attacked the homes of British officials, destroying the home of Deputy Governor Thomas Hutchinson, leaving only the walls standing. Mayhew was dismayed at the work his words had unleashed and wrote a letter of apology, but the damage was done. He could see the power of an unleashed pulpit and regretted his inflammatory message.[41]

Persuasive preaching must be power on a leash, God's leash. When we unleash the pulpit from God's ethical limitations, pulpit power dishonors God. When we leash the pulpit to God's ethical limitations, pulpit power honors God. Healthy pastoral influence is both effective and ethical.

38. Aubuchon, *Anatomy of Persuasion*, 18.
39. Kouzes and Posner, *Leadership Challenge*, 9.
40. Aubuchon, *Anatomy of Persuasion*, 18.
41. Stout, *New England Soul*, 262–63.

Persuasion is effective when the preacher motivates permanent and measurable changes in beliefs, attitudes, or behaviors. Effective persuasion accomplishes a willing, long-term change on the part of the person being persuaded. If the change in belief is against the person's will, such change will be short-term at best. Short-term change is not effective change. The only kind of change that is truly effective is change that is carried out over the long-term with a willing spirit. Such change is heart change, and that depends on the power of the Spirit of God to bring about the change.

Ethical persuasion respects the person in a relational context so healthy relationships are maintained even in disagreement. It is influence that does not abuse the person through either coercion or manipulation. It is influence that will not destroy a person to accomplish an agenda. Ethical persuasion cares about the truth more than the objective, the person more than the goal. The ethical preacher may choose a failure of persuasion—failure to secure the intended result—out of respect for the person being persuaded, leaving it to the Holy Spirit to do his persuasive work. Brembeck and Howell define what they call the EQ, or *ethical quotient,* as similar to an IQ, or *intelligence quotient.* We need to develop our EQ because we can become careless and forget our persuasive words can lead to unethical results. They attribute ethical failures to two potential causes—either the persuader neglects the ethical component of his persuasion, or there is insufficient accountability to guard against the unethical persuasion.[42]

Classical rhetoric involved three philosophies of communication. These competing philosophies emphasized results (the sophists), truth (Plato), and methods (Aristotle).[43] Healthy influence keeps the results leashed to truth and methods. It is not wrong to be intentionally results-oriented if the truth is not compromised and the methods employed are ethical. Motivating people without manipulating them means giving them water that truly quenches their thirst.[44] The healthy persuader will not force people to drink, but he will seek to make them thirsty for truth. The persuasive preacher provides the water which will quench their thirst, always testing it to ensure it is genuine and pure.

---

42. Brembeck and Howell, *Persuasion,* 25–27.
43. McLaughlin, *Ethics of Persuasive Preaching,* 44–46.
44. Smith, "Manipulation Game," 110–16.

# 2

# For the Love of Rhetoric

Pulpit power impresses people today as rhetoric did in Paul's day. Rhetorical skills inspire people in our modern churches like they swayed people in first-century Corinth. Unfortunately, like Corinth, gifted preachers often succumb to the seduction of pride, superiority, and a domineering, controlling manner of ministry.

The news broke as I was writing this book. The board of Acts 29 announced the removal of Steve Timmis as CEO because of spiritual abuse. Timmis was the former pastor of the Crowded House in England and co-author of the bestselling book *Total Church*. A gifted and widely acclaimed preacher, he was guilty of a bullying, intimidating, and controlling style of leadership that left many broken lives in his wake. Reports of his coercive leadership had appeared over many years. Five years earlier, staff members from the Dallas office had written a nineteen-page letter accusing him of spiritual abuse only to see the board dismiss their allegations and ask the staff to resign instead. Even after he was dismissed, pastors around the world spoke highly of his gifts as a preacher. Some say he is "still probably the best preacher" they have ever heard. The power of rhetoric breeds such popularity people will overlook proud and abusive behavior, just like Paul warned us about in Corinth.[1]

Timmis joins a growing list of orthodox, effective, and gifted evangelical preachers who have discovered they are not immune from the sins of pride and power. Mark Driscoll resigned from Mars Hill Church in Seattle for similar sins in 2014 after being removed from Acts 29. Darren Patrick was fired by The Journey megachurch in 2016 because of a manipulative and domineering style of leadership. Ironically, both Darren Patrick and Steve Timmis were on the board that removed Mark Driscoll only to face

---

1. Shellnutt, "Acts 29 CEO Removed," paras. 4, 32–33, 45.

similar charges later. Both Bill Hybels at Willow Creek and James MacDonald at Harvest Bible Chapel were removed from leadership at least partially because of the improper use of power and influence. C. J. Mahaney, president of Sovereign Grace Ministries, voluntarily took a leave of absence in 2011 because of accusations of pride, lack of accountability, and "heavy-handed" leadership. These are all gifted preachers who succumbed to the seduction of spiritual power.[2] Paul warned us to beware of the bully pulpit. Abusive power is a sin that rises out of the pride of rhetoric. If we are to understand the danger of spiritual abuse, we must comprehend the love of rhetoric Paul faced in early Christianity.

## Rhetoric: Then and Now

Rhetoric dominated the first-century world in which Christianity was born and flourished. More importantly, rhetoric was not exclusively the domain of the wealthy and highly literate elements of society, but "rhetors" could be found in all the major cities of the ancient world, including Tarsus and Jerusalem.[3] Any man interested in a professional or political career pursued training in rhetorical skills. Civic leaders in the local assemblies around the Roman Empire needed rhetorical training, as did lawyers and government officials. The path to professional success required training in public speaking.[4] The Greeks worshipped at the altar of rhetoric. One of the Greek goddesses was Peitho, the goddess of persuasion.[5]

### The Educational System

Rhetoric was the central feature of the Greco-Roman educational system by the first century BC, so rhetorical training became a universal characteristic of an educated man.[6] Rhetorical schools flourished for boys who began

    2. Stetzer, "Power and Pastors," paras. 2–3; Shellnutt and Lee, "Mark Driscoll Resigns from Mars Hill," para. 4; Moon, "Acts 29 Removes Mars Hill," paras. 47–55; Shellnutt, "Darrin Patrick Removed," para. 2; Shellnutt, "Willow Creek Investigation," para. 6; Ross, "Sex, Money . . . Pride?," paras. 3, 9; Perry, "Willow Creek and Harvest," para. 19; Wagenmaker, "Harvest Bible Chapel," paras. 5–6.

    3. Witherington, *Conflict and Community in Corinth*, 39–48.

    4. Winter, *Philo and Paul among the Sophists*, 5.

    5. Overstreet, *Persuasive Preaching*, 27. See also his thorough analysis of *peitho* in 227–34.

    6. Litfin, *St. Paul's Theology of Proclamation*, 88–89; Kinneavy, *Greek Rhetorical*

studying during middle adolescence because rhetoric was the surest way to fame and fortune in the Hellenistic period. After rhetorical school, a young man in his late teens and early twenties could attend the school of a philosopher. Rhetorical students would internalize the rules of rhetoric so they could easily adapt and even invent their rhetorical methods naturally.[7]

The rhetorical education of the Hellenistic world had even influenced rabbinical thought by 30 BC so the apostle Paul may well have been exposed to rhetoric as part of his early rabbinic training. While Paul may not have been formally educated in classical rhetoric, we know rhetorical education influenced the entire educational system of his day and would have informed his education.[8] A growing body of literature demonstrates Paul not only knew how to use rhetorical methods, but was skilled at using them. Many scholars today classify Paul's letters as examples of deliberative rhetoric.[9]

George Kennedy wrote, "The significance of oratory is as great in substance as in form. Wherever persuasion is the end, rhetoric is present." Isocrates saw speech, particularly "the power to persuade" as the basis of civilization. It was the ability to speak that sets us apart from the animal world. Quintilian considered rhetoric "the science of speaking well."[10] Cicero said the ability to move an audience was the speaker's greatest power. "This eloquence has power to sway men's minds and move them in every possible way. Now it storms the feelings, now it creeps in; it implants new ideas and uproots the old." The orator had the power, according to Quintilian to "sweep the judge from his feet," "call the dead to life," and "inspire anger and pity."[11]

Persuasion, linked inseparably with rhetoric in the public mind, pervaded the social world in which Christianity began. The Roman imperial state was a propaganda machine that linked persuasion and coercion into a single social force. Roman propaganda was so powerful that sometimes it was hard to distinguish where persuasion ended and coercion began. The Jews of the diaspora, on the other hand, were careful to distinguish coercion from persuasion. Josephus, for example, stressed that Moses created a

---

*Origins of Christian Faith*, 37.

7. Kennedy, *Art of Persuasion in Greece*, 270–72.

8. Kinneavy, *Greek Rhetorical Origins of Christian Faith*, 80–91; Winter, *Philo and Paul among the Sophists*, 228; Russell, "Rhetorical Analysis of the Book of Galatians," 346.

9. Witherington, *Paul Quest*, 115–27.

10. Kennedy, *Art of Persuasion in Greece*, 7–9.

11. Litfin, *Paul's Theology of Preaching*, 77.

theocracy founded on persuasion. They reacted negatively to the coercive power of Roman persuasion, rejecting it as tyrannical and despotic.[12] Here is but one of the many examples of the debate over the ethics of persuasion even in the ancient rhetorical world. Persuasion must function within ethical limits to qualify as healthy persuasion.

## Aristotle to Augustine

Rhetoric, particularly in its Aristotelian form, developed a universal appeal. Students of rhetoric identified three universal factors in any persuasive situation. Every rhetorical situation includes the speaker, the audience, and the message. Along with these universal factors, Aristotle's classic divisions of "ethos," "pathos," and "logos" dominated the rhetorical world.[13] These divisions were the means or proofs necessary for effective persuasion. Aristotle emphasized persuasion took place when the orator used these methods to move his audience toward the desired decision.

If Aristotle's focus was on methods, Plato's was on truth. Plato was not opposed to the methods of rhetoric. He believed in rhetoric. Plato grew alarmed by the rise of the sophists who used rhetorical methods for the pride of applause. Persuading an audience was an end in itself to the sophists. The power to move people was the goal of sophistry no matter what the result might be. Sophists, like Isocrates, sought to seduce the audience with the power of rhetoric. "If the orator played the audience, it was the audience who called the tune, and it was this overwhelming power of the crowd that Plato feared most." Unfortunately, Isocrates and the sophists would win the battle that truth would lose. The sophists would coopt the methods Plato's younger contemporary, Aristotle, would develop, and use them to control the schools of rhetoric that would dominate the Roman educational system in the first century.[14] Sophistry reigned by Paul's day.

Aristotle profoundly influenced Augustine, who in turn profoundly influenced the development of Christianity. Augustine adopted the methods of Aristotle in defense of Plato's desire for truth. It was Augustine who made the famous statement regarding the value of rhetoric for Christian leaders.

---

12. Elliott, "Romans 13:1–7," 198–99.
13. Kennedy, *New Testament Interpretation through Rhetorical Criticism* 15.
14. Litfin, *Paul's Theology of Preaching*, 82, 64–69.

For since by means of the art of rhetoric both truth and falsehood are urged, who would dare to say that truth should stand in the person of its defenders unarmed against lying, so that they who wish to urge falsehoods may know how to make their listeners benevolent, or attentive, or docile in their presentation, while the defenders of truth are ignorant of that art?

While the faculty of eloquence, which is of great value in urging either evil or justice, is in itself indifferent, why should it not be obtained for the uses of the good in the service of truth, if the evil usurp it for the winning of perverse and vain causes in defense of iniquity and error?[15]

## Rhetoric and Persuasion

What is rhetoric? Should preachers seek to persuade others using rhetorical skills, as Augustine argued? The subject is crucial as we consider our roles in calling people to follow Christ. Duane Litfin defines rhetoric as "a persuasive response to situations that are susceptible to influence."[16] Even he recognizes this definition is so broad it leads to confusion, particularly as it relates to preaching—a narrow sliver of the broader world of rhetoric. Larry Overstreet gives us a more useful definition of rhetoric, which can be adapted for preaching. "Rhetoric is persuasive communication in the service of Truth which should create an informed appetite for the Good."[17]

I believe the goal of preaching is to bring about change in the listeners. Preaching is intentionally persuasive, but all persuasion is not healthy persuasion. Persuasion by any means possible is not God-honoring, nor does it produce genuine spiritual change. Overstreet's definition lays out a general definition of rhetoric which helps us frame our persuasive preaching properly. It combines Plato's quest for truth with Aristotle's use of rhetorical methods while avoiding sophistry. The elements of truth, information, appetite, and good help frame rhetoric for persuasive preaching.

Rhetoric has shaped the way we communicate in the Western world. Kenneth Burke exhaustively analyzes rhetoric from the classical Greek period through Augustine and into the early twentieth century, demonstrating

---

15. Augustine, quoted by Cunningham, *Faithful Persuasion*, cover page. For a critique of Augustine's position, see Litfin, *Paul's Theology of Preaching*, 52. The topic will be addressed in a later chapter.

16. Litfin, *Paul's Theology of Preaching*, 37.

17. Overstreet, *Persuasive Preaching*, 13.

the traditional principles of rhetoric are still illustrated in our modern forms of communication.[18] Stephen Pogoloff writes, "Our world is inescapably rhetorical." No speaker can avoid persuasion because the speech both shapes the situation and is shaped by the situation. Language, by its nature, is "highly social."[19] Burke points out modern rhetoric "is rooted in an essential function of language itself."[20]

Democracies depend on persuasion over force as the means of social implementation of ideas and control of organizations. Persuasion is the form leadership takes in our Western society and is seen as essential for modern life.[21] The church, as it exists in the Western world, must deal with the issue of persuasion as it relates to life in general. Everybody is a persuader in some way.[22] The intentionality behind almost all communication makes it difficult to avoid being persuasive in our social relationships.

God's word has been communicated through human speakers from the beginning of Christianity. This means revelation is communicated in social and cultural contexts which shape the form of that communication from God through humans to humans. We must then seek to understand the dynamics of that human communication process through which such vital truths are revealed. Furthermore, Christians must try to communicate those eternal truths as effectively as possible, clothed as they are in the cultural forms and symbols of language. For this reason, Aristotle's model of communication has proven useful for twenty-three centuries.[23] Christianity has always submitted itself "to the marketplace of ideas," which is essentially a posture of persuasion.[24]

Persuasion was an essential feature of Christianity from the apostolic period onward. The early Christians lived in a world hostile to Christianity and ruled by imperial forces that controlled religion. They could not coerce others to believe but instead invited others to adopt the Christian faith and follow Christ. These are all elements of persuasion we can see in the

---

18. Burke, *Rhetoric of Motives*, 49–180.
19. Pogoloff, "Isocrates and Contemporary Hermeneutics," 342.
20. Burke, *Rhetoric of Motives*, 43.
21. Brembeck and Howell, *Persuasion*, 4–18. They call it the "cementing principle of modern civilization."
22. Maxwell and Dornan, *Becoming a Person of Influence*, 2.
23. Hunter, *How to Reach Secular People*, 74.
24. McLaughlin, *Ethics of Persuasive Preaching*, 181–82.

preaching of the early church.[25] Since persuasion cannot be avoided in the context of human relationships, we must use effective rhetorical principles in that process. I think it would be unethical, given God's call on our lives, for us not to use the best rhetorical methods possible.[26] Why would we not want to be the sharpest tools we can be in the service of Christ?

## Primary and Secondary Rhetoric

Historians have divided rhetoric into the categories of "primary" and "secondary." Secondary rhetoric utilized the tools of rhetoric for non-persuasive purposes. Secondary rhetoric focused on entertainment and aesthetics rather than persuasion, preferring artistic expression to influence.[27] Sophistry specialized in secondary rhetoric. Sophists became performing artists seeking the applause of audiences more than any persuasive goals. By the time of Philo and Paul in the first century, sophistry flourished across the Roman empire. The eloquence of the sophists won the admiration of large crowds in city after city.[28] Oratory became performance art with the rise of sophistry. Preaching becomes sophistry whenever the preacher pursues eloquence over influence. As the modern literary critic Denis Donoghue writes: "Eloquence, as distinct from rhetoric, has no aim: it is a play on words or other expressive means. It is a gift to be enjoyed in appreciation and practice."[29]

Primary rhetoric focused on persuasion—to move an audience so they changed their beliefs or direction. Aristotle wrote "the object of rhetoric was judgment."[30] The objective of the speaker is to call the audience to decide. The orator persuades the listener to choose. In healthy rhetoric, the speaker calls the listener to choose truth. The speaker desires to "create an informed appetite for the Good."[31] Unfortunately, the sophists corrupted primary rhetoric as well as secondary rhetoric. Sophistry, both ancient and modern, focuses so much on the intended result it loses sight of what is true and

---

25. Hunter, *How to Reach Secular People*, 35.
26. McLaughlin, "Ethics of Persuasive Preaching," 121.
27. Litfin, *St. Paul's Theology of Proclamation*, 32–33.
28. Winter, *Philo and Paul among the Sophists*, 4.
29. Donoghue, *On Eloquence*, 3.
30. Aristotle, *Art of Rhetoric*, II. B. 1–4.
31. Overstreet, *Persuasive Preaching*, 13.

good. Win the convert by any means possible. Sophists induce the audience to do what they want because the result is all that matters.

There was always a strong, almost magical connection between oratory and power in the ancient world.[32] Primary rhetoric came to emphasize persuasion—any persuasion—without apology. All that mattered, especially to the sophists, was effectiveness. They focused on adapting the methods to achieve the desired results.[33] Pragmatism ruled. Rhetoric began to move away from ethical considerations toward effectiveness, no matter what means were used. Greater emphasis was placed on how to persuade rather than why the speaker was persuading. The temptation of persuasion, then and now, is to neglect the truth in the pursuit of results. Rhetorical influence can seduce us into persuasion for the sake of persuasion. Why? Because it works. There is power in persuasion. We can become so obsessed with achieving results that we forget God's ethical limitations. Preachers can transfer the adulation they receive as speakers into a desire to control and dominate people in the church. Experts in the pulpit can think they are experts on all of life. Sadly, the temptation of spiritual abuse seems most prevalent among those who are most dogmatic in theology.

By the first century, there was a growing emphasis on displaying the skills of oratory. Quintilian, for example, had moved away from classical Aristotelian rhetoric to emphasize matters of style.[34] Orators considered style under three headings. Style was either "grand," "middle," or "plain," but all three could be present even when one was predominant.[35] The sophists emphasized the grand style leading to rhetorical pride. Preachers can easily take pride in their platform skills at the expense of their people. Cicero, however, taught that oratory had three functions: to teach, please, and move. He connected these three functions he called offices with the three styles of oratory (grand, middle, and plain), which corresponded to the three offices of the orator (to teach, please, and move).[36] Augustine built on this analysis as he later developed the concept of Christian rhetoric.[37]

---

32. Litfin, *Paul's Theology of Preaching*, 75–76.

33. Litfin, *St. Paul's Theology of Proclamation*, 34–35.

34. Kennedy, *New Testament Interpretation through Rhetorical Criticism*, 13.

35. Campbell, "Rhetorical Design in 1 Timothy 4," 194; Kennedy, *New Testament Interpretation through Rhetorical Criticism*, 25–28.

36. Burke, *Rhetoric of Motives*, 73.

37. Burke, *Rhetoric of Motives*, 75.

Our modern preaching styles owe much to the rhetoric of the ancient Greeks, whether we like to admit it or not. Some argue our dependence on ancient rhetoric demonstrates the corruption of preaching compared to the apostolic era. I argue, instead, that the ancient rhetoricians were skilled at observing human communication and identifying how social language works. God created humans as social beings, and language is the expression of social communication. The early Christians used the forms of communication inherent to their culture to preach Christ. We too use the forms of communication inherent to our culture to communicate the gospel. The means of communication are morally neutral. How we use those social methods determines the morality of the communication.

## Three Species of Rhetoric

Scholars have recognized three kinds of rhetoric: judicial, deliberative, and epideictic.[38] Judicial rhetoric seems to have been the first species to consciously develop in ancient Greece because of the growth of democratic juries dependent on the arguments of the lawyers to make the case. Judicial rhetoric was legal, or forensic, rhetoric oriented around the defense or prosecution of an individual before a jury of his peers. It required a strong presentation of evidence more than oratorical skill.[39] George Kennedy sees examples of judicial rhetoric in Paul's Second Letter to the Corinthians.[40]

The most common form of deliberative oratory took place at a meeting called a *contio*, which was used for legislative discussions in the Roman world. Deliberative speeches were mostly political in nature and were used to convince or dissuade others in the public forum regarding some matter under review. They had only three divisions: introduction, proof, and epilogue.[41] Since persuasion was a significant emphasis in deliberative rhetoric, the skillful use of the three proofs (*pisteis*)—ethos, logos, and pathos—were of the utmost importance.[42]

---

38. Church, "Rhetorical Structure and Design," 18; Watson, "Rhetorical Analysis of 3 John," 484; Kennedy, *Art of Persuasion in Greece*, 10; Reid, "Consideration of the Function of Romans 1:8–15," 186; Campbell, "Rhetorical Design in 1 Timothy 4," 192.

39. Kennedy, *Art of Rhetoric in the Roman World*, 7–18.

40. Kennedy, *New Testament Interpretation through Rhetorical Criticism*, 86–96.

41. Kennedy, *Art of Rhetoric in the Roman World*, 11, 18, 203–6.

42. Church, "Rhetorical Structure and Design," 19.

The traditional view of epideictic rhetoric was "oratory of display."[43] Richard Chase defines epideictic rhetoric as "oratory of praise and blame," which is "only secondarily for display."[44] In epideictic speech, the speaker does not need to persuade the audience. The speaker is seeking to enhance common values he shares with the audience. Thus, the speaker becomes an "educator." He is not so much interested in changing a value system as he is in developing adherence to that value system.[45]

The three species of rhetoric all rely on each other and are often directly related.[46] All three are considered joint creations between the speaker and the audience since in all three kinds of rhetoric the audience is required to pass judgment in some form upon the speech and speaker. There is a close connection between observation and understanding in a typical audience. Both are judgments in some sense which require the audience to respond intelligently. The formal judgment of judicial rhetoric certainly requires a decision by the audience, but the audience also must make judgments about the speaker and the object of praise or blame in epideictic speech.[47] Deliberative rhetoric requires the audience take some action or make some decision as a result of the speech.

## Invention: The Means of Persuasion

In Greco-Roman rhetoric, the category of "invention" (*inventio*) referred to the speaker's choice of resources to use in convincing his audience regarding the issue before them. The materials used were called proofs. A proof could be artificial, meaning it was taken from the speaker's own skills as an orator. A proof could also be evidential, meaning it was taken from existing evidence such as witnesses, documents, and court cases.[48] The distinction between artificial and evidential proofs is an important distinction to maintain. All proofs were part of invention, but not all proofs were equally dependent on the orator's efforts. Aristotle developed what he called rhetoric proper within the category of invention. Rhetoric proper is "the faculty

---

43. Oravec, "Observation in Aristotle's Theory of Rhetoric," 164.
44. Chase, "Classical Conception of Epideictic," 299.
45. Hester, "Placing the Blame, 294–95.
46. Watson, "Rhetorical Analysis of 3 John," 485.
47. Oravec, "Observation in Aristotle's Theory of Rhetoric," 166–68, 172.
48. Campbell, "Rhetorical Design in 1 Timothy 4," 193.

of discovering, in the particular case, the available means of persuasion."[49] The "available means" may be ones the rhetor constructs himself, but they may also be objective resources which the rhetor uses in the speech. For the preacher, artificial proofs would be logical or emotional arguments and anecdotes the preacher selects to make the point. Evidential proofs would be evidence drawn from the biblical text and systematic theology.

## The Proofs We Use

The word the rhetors used for "proof" is our New Testament word for faith (*pistis*). Proofs may be of three kinds—ethos, logos, and pathos.[50] In rhetoric proper, proof came from a demonstration (*apodeixis*), so the goal of the speaker was to prove his case by a demonstration of the evidence selected to elicit belief. In other words, we are more likely to believe what we can see. Demonstrations show us what we should believe. These terms, proof (*pistis*) and demonstration (*apodeixis*), become essential for our understanding of what Paul is saying in 1 Corinthians 2:4, which we will examine later in this book.[51] Cicero, and later Augustine, modified Aristotle's three modes of proof:

1. Pathos: the world to which preachers speak
2. Ethos: the character with which preachers speak
3. Logos: the word which preachers speak[52]

Aristotle considered ethos (moral character) the "most effective means of proof."[53] The ancient Athenian system disqualified any speaker who was "suspected of certain dishonorable acts . . . he could be prosecuted, not for the offense, but for continuing to speak in the assembly after committing the offense."[54] Perhaps if we held our politicians to the Athenian standard of

---

49. Cunningham, *Faithful Persuasion*, 18.

50. Aristotle, *Art of Rhetoric*, I. ii. 3; Campbell, "Rhetorical Design in 1 Timothy 4," 193; Cunningham, *Faithful Persuasion*, 18; Jowett and O'Donnell, *Propaganda and Persuasion*, 30; Kennedy, *New Testament Interpretation through Rhetorical Criticism*, 15.

51. Litfin, *Paul's Theology of Preaching*, 72–73; Litfin, *St. Paul's Theology of Proclamation*, 80; Winter, *Philo and Paul among the Sophists*, 158–59.

52. Adapted from Cunningham, *Faithful Persuasion*, x–xi; Kennedy, *New Testament Interpretation through Rhetorical Criticism*, 18.

53. Aristotle, *Art of Rhetoric*, I. ii. 4; Cunningham, *Faithful Persuasion*, 100–3.

54. Jowett and O'Donnell, *Propaganda and Persuasion*, 29.

ethos, we would see better results in our government! The Romans regarded a person as noble if he had strong character combined with brevity![55] We preachers could use that lesson. Quintilian, a first-century orator, expanded Aristotle's rhetorical proofs by combining moral character with verbal skills when he promoted oratory as good men speaking well.[56] Character and skill go hand in hand in the pulpit.

Aristotle wrote, "persuasion is produced by the speech itself (logos) when we establish the true or apparently true from the means of persuasion applicable to each individual subject."[57] Here is a fundamental distinction made in classical rhetoric. Although the speech is part of invention, it is still considered distinct from the means of persuasion which the speaker might use. Logos should be perceived as the content of the speech, which can be either true or false. The Stoic and Roman philosophy of rhetoric was summarized by the admonition, "seize the subject, the words will follow."[58] Logos was the central argument of the speech—the message itself. The speaker used topics to frame the speech. Topics were the places where the orator looked for his material from which to compose his arguments. This material did not require fabrication but constituted the necessary information for the audience to make a judgment.[59] Without accurate information—logos—the audience could not make an informed decision.

Pathos is often understood as passion, but it is more than mere emotion. Pathos referred to the world which the speaker addressed. Pathetic speaking is audience-centered speech. The audience functions as the judge in Roman rhetoric since they will approve or disapprove of the speech.[60] Tapping into the emotions, ideas, and needs of the listener is an essential tool in persuasion. Aristotle wrote, "the orator persuades by means of his hearers, when they are roused to emotion (pathos) by his speech." He calls this "putting the hearers in a certain frame of mind."[61] Litfin emphasizes that rhetorical adaptation to the audience was the "genius of rhetoric." The

---

55. Kennedy, *Art of Rhetoric in the Roman World*, 6.

56. McLaughlin, *Ethics of Persuasive Preaching*, 48; Jowett and O'Donnell, *Propaganda and Persuasion*, 31.

57. Aristotle, *Art of Rhetoric*, I. ii. 6; For a fuller discussion, see Cunningham, *Faithful Persuasion*, 148–55 and 164–75.

58. Kennedy, *Art of Rhetoric in the Roman World*, 4.

59. Campbell, "Rhetorical Design in 1 Timothy 4," 193.

60. Litfin, *St. Paul's Theology of Proclamation*, 94–95; Cunningham, *Faithful Persuasion*, 82–89.

61. Aristotle, *Art of Rhetoric*, I. ii. 3, 5.

speaker must adapt himself to the opinions and needs of the audience in order to win the approval of the audience. Their needs shape the speaker's methods.[62] Even though a key element of rhetoric has always been adapting to the needs of the audience, this does not mean such a pathetic focus automatically involves a "total disregard of truth," particularly "where absolute truth is available."[63] Cunningham notes:

> The challenge for rhetoric, then, is to tread a fine line between a desire for sheer identification (which simply panders to the audience's assumptions and thus fails to effect a change) and an absolute demand for instant movement and realignment (which may alienate the audience completely). When the argument unfolds between these two extremes, persuasion is possible.[64]

## All Proofs are Not Equal

Pathos, ethos, and logos work in concert with one another, but the three proofs are not equal. Therein lies the ethical danger for every preacher. Pathos is the judgment the audience delivers after evaluating the ethos or moral character of the preacher as seen through the logos or actual content of the message. Classical rhetoric argues persuasion is produced (they believe) by the speech (word) using persuasive means. Paul adapts the model of Aristotle by stressing faith comes by the power of the Spirit using the word to change humans and not by human ingenuity or techniques (1 Cor 2:1–5). The logos takes precedence. Ethos is next, and pathos is last. Passion alone cannot produce lasting faith. The centrality of the word is vital to biblical preaching. God uses his word (logos), communicated through the character of his preacher (ethos), using his passions and skills (pathos), to reach people. The apostolic model for preaching stressed message over method, the Spirit over emotions, and so avoided pathetic preaching.

Duane Litfin has correctly warned us we can go too far in our pursuit of results whenever we adjust the message to manipulate the audience.[65] Pathetic preaching starts with the audience and caters to their needs to produce faith. Sophistry used rhetoric to manipulate people by pandering

---

62. Litfin, *St. Paul's Theology of Proclamation*, 65–66, 92–93, 104–8.
63. Litfin, *St. Paul's Theology of Proclamation*, 30–31.
64. Cunningham, *Faithful Persuasion*, 48.
65. Litfin, *St. Paul's Theology of Proclamation*, 246.

to the needs of the audience. The speakers elevated pathos—human feelings and needs—to the highest means of persuasion. Pathos, more than logos or ethos, is all about moving the audience by our passion.[66] The danger is preachers develop an "idolatry of method" over message in their desire to be relevant to people.[67] I fear we can be quick to shape our message to fit our method. We need to return to the model of apostolic preaching on which Christ founded his church and avoid allowing audience appeal to determine the message. Logos comes first and ethos second. Whenever pathos drives the sermon, our preaching becomes pathetic. Pathetic preaching is audience-driven instead of text-driven, results-oriented instead of truth-centered.

## Is the Sermon Pagan?

Frank Viola and George Barna popularized the charge calling the sermon a pagan invention by the church fathers who adopted Greek rhetoric as the form of their sermons. They wrote, "the stunning reality is that today's sermon has no root in Scripture. Rather, it was borrowed from pagan culture, nursed and adopted into the Christian faith."[68] As is often the case with sensationalized and hyperbolized writing, there is a kernel of truth behind the charge. The deterioration of Christianity after the first century is well documented.[69] Greco-Roman culture secularized the church leading to the hierarchical role of clergy and the allegorical interpretation of Scripture. The flourishes of ornamental rhetoric turned the sermon into oratory in contrast to the apostolic church of the New Testament. With the grand style of rhetoric came the pride of position and the dominance of eloquence. Preachers grew powerful by using the bully pulpit as a platform to influence people. Sophistry ruled the world of rhetoric by the first century and infiltrated the church by the second century. We see the seduction of sophistry developing in Paul's battle with the sophists of Corinth, which is why we must take his warning seriously.

Many social scientists are openly critical of Christianity with its emphasis on conversion and evangelism largely because of the persuasive nature of these activities. The crusade methodology of Billy Graham has

---

66. Overstreet, *Persuasive Preaching*, 58.
67. Hull, "Is the Church Growth Movement Really Working?," 141–42.
68. Viola and Barna, *Pagan Christianity?*, 86.
69. Stitzinger, "History of Expository Preaching," 5–32.

been criticized as proof conversion rests on social proof principles of mass persuasion.[70] Many argue the rise of Christianity in the first four centuries is a classic example of the power of propaganda and can be attributed to rhetorical methods. They consider the growth of Christianity to be "one of the great propaganda campaigns of all time."[71] Critics today argue "televangelism and born-again politics" are case studies in propaganda.[72] Robert Lifton considers any organized religion to be an example of "thought reform" and "religious totalism" whenever it emphasizes "exaggerated control and manipulation of the individual."[73] Unfortunately, the stunning cases of spiritual abuse by celebrity preachers today exacerbate the problem and illustrate the seductive power of rhetoric to corrupt and destroy.

Many view evangelical preachers as manipulative in our methods of evangelism. I sat in a symposium of civic leaders who were gathered to discuss the matter of discrimination with respect to racial differences and gender identity. I was the token evangelical in the group, which quickly attacked all evangelical preaching as manipulative. The central theme was that any moral persuasion was wrong. I could express my perspective as long as I stopped at information and did not seek to persuade anyone else to join me in my faith. The group considered all persuasive preaching to be thought reform and propaganda, and therefore unethical and immoral. I attempted to show them love does not require moral neutrality. We can disagree with someone and still love them. In fact, if I truly love someone who is drowning, the most loving act I could do for them would be to persuade them to grab the life jacket I offered them. At the end of the symposium the young man sitting next to me said that idea was the most important idea he would take with him as he left the meeting. I rejoiced in the persuasive success of that tiny movement of thought!

Christianity was born in a rhetorical world and has always been closely connected with rhetorical values. Christians present a viewpoint of reality in spoken and written form which inevitably involves them in a socially persuasive activity.[74] Many Christian apologists, preachers, and leaders have been heavily influenced by classical rhetoric from the earliest days of Christianity. Such thinkers as Tertullian, Gregory of Nazianzus, Eusebius,

70. Cialdini, *Influence*, 118.
71. Jowett and O'Donnell, *Propaganda and Persuasion*, 42.
72. Jowett and O'Donnell, *Propaganda and Persuasion*, 180–86.
73. Lifton, *Thought Reform and the Psychology of Totalism*, 419–20.
74. Pogoloff, "Isocrates and Contemporary Hermeneutics," 344.

Basil the Great, Gregory of Nyssa, John Chrysostom, Augustine, John Calvin, and John Henry Newman, to name a few, have openly expressed their admiration and appreciation for classical rhetoric.[75]

While it is true that sophistic elements of rhetoric heavily influenced the church in the first few centuries, it is also true that many Christian thinkers rejected the excesses of sophistry and carefully adapted the principles of rhetoric for the church. Augustine, for example, adapted the model of Cicero, emphasizing the three responsibilities of a preacher to instruct, to please and to persuade.[76] He understood the best human efforts cannot accomplish what only God and his power can accomplish in persuading souls to follow Christ. In this way, Augustine rejected the sophistic elements of rhetoric and trusted in God for the results. However, he still believed rhetoric held value for the preacher if it was kept in its proper place. Augustine argued that rhetoric, like medicine, "administered to men by men, is of no avail except to those whom God restores to health," yet we still administer medicine. God does not need our medicine, but we still rightly look to doctors for medical help. So too, rhetorical methods, when used "by men, are of help to the soul when God makes them of help, who could have given his Gospel to man even without man's agency or help."[77]

No, the sermon is not pagan, but how we deliver the sermon could be! Sophistry, both ancient and modern, corrupts the preacher and the preaching. Preachers should not preach with a superior attitude or from a hierarchical position of authority. We must not put our trust in our methods, techniques, and skills. Our preaching skills must not become the platform we use to control our people. Rhetorical power without spiritual accountability is a recipe for ministry disaster. It is but a small step from effective preaching to thinking others should follow our every directive without holding us accountable before God. Preachers should strive to hone their skills to be the best they can be in the service of Christ while following Augustine's example of dependence on God to change lives. We preach the word of God, by the power of God, to the people of God, who hold us accountable to the truth of God.

---

75. Cunningham, *Faithful Persuasion*, 34–35.
76. Litfin, *Paul's Theology of Persuasion*, 52.
77. Litfin, *Paul's Theology of Persuasion*, 52.

# 3

# Sophistry and the Cross

WAITING IN LINE AT a local coffee shop before heading into the church office, a local pastor of a rapidly growing church in our area greeted me. Our church had been involved in a building program, and he had noticed the new worship center nearing completion. We had been at two services for four years while raising funds to build the new building, and I was excited to see the project coming to fruition. The pastor asked me how many people the new worship center would seat. I told him 300, to which he quickly replied, "Oh, that's too bad. You built it too small. You should have built it at least twice that size." I responded that we built what we could afford in agreement with our vision for what we believed God wanted to do through our ministry. It was a step of faith for our small church. He said:

> I have done my doctoral work under Peter Wagner on church growth principles, and I can tell you based upon extensive research, that if you follow the right sociological principles in my manual, given the demographic information for this area that a church should grow to at least 2,000 in the near future. This would be true if Donald Duck were pastor. Of course, Donald Duck should be born again![1]

I think this story is a modern example of an ancient problem infiltrating the church today. The problem of sophistry is not new. Paul dealt with sophistry in Corinth and addressed the problem directly in his letter to the Corinthians. Who were the sophists? Initially, the term referred to the wise men of the ancient world, but by the first century the word described speakers skilled in rhetoric who could attract large followings of people. They taught their methods and skills in schools of rhetoric for

---

1. Personal conversation.

profit and applause.² Sophists were the epitome of success in the Hellenistic world of the first century.

Sophistry as a movement was already popular by Paul's day. Sophists specialized in pragmatic persuasion, which employed established methods to achieve predetermined results. The movement of orators often focused on self-promotion, manipulation, style without substance, and financial reward for entertaining audiences. Philo called it "shadowboxing."³ The Greek sophists from the fifth century BC on devoted themselves to philosophical relativism. Absolute truth was nonexistent for them. Since man was the measure of all things, then rhetoric was highly important. Only as two sides were persuasively presented by skilled orators could a choice be made.⁴ Sophists functioned much like lawyers today. They were paid to present one side of a controversial issue, whether it was in the courtroom or on the public stage.

Sophistry came to dominate the field of rhetoric. Rhetoric soon was perceived as the art of persuading people to accept something as true, whether it was true or not. Such a position left rhetoric open to manipulation because the less-educated masses could be moved by skillful practitioners to accept falsehoods presented in attractive ways.⁵ Plato, following Socrates, opposed the sophists, arguing that sophistry was propaganda oriented around trickery, deceit, and superficiality.⁶ Philo criticized the sophists as masters of illusion. He considered them tricksters who seduced people with their confident style of speaking so they could manipulate the audience to their persuasion. Philo contrasted the sophists with Moses, who won his victory by God's power and not by deceptive methods.⁷ Paul's argument for the power of God over the wisdom of men in 1 Corinthians is similar to Philo's critique of sophistry.

Plato criticized the sophists for self-promoting greed, saying the sophist is a merchant who sells the "provisions on which the soul is nourished . . . hawking them about to any old purchaser who desires them." Philo leveled

---

2. Winter, *Philo and Paul among the Sophists*, 3–4.

3. Witherington, *Conflict and Community in Corinth*, 42.

4. Kennedy, *Art of Persuasion in Greece*, 13–14.

5. Betz, *Galatians*, 24. He wrote, "rhetoric works only as long as one does not know how it works." See also, Kennedy, *Art of Persuasion in Greece*, 14.

6. Jowett and O'Donnell, *Propaganda and Persuasion*, 30; Litfin, *St. Paul's Theology of Proclamation*, 46; Kennedy, *Art of Persuasion in Greece*, 15.

7. Winter, *Philo and Paul among the Sophists*, 88–89.

the charge that they "sell their tenets and arguments like any bit of merchandise in the market." The cynics, by contrast, offered their rhetorical skills for free to highlight the differences between good and bad rhetoric.[8] The sophists were marketing experts, and truth was collateral damage. However, Plato said, true rhetoric demonstrates truth via true principles. Aristotle agreed with both Plato's criticisms of sophistry and that rhetoric was a useful tool. He argued those who know truth have an "obligation to be persuasive,"[9] an argument later promoted by Augustine.

Therefore, long before the time of Paul, philosophers criticized sophistry as unethical rhetoric. It had become a form of entertainment, and such oratory was cause for alarm. Rhetoric degenerated into the sophistic "rhetoric of flattery" instead of the Aristotelian rhetoric of persuasion.[10] Gaius Gracchus, a great political orator, employed a servant with a pitch pipe to stand beside him so he could modulate his voice properly when speaking to a crowd.[11] The debate about ethics centered around the pragmatism of the sophists. Rhetoricians hotly debated whether a speaker could be effective and successful without regard to ethics or truth.

Sophistry degenerated into a rigid system of rules which promised success to the orator based upon certain techniques or methods. By the fourth or fifth century AD, sophistry had permeated Roman society with *paideia*, a popular form of education. The early Christian monks radically opposed these persuasive methods as unethical.[12] Sophistry was results-oriented, audience-driven to the point where truth was manipulated to fit the listener, and dependent on the skills of the orator with a strong faith in the power of the spoken word to accomplish predetermined goals. The goal of the orator was to achieve professional and financial success by attracting large followings.

## What is Sophistry?

Sophistry is the ability to attract large followings of people by the intentional use of persuasive methods to induce the will to choose what the speaker wants without regard to truth or love. Sophistry elevates method

---

8. Winter, *Philo and Paul among the Sophists*, 91–92.
9. Kennedy, *Art of Persuasion in Greece*, 16, 18.
10. Witherington, *Conflict and Community in Corinth*, 41–42.
11. Judge, "Paul's Boasting," 44.
12. Brown, *Power and Persuasion in Late Antiquity*, 40–60.

over message, pride over humility, technique over truth, clever arguments over honest reasoning, and direct pressure on the will of the listener to achieve the results the speaker wants without caring about what is best for the listener. Ancient in origin, sophistry is modern in application. Examples of sophistry can be found in many modern texts on persuasion, particularly texts that cater to marketing and sales. Whenever marketers write about influence in terms of "secrets," "the technology of influence," or "competencies," which "make a person able to influence or persuade others," they border on, if not practice, sophistry.[13] Bestselling author and professor of marketing, Robert Cialdini, argues persuasion is really "pre-suasion" in his popular sequel: "The best persuaders become the best through pre-suasion—the process of arranging for recipients to be receptive to a message before they encounter it."[14]

An explosion of books in recent years has informed consumers about scientifically proven ways to influence people. Getting people to say "Yes" is a popular topic. To get what you want in life, you must learn the secrets of mind control or master the art of manipulating others. Courses in neurolinguistic programming help you achieve your goals and persuade others. You can learn the secrets of body language to influence people. Social media influencers build up online credibility with followers who listen to their views on specific topics. Advertisers pay them to sell products to niche markets. Marketing power dominates our economic world. Power politics, power brokers, and power leaders influence our culture through power lunches, power corporations, and power meetings. These modern magicians of rhetoric claim to know the secrets to the power of persuasion. The key to success in life is to get people to do what you want them to do.[15]

Modern sophistry in the marketing world has spawned a debate among secular researchers, much like the early debates about rhetoric in the first century. Numerous writers have raised warning flags about the ethics of persuasive techniques and how to avoid succumbing to unethical influence.[16] Vance Packard questioned the morality of manipulating consumers through

---

13. Zuker, *Seven Secrets of Influence*, 16; Dawson, *Secrets of Power Persuasion*; Haass, *Power to Persuade*; Spence, *How to Argue and Win Every Time*.

14. Cialdini, *Pre-suasion*, 4.

15. Aubuchon, *Anatomy of Persuasion*, 1.

16. Cialdini, *Pre-suasion*, 209–23; Ehninger, *Influence, Belief, and Argument*; Rusk, *Power of Ethical Persuasion*.

unethical advertising as far back as 1957.[17] His prescient warnings about the rise of consumerism ring true today. Responsible persuasion functions within certain ethical boundaries that researchers identify as an antidote to manipulation and propaganda. Everett Shostrum wrote his popular book, *Man the Manipulator*, to counteract the power of modern sophistry. He argued all humans are manipulators, so we need to learn how to be healthy persuaders.[18] We can hear the echoes of Plato, Aristotle, and Philo in these modern voices warning us about unethical persuasion.

## Evangelical Sophistry

Unfortunately, the sophistry of method over message has invaded the evangelical church as well. Consumerism has infected the methods of evangelical ministries today. Persuasive preachers can become dependent on the secrets of success that will draw large crowds to hear them preach. Sophistry is still sophistry even when dressed in evangelical garb! What is evangelical sophistry? Evangelical sophistry is the ability to attract large followings of people by the intentional use of persuasive methods to induce the will to choose what the preacher wants without regard to truth, love, or the Holy Spirit.

The church growth movement has much in it to commend, and there are many good methods pastors can learn to implement in our modern world. However, local pastors face the temptation to develop an "idolatry of method" over message, just as Bill Hull predicted in 1992, and the result is evangelical sophistry. We can now see the results which Hull wrote about so prophetically:

> We are in danger of having an entire generation of pastors committed to clever programming instead of Scripture. That, of course, will not happen with any official declarations; in fact, those who engage in this idolatry of method will not even really think they are doing so. Still, the simple proclamation of God's word and care of souls will take a back seat in church life to programs and strategies that have more in common with big business than with Christ's kingdom.[19]

---

17. Packard, *Hidden Persuaders*, 153–59.
18. Shostrum, *Man the Manipulator*.
19. Hull, "Is the Church Growth Movement Really Working?," 147.

Evangelical sophistry is not confined to church growth methods, however. John MacArthur Jr. identified sophistry under what he calls the rise of "Neo-Gnosticism." He wrote of three deadly influences on the church today under the headings of "psychology," "pragmatism," and "mysticism."[20] Others have warned preachers to beware of the seductions of modern sophistry. Raymond McLaughlin applied ethical guidelines to persuasive preaching.[21] Larry Overstreet's book, *Persuasive Preaching*, balances the battle between effective and ethical persuasion. His chapter on giving a public invitation is helpful.[22] Duane Litfin warns us to focus on proclamation instead of persuasion because of the inherent dangers of using persuasive methods to preach God's word. His chapter on the church growth movement is an irenic and balanced analysis.[23] Sadly, however, evangelical authors in recent years have mostly ignored the topic of ethics in persuasive preaching. Ancient sophistry is alive and well in modern America, and it has a significant effect on the church today as it did in Paul's day.

## Does the Cross Eliminate Rhetoric?

The crux of the debate over rhetoric is 1 Corinthians 2:4–5. Paul states when he came to Corinth he determined "to know nothing among you except Jesus Christ and Him crucified." The cross is central to preaching. He went on to say, "my message and my preaching were not in persuasive words of wisdom, but in demonstration of the Spirit and power." Scholars have disagreed over the impact of these words for preaching. Since rhetoric is persuasion, does the cross eliminate all persuasion?

Duane Litfin argues—some might even say persuasively—against persuasion![24] Paul adopted proclamation as his "modus operandi" to avoid "usurping the power of the cross."[25] Any persuasive method the preacher might use is the fruit of a poisonous tree. The poisonous tree is

20. MacArthur, *Our Sufficiency in Christ*, 29–34.
21. McLaughlin, *Ethics of Persuasive Preaching*, 137–68.
22. Overstreet, *Persuasive Preaching*, 193–207.
23. Litfin, *Paul's Theology of Persuasion*, 350–59.
24. Duane Litfin first argued against persuasion in 1977 in an article entitled "The Perils of Persuasive Preaching." He later substantiated his arguments in his book entitled *St. Paul's Theology of Proclamation: 1 Corinthians 1–4 and Greco-Roman Rhetoric*, (1994). Litfin has refined and updated his position in his book entitled *Paul's Theology of Persuasion: The Apostle's Challenge to the Art of Persuasion in Ancient Corinth* (2015).
25. Litfin, *St. Paul's Theology of Proclamation*, 247.

the natural paradigm of intentional persuasion that formed the core of Greco-Roman rhetoric. The speaker determined a desired response and then created a strategy to achieve that response. All rhetoric was tainted by the poison of persuasion. Litfin writes, "what Paul rejected was the results-driven dynamic of Greco-Roman persuasion itself; that is, the use of human psychological techniques sophistic or otherwise, to generate *pistis* in his listeners."[26]

The argument Litfin develops is based on five foundational affirmations. 1) Rhetoric was result-driven because the speaker was intentionally persuasive. 2) Rhetoric was audience-driven rather than truth-driven. 3) Rhetoric was dependent on the skill of the speaker for results rather than God. 4) Rhetoric placed its faith in the magical power of words and methods to accomplish its goals. 5) Rhetoric was the means by which the speaker achieved financial and social success.[27] Because of these characteristics of rhetoric, Paul adopted a distinctly different methodology for preaching the cross.

> The crucified Christ would be his constant, unchanging, inexhaustible theme, simply placarded before all. He would avoid artful argumentation with a view to engendering belief by rendering the message somehow impressive and compelling, indeed, irresistible. The matter of the listeners *pistis* must be left to the Spirit alone. Thus the herald's proclamation would constitute the essence of Paul's modus operandi as a preacher.[28]

## Two Spheres of Wisdom

Litfin's warning is commendable, but it raises several questions. Does his description fit all rhetoric or only sophistic rhetoric? Did Paul reject rhetoric totally, or was he qualifying rhetoric with theological parameters? Is Paul truly rejecting all rhetoric as antithetical to Christian preaching, or is he qualifying rhetoric and infusing Christian rhetoric with a Christian theology? To put it another way, is Paul in 1 Corinthians contrasting two spheres of wisdom (*sophia*), God's versus man's, or is he contrasting the method of proclamation (*kērygma*) with the method of persuasion (*peithoîs*)? If it is the latter, then Litfin is correct to reject all forms of rhetoric as antithetical to Christianity; but if it is the former, then there

26. Litfin, *Paul's Theology of Preaching*, 153, cf. 47.
27. Christensen, "Healthy Pastoral Persuasion," 12–16.
28. Litfin, *Paul's Theology of Persuasion*, 265.

could be rhetorical aspects of God's wisdom which are distinct from and qualify the rhetoric of man's wisdom.

Paul's conclusion would indicate he was contrasting two spheres of wisdom which he calls the "wisdom of men" versus the "power of God," upon which faith (*pistis*) must be grounded (1 Cor 2:5–7). Some writers are careful to note the real issue in this passage is between human wisdom and divine wisdom and that Paul is rejecting any dependence on human wisdom to produce genuine, saving faith.[29] The world's wisdom and God's wisdom form a dichotomy, and rhetoric functions on a continuum between those two fountainheads. The more dependent we are on one source or the other, the more our rhetoric is either worldly or godly. Grosheide wrote, "Paul has no objection to persuading words, on the contrary he used them himself, but he objects to persuading words dictated by worldly wisdom."[30] MacArthur places the emphasis not on a rejection of all rhetoric, but on the issue of "calculated theatrics and techniques to manipulate response."[31]

Bruce Winter disagrees with Litfin's conclusion that Paul rejected all rhetoric and suggests Litfin did not consider all the available evidence.[32] Paul rejected the grand style of sophistic rhetoric that was common in the secular assemblies of Greco-Roman culture in favor of a plain style of speech that was less impressive to the Corinthians. Sophistic rhetoric dominated the secular world at the time. Known as ecclesial rhetoric, the confusion for the church as a spiritual ecclesia is readily apparent. The Corinthians wanted to use the grand style of the secular ecclesia and apply it to the church. They considered Paul to be deficient because he spoke in a plain style without the trappings of sophistic rhetoric.[33] Paul opposed the sphere of worldly wisdom. He operated in the sphere of Christ, which led him to trust in the methods of the spiritual sphere (2 Cor 10:4–5, 7–8, 12–15).[34] He intentionally avoided the use of sophistry because genuine faith cannot come by human wisdom. Paul

---

29. Morris, *First Epistle of Paul to the Corinthians*, 52; Clark, "Wisdom in First Corinthians," 203–4; Hodge, *Exposition of the First Epistle to the Corinthians*, 32.

30. Grosheide, *Commentary on the First Epistle to the Corinthians*, 61.

31. MacArthur, *1 Corinthians*, 56; Fee, *First Epistle to the Corinthians*, 94.

32. Winter, *Philo and Paul among the Sophists*, 8.

33. Winter, *Philo and Paul among the Sophists*, 178–79, 251; Overstreet, *Persuasive Preaching*, 52.

34. I am indebted to David Deuel for this insight in his private correspondence with me. See also, Deuel, "Disability and Biblical Weakness," 14–15.

"would not modify his 'plain' style to elicit praise, instead striving to highlight the message rather than the messenger."[35]

## The Centrality of the Message

The message must be central, not the methods or the messenger. The messenger and his methods must never take away from the centrality of the cross. To the degree we use methods—and we cannot avoid using methods—the persuasive preacher will use them to point back to the central message. Paul writes that his "message" (*logos*) and his "preaching" (*kērygma*) were not with persuasive wisdom (1 Cor 2:4). The *logos* is the central message of Christianity: the cross. The *kērygma* is the way in which the message is communicated.[36] Preaching the cross is a proclamation focusing attention on the received message which we do not invent. A *kērygma* was an announcement of truth entrusted to heralds (Titus 1:3). The centrality of the message is essential to ethical persuasion.

Interestingly, Paul goes on to use words freighted with rhetorical baggage (1 Cor 2:5) to establish his approach to preaching. We have already seen the word *logos* used, which was important to classical rhetoric. Paul says his *logos* came in a demonstration (*apodeixei*) of the Spirit and power. His purpose in preaching this way was so their faith (*pistis*) would not depend on man's wisdom but God's power. The words for demonstration (*apodeixei*) and faith (*pistis*) were both significant words in classical rhetoric. A demonstration, according to Aristotle, implied an argument was true and the result certain. Faith was actually "proof" in classical rhetoric.[37] So the proof God gave to the Corinthians (their faith) was demonstrably true and certain because it was based on the proclamation of the word by the power of the Spirit. Paul intentionally uses rhetorical words to argue for the central message of the cross!

---

35. Winter, *Philo and Paul among the Sophists*, 164.
36. Overstreet, *Persuasive Preaching*, 53–54.
37. Winter, *Philo and Paul among the Sophists*, 159–60.

## Pastoral Preaching

Greek society was dependent on oral communication.[38] Literacy in the Greco-Roman world was "at most between 10%–20% of the entire population."[39] Letters were really "extensions of oral speech" for Paul.[40] The New Testament Epistles were designed to be heard more than read, since few would have the opportunity or ability to read them for themselves. As such, they retain much of the flavor of oral communication. Paul gave serious attention to his letters as vehicles of oral communication and may have even entrusted them to be read by co-workers whom he knew could communicate orally the ideas he wanted to get across to his audience. The written word was designed to be "heard as persuasive, not merely seen as persuasive."[41]

Therefore, Paul's letters are the best examples we have of pastoral preaching, and the evidence demonstrates Paul used rhetorical forms in which to communicate to the churches.[42] While Paul may not have been a professional rhetor, he was almost certainly acquainted with the rhetorical methods of his day.[43] The appeals we see in the New Testament Epistles show remarkable similarities to the appeals made in classical rhetoric.[44] Litfin acknowledges Paul's communication is certainly rhetorical in the "broader sense" of the term, meaning the speaker intended to influence the listener in some way.[45]

Paul limited, qualified, and even rejected the philosophical foundations of sophistic rhetoric when they collided with the theological foundations of Christianity. Yet this does not mean Paul rejected rhetoric or refused to exercise the methods of human influence intrinsic to classical rhetoric. Paul sought to establish important boundaries on human influence for the practice of Christian persuasion while at the same time using rhetorical principles in his persuasion. Paul was not rejecting classical rhetoric but was reformulating it in Christian terms.

38. Kennedy, *Art of Persuasion in Greece*, 3.
39. Witherington, *Paul Quest*, 92.
40. Witherington, *Paul Quest*, 45; Betz, *2 Corinthians 8 and 9*, 128.
41. Witherington, *Paul Quest*, 93; Witherington, *Conflict and Community in Corinth*, 45.
42. Witherington, *Paul Quest*, 39; Horsley, "Building an Alternative Society," 211, 252.
43. Judge, "Paul's Boasting," 40–41.
44. Kinneavy, *Greek Rhetorical Origins of Christian Faith*, 106–20.
45. Litfin, *St. Paul's Theology of Proclamation*, 254–62.

Classical rhetoric had greatly influenced the Jewish system of education by the time of Paul.[46] The Jewish educational system in Palestine was heavily influenced by Hellenistic models, particularly in the fields of law and rhetoric. Paul was very likely to have come into significant contact with Greco-Roman rhetoric.[47] Emil Schurer wrote: "the rabbis possessed an undeniable but limited knowledge of Greek culture," which was "centered on Gentile legal studies and their methods of rhetoric."[48] Paul could not have been ignorant of the subject even if he was not formally schooled in rhetoric. He studied under Gamaliel the Elder (Acts 22:3). The Talmud indicates 500 of Gamaliel's 1,000 students were trained in the wisdom of the Greeks.[49]

A growing body of literature devoted to the rhetorical analysis of the New Testament clearly demonstrates Paul knew how to use rhetorical methods in his Epistles.[50] Scholars today are classifying Paul's letters as examples of deliberative or epideictic rhetoric.[51] There are many parallels between the techniques Paul uses in his letters and the rhetorical devices described by philosophers in the Greco-Roman world.[52] The use of rhetorical methods and strategies by Paul cannot be limited to mere form or peripheral matters. The modus operandi of his letters, which are the best examples of his pastoral preaching, involves much more than information. Paul uses these methods to influence his listeners to take action. They are designed to move the emotions, not just inform the intellect.

Ironically, Litfin acknowledges the rhetorical elements of Paul's letters but argues preaching to Christians is different than preaching to non-Christians. Christians possess the Holy Spirit, but non-Christians do not. Therefore, Paul would use rhetorical methods in his pastoral preaching but not in his evangelistic preaching.[53] His argument is highly suspect theologically. The Holy Spirit's influence is no less important when preaching to

---

46. Russell, "Rhetorical Analysis of the Book of Galatians," 345–46; Merrill, "Isaiah 40–55," 7.

47. Kinneavy, *Greek Rhetorical Origins of Christian Faith*, 80–91; Witherington, *Paul Quest*, 94–98.

48. Schurer, *History of the Jewish People*, 1:78.

49. Judge, "Paul's Boasting," 40; Kinneavy, *Greek Rhetorical Origins of Christian Faith*, 90.

50. Witherington, *Paul Quest*, 118–27.

51. Horsley, "Building an Alternative Society," 252; Watson, "1 Corinthians 10:23—11:1," 302; Watson, "Paul's Speech to the Ephesian Elders," 192.

52. Watson, "1 Corinthians 10:23—11:1," 303–8; Danker, "Paul's Debt," 262–80.

53. Litfin, *Paul's Theology of Preaching*, 306.

believers than when preaching to nonbelievers. The only way to influence anyone spiritually is by the power of the Spirit, whether that power is external or internal to the listener. Pastoral preaching is just as dependent on the Holy Spirit as evangelistic preaching. The gospel is not merely to get people saved but is foundational to the whole Christian life.

Paul describes his pastoral preaching style in Colossians 1:28–29. Pastoral preaching proclaims Christ to believers. Paul's goal in pastoral proclamation is to present every man complete in Christ. Paul labors to preach. He strives, agonizes with great effort while admonishing and instructing believers. The Spirit's power is at work in Paul, the speaker, to influence the listener. Proclamation is persuasive. The intention and even the effort to persuade do not make the preaching unethical. Therefore, Paul cannot be rejecting all rhetoric—human persuasive effort. He must be using rhetoric within certain theological and ethical boundaries.

Paul opposed the use of "sophistic or ornamental rhetoric" in all his preaching, whether evangelistic or pastoral, because he wanted his audience to focus on the content of the message and not the form.[54] He refused to use tricks or manipulation, as was common among the sophists in his day, while using an appealing style to reach people.[55] Paul did not want the gospel connected with theatrical, entertaining, and contrived techniques of persuasion. He desired for the Corinthians to focus on the central issues of the faith—the substance—and not the style of communication. For this reason, he disavowed any connection to "persuasive words of wisdom." There are ethical and theological boundaries for the use of persuasive methods by preachers, and these parameters are vital to Christianity.

## The Spirit of Wisdom

Paul is not contrasting proclamation and persuasion in 1 Corinthians 2:4–5. The contrast is between two means by which proclamation produces faith. Paul draws a contrast between "in persuasive words of wisdom" and "in demonstration of the Spirit and of power." The contrast is further elaborated in verse 5 as a contrast between "the wisdom of men" and "the power of God." Paul contrasts "God's wisdom" with the wisdom of "this age" (1 Cor 2:6–7). Therefore, the contrast is between the wisdom of men,

---

54. Witherington, *Conflict and Community in Corinth*, 46; Piper, *Expository Exultation*, 145–48.

55. Robertson, *Grammar of the Greek New Testament*, 1206.

characterized as persuasive, and the power of God, characterized as proof. The success of the message is in the proof produced by the Spirit of God, not the persuasive words of the speaker.

The Holy Spirit is the efficient cause of faith. His work in changing the human heart is the ultimate proof that produces faith. The question is: How does the Holy Spirit do his work? There were two traditions regarding the Holy Spirit in early Jewish texts, which antedate 135 CE. First, the Spirit works by overcoming the human speaker in power, and second, the Spirit works by equipping the speaker with wisdom. Philo and Josephus both saw prophetic rhetoric taking place when the Spirit overcame the reason of the speaker so the speaker did not know the Spirit was at work. Another tradition within Judaism was the Spirit of wisdom tradition, where God equipped humans with the wisdom to be persuasive based on the wisdom found in the revealed Scriptures.[56]

Since Paul planned what he wrote in 1 Corinthians and was very much aware of the force of his message in human terms, it is most likely he viewed this process according to the Spirit of wisdom tradition. If that is the case, then Paul is not disavowing all rhetoric but is teaching that the theological foundation for faith—the proof which produces faith—comes from the Holy Spirit working through the abilities of the human preacher, not by overcoming him supernaturally.

Paul places clear limits on the use of rhetorical skill in persuasion. Human methods are not wrong as long as the preacher understands faith comes from the Spirit and not the methods. The proof must come from the Holy Spirit. Perhaps Paul deliberately avoided rhetorical methods at Corinth precisely because the Corinthians were so enamored with sophistry and would attribute the result to rhetoric, not the Spirit. In those cases, the preacher must avoid using any methods which would detract from the work of the Holy Spirit. The preacher must avoid manipulating or manufacturing a result based on human methods. This forms an important ethical boundary for Christian rhetoric but does not mean all rhetoric is antithetical to Christianity.

---

56. Levison, "Did the Spirit Inspire Rhetoric?," 28–34.

# 4

# Informers or Persuaders?

"Would you give me five dollars to buy gas for my car?" Lloyd asked the first-time visitor to our church.

I happened to be walking by him in the lobby and overheard the conversation. I stopped, put my arm around Lloyd's shoulder, and gently but firmly said, "Now Lloyd, you know that you can come to the Deacons if you have a need and shouldn't be asking other people here at church for money."

The visitor shot me a relieved glance, and Lloyd quickly responded, "Yes, yes, Pastor. I know. I won't do it again."

Lloyd was a middle-aged alcoholic with limited intellectual capacity. He liked coming to church because he felt loved, and we often helped him, albeit carefully so as not to feed his alcohol addiction. We worshiped in a multipurpose room that was full to overflowing with narrow aisles and lots of young families. Lloyd sat near the front but would get up to walk out partway through the sermon every week, winding his way through the people. He would usually go into one of the back hallways and wander around until he met a woman. Blocking her path, he would engage her in a conversation. The women of our church quickly became uncomfortable with these situations even though Lloyd was relatively harmless. So, we set up a schedule of Deacons who were on "Lloyd duty." The Deacon would follow Lloyd out and make sure he didn't make any of the women feel uncomfortable while seeking to treat him graciously.

Because Lloyd's weekly excursions from the front of the church through the audience were disruptive, the Deacons and I came up with an idea. We had someone sew a "Reserved for Lloyd" chair cloth and put it on one of the chairs in the back row. We showed him the sign and explained to him that we had a special seat for him. Lloyd was excited to sit in his seat, and it was much easier for the Deacon on "Lloyd duty" to keep tabs on him, plus he was much less disruptive. It seemed like a win/win solution that worked well for some weeks.

I was preaching through the book of James and came to James 2:1–6 about not preferentially treating the wealthy in their fine clothes by seating them in the best seats and giving the less desirable seats to the poor in their shabby clothes. I taught the congregation about the social context of James and the biblical principles that should inform our treatment of others in the church. I also sought to persuade people to implement these principles in our church. I passionately appealed to them with stories and illustrations designed to move their hearts. You guessed it! After the service, numerous church members accosted the Deacons to demand we do away with Lloyd's special seat! "Pastor Dave called us to treat everyone the same, so we can't make Lloyd sit in the rear of the church!" We removed the sign, and Lloyd sat wherever he wanted to sit after that!

I had preached a persuasive sermon, but the result was not what I had intended. Perhaps I should have informed the people about the passage without appealing to them to take any action. Dispassionate informative messages keep everything neutral and avoid unpleasant and awkward implementation. The Deacons let me know, tongue in cheek, that I should not be so persuasive in the future! My persuasive preaching became the topic of numerous jokes after that. Should preachers stick to information without persuasion? Are we informers or persuaders?

## The Communication Pyramid

Communication theorists break down the process into measurable steps, each building on the previous step as you reach a higher level of communication. Commonly the model identifies five steps.[1] I have adapted the normal five-step model into a four-step pyramid.

---

1. Litfin, *Public Speaking,* 131–32; Litfin, *Paul's Theology of Preaching,* 278–79. Litfin follows a five-step model: attention, comprehension, yielding, retention, and action.

## THE COMMUNICATION PYRAMID

```
        IMPLEMENTATION
   Need: Action   Response: To Behave
        Purpose: To Motivate

             PERSUASION
      Need: Proof   Response: To Believe
           Purpose: To Persuade

              COMPREHENSION
    Need: Explanation  Response: To Understand
              Purpose: To Inform

                 ATTENTION
      Need: Enjoyment        Response: To Enjoy
              Purpose: To Entertain
```

The preacher cannot accomplish a higher level on the pyramid without accomplishing the lower levels first. We cannot motivate until we persuade. We cannot persuade until we inform. We cannot inform until we get attention. The preacher starts at the bottom and moves up the pyramid in the persuasive process.

Duane Litfin argues Paul was a proclaimer, not a persuader. He recognizes Paul wanted his listeners to be persuaded by his preaching. He wanted them to climb to the top of the pyramid. However, Litfin asks the question, "What limited role did the Apostle play within that persuasion process?"[2] He argues Paul believed his role as a herald was to announce the information. It was the role of the Holy Spirit to persuade and motivate. In other words, Paul consciously stopped at the level of comprehension. Paul wanted to guard the persuasion process from human influence so the result would be of God and not of man. The preacher is an informer, not a persuader, according to Litfin's view of Paul's methodology.

Litfin uses the famous, perhaps mythical, illustration of D. L. Moody to prove his point. A drunk supposedly confronted the famous evangelist on the streets of Chicago and said, "Aren't you Mr. Moody? I'm one of

---

2. Litfin, *Paul's Theology of Preaching*, 281, see also 278–84, 303.

your converts!" To which Moody replied, "You must be right because you aren't one of the Lord's!"[3] There is no doubt great danger in persuasive preaching, and Litfin is correct to warn us about the danger. I remember going to the home of a man who was well known in the small town for his immoral and carousing ways. He had asked me to visit him to talk about spiritual matters. I explained to him the gospel and how he could know Christ as his Savior. He quickly replied, "Oh, I know all about that. I went forward at a Billy Graham Crusade many years ago. I'm saved and going to heaven." I don't know his heart. That is between this man and God, but he saw no need to repent of his sin. He was safe in his mind. I would say, with Moody, this man may have been a convert of the evangelist, but he was not a convert of the Lord!

It is surely possible to superficially persuade humans of spiritual truth by human methods, but the persuasion is not God's persuasion unless the Holy Spirit does the persuading. Human persuasion is temporary at best. God's persuasion is eternal. If the Holy Spirit does not persuade, then no true persuasion takes place. However, does that mean we must avoid going beyond comprehension in the persuasive process? Must we be informers only and not persuaders because of the inherent danger of human persuasion? Let's peel back the layers and examine the theological issues behind persuasion more precisely.

## Information-Only Idealism

"If I hadn't spotted that the sea was fizzing, then my parents, sister and me would all be dead," Tilly remembers ten years later.

In 2004, a tsunami struck southeast Asia killing 230,000 people. Her parents, Colin and Penny, had taken Tilly and Holly to Thailand for a vacation. It was about 8:30 in the morning, and they were all walking on the beach when Tilly noticed something strange. She had watched a video about the warning signs of a tsunami a couple of weeks earlier in her geography class in Oxshott, Surrey, England. She noticed all those signs as they walked on the Mai Khao beach in front of their Phuket hotel, so she told her parents. Her parents said, "Don't be silly, Tilly, the weather's just bad."

Tilly argued, "Tsunami, there's going to be a tsunami. We have to get off; we have to run."

---

3. Litfin, *Paul's Theology of Preaching*, 345.

Holly started to cry, so her dad took her back to the hotel, but her mom kept walking. By now, Tilly was screaming, "Please, mum, please come back with me. If you don't come back with me, you won't survive."

She remembers seeing people kayaking on the sea, lying on the beach, and thinking, "We're all going to die." Tilly ran back to the hotel. She and her dad found a security guard, and they all began shouting to people to get off the beach.

"Run. Run. Get off the beach," she screamed to everyone. They called to her mother, who was now running off the beach as the wall of water was forming in the ocean. The tsunami hit just as everyone reached the high ground. Tilly's warning saved 100 lives that day including her family.[4]

Announcing a tsunami is persuasive! Tilly delivered information, but her intention was implementation. "Run! Run!" She informed people, persuaded them to believe, and called for action. She covered the entire pyramid in the persuasive process. Her announcing was persuading. Proclamation is persuasive. The herald becomes a motivator. Teaching morphs into preaching. When it comes to matters of life and death, can we stop at disseminating information like an airline stewardess explaining the emergency procedures? When it comes to matters of eternal consequence, the arbitrary line between informing and persuading blurs.

Human language is inherently rhetorical. Litfin acknowledges preaching is persuasive when he writes, "we may be certain that Paul wanted his missionary audience to be 'persuaded' by his message; that is, he wished as fervently as did any of the orators that his listeners might proceed through all five steps of the persuasive process. . . . He was the human agent through whom they came to faith. So, in this sense, Paul was a persuader."[5] The intent to persuade makes the message persuasive. Purposeful words are rhetorical. Biblical words are always purposeful, so they are rhetorical. Communication is purposeful since when we speak we usually want something to happen. It is theoretically possible to speak without purpose to enjoy the sound our words, but most often, we seek to get someone else to change in some way. Teachers seek cognitive change at the very least, but cognitive change is still a change and so persuasive.

Even at the comprehension level, there is, in effect, persuasion taking place. The very act of gaining the listener's attention, the lowest level of communication, "pre-loads" the message "with importance." That

---

4. Lazzeri, "If I Hadn't Spotted that the Sea was Fizzing," paras 1–2, 16–21, 24–26, 33.
5. Litfin, *Paul's Theology of Preaching*, 293.

moment after initial attention, it turns out, is the most persuasive moment of all.[6] Humans rarely function only on the comprehension level of communication. We can do so when it concerns matters to which we are indifferent, but even the process of seeking to be understood involves persuasion. We want others to understand and, hopefully, agree with our perspective. Giving reassurance to others is a form of persuasion. Certainly, giving unsolicited advice—which pastors do every Sunday morning—is a strong form of persuasion.[7]

What is the difference between teaching and preaching? There has been much discussion over the years regarding this question. Some have tried to prove teaching is focused on believers and preaching on unbelievers, but the distinction does not stand the test of biblical scrutiny. The verb "to teach" (*didaskō*) and the verb "to proclaim" (*kēryssō*) are both used to describe messages delivered to unbelievers (Matt 4:23; 11:1; Acts 28:30–31). Paul is called a preacher and a teacher of the gentiles (1 Tim 2:7). Preaching (*euangelizō*) and teaching (*didaskō*) are combined descriptions of messages given to unbelievers (Luke 20:1; Acts 5:42; 15:35). Paul also describes his ministry to believers as one of preaching the gospel (Rom 1:13–15). John Piper writes it would "probably be artificial to draw a hard line between preaching and teaching" in these contexts because teaching and proclaiming are often "interwoven" with one another.[8]

Others have tried to maintain a distinction between teaching and preaching by saying teaching is informative while preaching is persuasive, but this distinction cannot stand either. For example, the verb "to teach" (*didaskō*) is linked to both "proclaim" (*katangellō*) and "to preach the gospel" (*euangelizō*) (Acts 4:2; 15:35). Paul uses poetic parallelism to treat teaching (*didaskō*) and "proclaiming" (*kēryssō*) as synonyms (Rom 2:21). Furthermore, after Jesus' Sermon on the Mount, we are told "he was teaching (*didaskō*) as one having authority, and not as their scribes" (Matt 7:28–29).

Preaching and teaching are not identical, but they are not radically distinct either. The difference is one of emphasis. Teaching emphasizes information while preaching emphasizes application. Teaching emphasizes content, while preaching emphasizes commitment. In other words, we cannot preach without teaching, but we can teach without preaching. We can easily blur

---

6. Cialdini, *Pre-suasion*, 4, 33.

7. Nirenberg, *Breaking through to Each Other*, 191–98; Woodward, *Persuasion and Influence in American Life*, 2.

8. Piper, *Expository Exultation*, 56–58.

the line between the two, however. If we stop at comprehension, with no attempt to frame the message persuasively, then we are teaching. However, the moment we start to reason, admonish, exhort, or encourage listeners, we are moving into preaching. Teaching morphs into preaching when we intend the information to change the listener in any way. Many a classroom instructor becomes a preacher in that moment of influence.

Unfortunately, many pastors fail to preach when they focus the message on information without application. There is an idealism that creeps into our theology of preaching. We can think information by itself is enough. I attended two different churches on successive Sundays, demonstrating a marked difference in the sermons. The first preacher explained the text clearly but spent large amounts of energy and time on how that text relates to our lives. He was preaching. The second preacher gave us volumes of information about the text but barely touched on how it relates to our lives today. The sermon was all about what happened to those people back then in their situation. He was not preaching. I have listened to many sermons during my years of teaching homiletics, and often I wrote "So what?" in my critique of the student's message. True proclamation of the word answers that fundamental question for the listener. Preaching should be persuasive.

## Announcing Persuasively

There are at least thirty-three Greek verbs used in the New Testament to picture the richness of biblical preaching.[9] Three word groups in particular are helpful to a theology of preaching. The first word group is translated "reasoning" (*dialegomai*). We get our English word "dialogue" from this word. Preaching is dialogical in nature, if not always in practice. Greek philosophers used this word to describe dialogue that was intended to teach students in a classroom. The verb stresses organized reasoning often in the context of dispute or debate. It can also mean to argue, contend, or dispute (Jude 9). The verb is only used thirteen times in the New Testament. However, Luke uses the verb eleven times to describe Paul's preaching ministry in Acts 17–24. Therefore, the verb became almost a technical term for Paul's preaching ministry.[10]

Luke used the term five times in Acts 17–19 to describe Paul's reasoning (*dialegomai*) with his listeners in a synagogue service (Acts 17:2,

---

9. Friedrich, "kēryx," 3:703.
10. Furst, "Think, Mean, Consider, Reckon," 3:820–21.

17; 18:4, 19; 19:8). Paul "reasoned with them from the Scriptures, explaining and giving evidence" about Christ, whom he was "proclaiming" (Acts 17:2–3). Then Luke adds, "some of them were persuaded" (Acts 17:4). His proclamation was persuasive as he reasoned, explained, and gave convincing evidence. Three times Luke used the term for reasoning in the church, the body of believers (Acts 19:9; 20:7, 9). The unbelieving Jews forced Paul to withdraw from the synagogue, so he moved his teaching to the lecture hall of a man with the rather distinctive nickname of Tyrannus (Acts 19:8–9). A textual variant of Acts 19:9 indicates Paul taught from eleven in the morning until four in the afternoon each day.[11] Paul preached like this for two years so all of Asia heard the word of the Lord, indicating his preaching ministry trained many who took his teaching to other parts of that region. Paul was reasoning extensively and deeply from the Scriptures so many were equipped to carry out the ministry. The same deep preaching took place in the church at Troas (Acts 20:7, 9) where Paul was still preaching after midnight. Paul's discourse was so heavy a young man fell to his death after succumbing to sleep.

This word for preaching carries the sense of arguing or disputing. Paul argued with Governor Felix about righteousness to the point that Felix became frightened and ordered Paul taken away (Acts 24:25). Michael the Archangel argued with the devil for the body of Moses (Jude 9). The disciples argued among themselves as to who was the greatest (Mark 9:34), and our Heavenly Father contends or exhorts us as sons (Heb 12:5). All these uses demonstrate the persuasive element of reasoning with others about spiritual truth. There was, and is, often a polemic or apologetic spirit in preaching. Sermons are persuasive speech.

The second word group is translated "herald" (*kēryssō*). The verb is used sixty-one times in the New Testament. It means to announce or proclaim and comes from the noun meaning "a herald." The idea is to proclaim or announce forcefully and authoritatively like an ancient herald announced the news to the city.[12] The word is used of the proclamation of the gospel (Mark 16:15); of the proclamation of God's commands that demand obedience (Rom 2:21); and of proclamation that demands total commitment in all areas of life, both for the preachers and the listener (1 Cor 9:27; 1 Thess 2:9). This kind of preaching is not weak and wimpy. This kind of preaching is authoritative and powerful. Therefore, the word emphasizes the delivery of

11. Bruce, *Paul*, 290.
12. Brown, "Proclamation," 3:48–67.

our message. Preaching is to be done in a manner that proclaims the word with all its demands for obedience and submission.

New Testament preachers understood the proclamation (*kērygma*) as a set of truths to be proclaimed to this world. Paul stated he was entrusted with the *kerygma* according to God's commandment (Titus 1:3). Many have tried to distinguish between the missional proclamation (*kērygma*) of apostolic preaching and the pastoral teaching (*didachē*) of the early church. The proclamation and the teaching were closely intertwined, so significant distinctions between preaching and teaching should not be emphasized. The *kērygma* of Paul's preaching in the New Testament centered around six core doctrines of the early church: 1) the messiahship of Jesus, 2) his death on the cross, 3) his resurrection to new life, 4) his exaltation as Lord, 5) his salvation of humanity from sin, and 6) his return to earth to start the new age.[13] These are the core doctrines proclaimed with authority by the apostles and taught to believers in the early church. Unlike the sophists, we are not free to invent the message. The *kērygma* is entrusted to us as preachers, and we are called to proclaim it.

The third word group means "announce" (*angellō*). Whereas the word translated "herald" (*kēryssō*) carries the sense of an authoritative proclamation demanding compliance, the word translated "announce" (*angellō*) communicates the idea of an informative offer to the listener. Coming from the word for "messenger" (*angel*), the announcement is a message. The apostles communicated the message of the risen Christ, so the word becomes almost a synonym for their witness regarding the resurrection (*apangellō*, Matt 28:8, 10; Mark 16:10, 13; Luke 24:9; *angellō*, John 20:18).[14]

Perhaps my favorite passage for describing expository preaching is Colossians 1:27–29. Here Paul announces (*katangellō*) Christ. We are messengers, and Christ is the message we preach. He is the hope of glory! Paul goes on to describe with two key verbs how we announce this message. We do so admonishing (*noutheteō*) and teaching (*didaskō*). The first descriptor (*noutheteō*) means to warn someone. When we preach, we are warning others that decisions must be made. Preaching calls people to decide to believe or to obey. All good preaching starts with teaching, but all good preaching calls for response. The goal of our preaching is to present our listeners complete in Christ. We are agents of change in the hands of God every time we preach. Our purpose is to work hard at preaching

---

13. Brown, "Proclamation," 60, 62.
14. Brown, "Proclamation," 44–48.

while acknowledging that Christ's power is the power that is working in and through us as we preach.

John Piper writes:

> The message of the preacher, the herald, is not merely a body of facts to be understood. It is a constellation of glories to be treasured. It is, at times, a tempest of horrors to be fled. Any thought that the message of a preacher can be delivered as a detached explanation fails to grasp the significance of Paul's use of the phrase, 'Herald the word!' . . . Preaching is both accurate teaching and heartfelt heralding. It is expository exultation.[15]

## What is Persuasion?

The question is not so easily answered. I culled nearly a dozen definitions from my research in the literature. Apparently, defining persuasion in a precise manner can be difficult.[16] Here is the best working definition of persuasion I have found:

> Persuasion is an activity or process in which a communicator attempts to induce a change in the belief, attitude or behavior of another person or groups of persons through the transmission of a message in a context in which the persuadee has some degree of free choice.[17]

According to this working definition, there are five basic characteristics necessary for persuasion to take place.

1. Both the sender and receiver are active.
2. The source of persuasion intends to bring about change.
3. There must be a willing change, or private acceptance of a change, in beliefs, attitudes, or behaviors by the recipient.
4. The change is predicated on the transmission of a message containing specific content.

---

15. Piper, *Expository Exultation*, 66. See also his extended discussion of the words for preaching in the New Testament (51–71).
16. Christensen, "Healthy Pastoral Persuasion," 189–91.
17. Perloff, *Dynamics of Persuasion*, 14.

5. The receiver must be free to accept or reject the message on some level.[18]

Emory Griffin adds two more tests for "significant persuasion."

6. The change must be "long-lasting."
7. A change in one area of life brings change in another area of life because attitudes are "interrelated."[19]

Larry Overstreet carefully analyzed the use of the word "persuade" (*peithō*) in both secular Greek and the New Testament. The overwhelming emphasis of persuasion was not on comprehension but on action. He writes, "the words stress a change of mind with resulting action, which comes from the persuasive influence of one person upon another."[20] Persuasion (*peithō*) in the New Testament stressed results demonstrated in life, not merely information acquired for the sake of knowledge. Persuasion meant a "winning over" of the listener, resulting in "being convinced" of the truth. The results of persuasion in the New Testament were obedience, trust, and confidence on the part of the receiver.[21] New Testament preachers were persuasive because they knew their message was transformative.

Paul baldly declared he intended to persuade people. "Knowing the fear of the Lord, we persuade men," he wrote (2 Cor 5:11). Here is a simple, declarative statement of Paul's intention in preaching. The verb translated "persuade" (*peithō*) means to convince or appeal to others. It can also mean to depend on, trust in, or put confidence in someone or something.[22] John Calvin defined faith as a "sure persuasion" of God's truth.[23] Paul knew the fear of the Lord, and he sought to persuade others to fear the Lord. It is probably best to take the verb as a conative present. The persuasion is incomplete. A conative present emphasizes the attempt while leaving the result unknown.[24] Living with the knowledge that God will judge us for how we invest our lives, we try to persuade men. We make every attempt

18. Perloff, *Dynamics of Persuasion*, 14–16.
19. Griffin, *Mind Changers*, 4–5.
20. Overstreet, *Persuasive Preaching*, 33. See also 32–56.
21. Overstreet, *Persuasive Preaching*, 41–48.
22. Arndt and Gingrich, *Greek-English Lexicon of the New Testament*, 639.
23. Calvin, *Institutes*, 3.2.12.
24. Moulton, *Grammar of New Testament Greek*, 3:63; Overstreet argues the verb is not conative but durative. Paul is saying he was actually persuading men in this verse (*Persuasive Preaching*, 48).

to appeal to people. We constantly seek to convince people. Yet we leave the result to God. We call people to the point of decision but recognize the decision is between them and God.

Once again, Overstreet points us in the right direction. The testimony of others indicates Paul was a persuasive preacher. Luke records that in Thessalonica, "some were persuaded and joined Paul and Silas" (Acts 17:4). Demetrius, as a silversmith for the shrine of Artemis, argued "Paul has persuaded and turned away a considerable number of people" in Asia from following the goddess (Acts 19:25–26). King Agrippa famously said to Paul, "in a short time you will persuade me to become a Christian," to which Paul replied that he "would wish to God" that Agrippa and others would join him in his faith (Acts 26:28–29)! Paul intended to be persuasive, and the persuasion he sought was change in both belief and behavior. Paul and Barnabas were speaking to people, "urging them to continue in the grace of God" (Acts 13:43). Urging is persuading (*epeithon*). The imperfect tense indicates an ongoing persuasion by Paul and Barnabas. Under house arrest in Rome, Paul continually tried to persuade (*peithōn*) people concerning Jesus, and some "were being persuaded" (Acts 28:23–24). Paul is the portrait of a persuasive preacher.[25]

Persuade is an action word. One of the more interesting connections that demonstrates this truth is the relationship between obedience and faith. We obey because someone convinces us—persuades us. To disobey is to be unpersuaded. The word "disobey" (*apeitheō*) is part of the persuasion word group (*peithō*). To disobey in the New Testament means to disbelieve. Disobedience is used as a synonym for unbelieving and an antonym for believing (John 3:36; Acts 14:1–2; 1 Pet 2:7–8; Heb 3:18–19).[26] Unbelievers are disobedient to God because they are not persuaded to follow God's commands. Paul rebukes the Galatians for turning away from the gospel and asks them, "who hindered you from obeying (*peithō*) the truth?" He then adds, "this persuasion (*peismonē*) did not come from him who calls you" (Gal 5:7–8).[27] The persuasive preacher calls people to trust and obey. Phillip Jensen and Paul Grimmond write, "Because it is impossible to preach the gospel without calling on people to respond, it is impossible to preach any part of God's word without calling on people to obey it."[28]

---

25. Overstreet, *Persuasive Preaching*, 38–39.
26. Bultmann, "Peithō," 6:1–11.
27. Overstreet, *Persuasive Preaching*, 42.
28. Jensen and Grimmond, *Archer and the Arrow*, 31.

On the other hand, some calls to action will be rejected. For example, Paul was under arrest and held in the barracks in Jerusalem when his nephew heard of plans to ambush Paul. He told Paul, who asked the centurion to take his nephew to the commander. The young man urged the commander not to listen to—literally be persuaded by (*peisthēs*)—the Jewish leaders, and to refuse to bring Paul to the council. Paul's nephew won the argument. The commander was unpersuaded by the Jewish leaders (Acts 23:21). The debate was over more than mere comprehension. The persuasion required action. In another example, Paul tried to convince the centurion to remain in the harbor, but he was "more persuaded (*epeitheto*) by the pilot and the captain of the ship," so they set sail into a massive storm (Acts 27:11).

One final example will help us strike the right balance in Christian persuasion. Paul had set his mind to go to Jerusalem when he arrived in Caesarea at the house of Philip the Evangelist. Agabus, a prophet from Jerusalem, arrived to predict what would happen to Paul if he went to the city. The believers began begging Paul with many tears not to go to Jerusalem, but Paul disregarded their arguments. Luke records that since Paul "was not persuaded" (*peithomenou*) they "fell silent," remarking, "the will of the Lord be done" (Acts 21:14). As ethical persuaders, we must always strike this delicate balance between our persuasive intentions and our faith in the will of God. We can seek to persuade others of what we believe is right, but we must always back off if we are not successful in our persuasion because we trust ultimately in God as the great persuader. "May the will of God be done" must be our refrain of faith.[29]

Circling back to Paul's classic warning about faith and persuasion, Paul wrote, "my message and my preaching were not in persuasive (*peithois*) words of wisdom, but in demonstration of the Spirit and of power so that your faith would not rest on the wisdom of men, but on the power of God" (1 Cor 2:4–5). Paul is reacting to the sophists in Corinth who used grand eloquence, celebrity status, and style points to influence Christians to follow their methods. Paul warns against the sophists because their approach to persuasion "empties the cross" as John Piper puts it:

> The wisdom in view is not any deep worldview over against Christianity; it's the sophistry of using language to win debates and show oneself clever and eloquent and powerful. The eloquence Paul is rejecting is not so much any particular language

---

29. Overstreet, *Persuasive Preaching*, 37–38.

conventions, but the exploitation of language to exalt self and belittle or ignore the crucified Lord.[30]

The risk of persuasion is we place our faith in our eloquence and empty the cross of his glory. We exalt self over Christ, our abilities over his cross, our wisdom over his word, and our methods over his message. The seduction of persuasion is subtle. The trappings of our success can overshadow the humility of his sacrifice. How easy it is to be wowed by the messenger instead of the message. Seduced by the pride that comes from people hanging on my words, I can empty the cross of his glory even as I preach the cross with my eloquence.

Persuasion's mistress strokes our egos. The power of influence craves the approval of others. Everyone, including preachers, wants to be liked. How often have you been listening to a sermon—or worse, preaching a sermon—when the focus subtly moved from message to messenger? It became more about winning over the people than pleasing the Lord. Avoid offense to attract the crowds. Frame the message to sell ourselves. Preacher, you know the temptation. I know I do.

Do we preach to persuade others or to please others? Paul has just cursed the false preachers with anathema. Then he writes, "Am I now seeking the favor of men, or of God? Or am I striving to please men? If I were still trying to please men, I would not be a bond-servant of Christ" (Gal 1:10). The word translated "seeking the favor" is the word to persuade (*peithō*). Paul draws a contrast between persuading others and pleasing others. The twin questions are opposites, not parallel. The first question expects a "Yes" answer, and the second question a "No" response. Paul is saying we seek to persuade men, for we surely wouldn't be seeking to persuade God! Trying to persuade God would be anathema to Paul.[31] But we don't seek to please men because that becomes manipulative. Persuading others God's way is antithetical to pleasing others. Controlled by the desire to please God, we can be "all things to all men" (1 Cor 9:22) without being unethical. We are agents God uses for change, not marketers selling ourselves.

---

30. Piper, *Expository Exultation*, 147.

31. Bruce, *Epistle to the Galatians*, 85. While it is true that *peithō* can mean "to pacify" or "conciliate others" in secular Greek, it would be a rare usage in New Testament Greek. There are only two possible texts that might have this meaning (Matt 28:14; 1 John 3:19), and both could easily be translated with the more usual sense of "to convince." Paul is trying to persuade the false preachers to give up their false doctrine, which means he is not pleasing them. However, he is pleasing God by trying to persuade men to reject the false gospel.

## Agents of Change

Thom Rainer, in his book *Eating the Elephant,* tells the tale of two pastors. Pastor Bulldozer aggressively took charge of the church, pushing for changes in everything from the style of worship to the committee structure of the church. The constitution of the church hindered the work of God, he argued, as he took control of all ministry decisions. The last straw for the congregation came one Sunday morning when they showed up for worship, and all the hymnals were gone, replaced with contemporary worship songs on a screen. Pastor Bulldozer lasted five months before he resigned from the church.

Pastor Passive was the opposite. The church had called him to come with the goal of change, but change was messy. He avoided conflict because people's feelings got hurt. He would not push his agenda on anyone, choosing instead to love the people where they were. Pastor Passive was content to tend the garden of the church, making it beautiful, but fruitless. Fifteen years later, change was long forgotten. People drifted away. Attendance declined. The church was aging out and dying off.[32]

"We are supposed to see transformation, but too often we see stagnation," Ed Stetzer and Thom Rainer write in their book *Transformational Church.* They call it the "merry-go-round approach to church."[33] Pastors are content to keep the church moving, music going, and programs spinning because it pleases the people. The result is a slow death. Change is necessary for transformation to happen. Persuasive preachers are agents of change. We are persuaders, not merely informers. Yet the danger of bulldozing people into artificial change is real. True transformation only comes by God's power, not our prowess. Every pastor should seek transformation without coercion or manipulation. Effective persuasion must also be ethical persuasion.

"How do you eat an elephant?" Thom Rainer asks. "One bite at a time!" How do we bring about change to our churches? One bite at a time! Neil Hudson, in *Imagine Church,* writes that we shift the church slowly over time. He uses the analogy of a compass. We bring about effective change in a church through "one-degree shifts." Change comes one degree at a time.[34] We can become frustrated with this process, but long-term ethical change

---

32. Rainer, *Eating the Elephant,* 36–37.
33. Stetzer and Rainer, *Transformational Church,* 2–3.
34. Hudson, *Imagine Church,* 97.

requires the right balance of patience and vision. Persuasive preachers keep their eyes on the transformation goal while trusting in the wisdom of God's process. We must not stop challenging and exhorting our people to change while trusting God to bring about the growth. This combination of ambition and patience characterizes an ethically persuasive preacher.

Capital campaigns test the persuasive skills of pastors to the limit. They represent the part of ministry we all love to hate. While I was writing this section of the book, I met with a pastor who shared he was currently immersed in a capital campaign for his church. He said, "I didn't want to implement a capital campaign, but we had to do it." He went on to share some of the ongoing decisions that made the process so onerous, though necessary. My thoughts turned back more than two decades to the capital campaign I had led to build a new worship center for our church.

I accepted the call to pastor Galilee Baptist Church in 1990 while still Academic Dean at New England Bible College. I agreed to pastor the church with the understanding that I would continue in ministry at the college. The church grew steadily, and we started a second service within a few years. We were holding two services in a multipurpose room, so it wasn't long before we formed a building committee to plan for a new worship center. We paid off a small mortgage in one Sunday of giving as our first step of faith. For a year and a half, the committee worked our way through various problems to lay a solid foundation for our building proposal to the church body. I remember at one meeting when we reached an impasse, one of the leaders looked across the table at me and said, "Now what are you going to do, Pastor?" I replied that I didn't know, but we would pray about it and reconvene in two weeks. By that time, we were able to see a solution and move ahead. Plans were drawn up with the architects after various iterations of ideas. We held a business meeting/prayer meeting to launch the process.

The capital campaign followed in the fall of 1995 with the theme, "We are building to celebrate him!" Kickoff Sunday was October 15. I preached a sermon entitled "Moved to Give" on Exodus 35:20—36:7. I challenged our small church that this was a "spiritual enterprise from start to finish." I said, "God is testing Galilee. Will we trust him to provide what we need to give back to him? That is the real test! He is testing our motivation to give to him." We divided our congregation into nine prayer groups. We disseminated the plans to the people. I prepared a video that would be shared with the small groups. I concluded the video with these words. "Right now, I am going to ask you as a group to spend a few minutes in prayer together. This is truly as spiritual a decision as any decision our church will make in the next twenty years because the mortgage, like an 800-pound gorilla, will sit wherever it wants in our budget. Will you pray together about this decision and then go your separate ways in that same spirit of prayer?"

On November 5, I preached another sermon from Exodus 29–30 entitled "Consecrated to Him." Collection Sunday was November 12, and I preached a sermon entitled "Selling Out!" from Exodus 32:1–10. Our small congregation took a big step of faith in pledging enough money over and above regular giving to launch construction. Our capital campaign culminated on Celebration Sunday, November 19, 1995, with a sermon from Exodus 40:34–38 entitled "Giving for His Glory!" A year later, we expanded and converted those pledges into cash with the purchase of bonds to cover the mortgage. The bond sales took place over a weekend in November that culminated in a terrible hurricane. I drove through flooded roads to get to the church office, where the broker was selling the bonds. Not one person missed their scheduled appointment despite power outages and flooded roads. We raised enough money to self-fund most of the mortgage. However, the most important thing to me was the unity we experienced as a church trusting God to lead us forward for him. A small church that doubted it could do anything very big had stepped out in faith and found God more than able to provide what we needed to do what he wanted.

Was I wrong to be so persuasive? Some would say I was. Much human planning using human methods went into the capital campaign. Is it wrong to invoke biblical principles in the pursuit of financial goals? If not a building program, what about missions? Is it wrong to use human skills to raise money for missions? Some would say it is. According to some, we exhibit a lack of faith in God when we raise funds to do God's work. Informing people of the need is acceptable but don't persuade people to respond. Leave the persuasion to God—that is his job, not ours!

At a meeting of Baptist pastors in the 1700s, William Carey rose to challenge the other pastors to develop plans for sending missionaries overseas. One of the older pastors quickly stood up and famously said, "Young man, sit down! You are an enthusiast. When God pleases to convert the heathen, he'll do it without consulting you or me."[35] As John Piper correctly notes, there is a hyper-Calvinism that thinks God does his work without

---

35. "William Carey," lines 1–8.

using human means. Such a notion is theologically wrong.[36] In 1792, William Carey, the father of modern missions, responded with an eighty-seven-page booklet entitled *An Enquiry into the Obligation of Christians to Use Means for the Conversion of the Heathens.* Carey wrote:

> It has been said that we ought not to force our way, but to wait for the openings, and leadings of Providence; but it might with equal propriety be answered in this case, neither ought we to neglect embracing those openings in providence which daily present themselves to us. What openings of providence do we wait for? We can neither expect to be transported into the heathen world without ordinary means, nor to be endowed with the gift of tongues, &C. when we arrive there. These would not be providential interpositions, but miraculous ones.[37]

How does God bring about change? How does God persuade? The genius of God is to use natural means to achieve supernatural results. Repeatedly in biblical history, God used the personalities, abilities, and ambitions of humans to accomplish his objectives. Sometimes God performed miracles, but often he used natural means. God must always get the glory whether he works through natural or supernatural methods. God is the initiator, God is the energizer, but God uses us to do his work in this world.

God used humans to write the Bible, but God was the author.

God uses doctors to heal the sick, but God is the healer.

God uses preachers to persuade people, but God is the persuader.

## The Altar of the Heart

The altar in Scripture is the place where man meets God. Persuasive preachers bring men and women to the altar of the heart. We call our listeners to a fresh encounter with God on the altars of their hearts every time we preach. What our listeners do at the altar is between them and God, but it should be a point of decision, a fork-in-the-road moment for our audience. It is not enough to merely inform them of the choices; the altar is a call to commitment, not a place of education. We must appeal, exhort, and encourage them to respond to the message. However,

---

36. Piper, *Desiring God*, 197.
37. Carey, *Enquiry into the Obligations of Christians*, 10–11.

persuasive preachers must be ready to stop short—to limit—the persuasion so the result is of God and not man. Ultimately, the decision is between the listener and God on the altar of the heart.

It was Sunday morning, December 5, 1858, at the Music Hall, Royal Surrey Gardens. His text was Luke 14:23. C. H. Spurgeon introduced his sermon with these words:

> Children of God, ye who have believed, I shall have little or nothing to say to you this morning; I am going straight to my business—I am going after those that will not come—those that are in the byeways and hedges, and God going with me, it is my duty now to fulfil this command, "Compel them to come in." First. I must find you out; secondly, I will go to work to compel you to come in.[38]

There was no doubt about Spurgeon's intent to persuade unbelievers to heed Christ's call. He couldn't have been more open and transparent about his objective. In the words that followed, Spurgeon pulled out all the stops to invite people to trust Christ. First, he "found out" the spiritually poor, maimed, halt, and blind by describing them in graphic terms. For example, he spoke to the halt this way: "Ah, limping brother, to you also is the word of this salvation sent. Though you halt between two opinions, the master sends me to you with this message: 'How long halt ye between two opinions?'" Spurgeon spoke openly about the "herculean labour" that lay ahead of him. He must "compel" them to come in "with a groaning, struggling, and weeping heart." He would "accost" them "in the highways of sin" to deliver the King's invitation. He imagined some of his listeners would put him off. They might say they would hear him "by-and-bye" but right then they had to "attend to" their "farm and merchandise." Spurgeon shot back. "Stop brother, I was not told merely to tell you and then go about my business. No, I am told to compel you to come in."[39]

Spurgeon was a master of word pictures. He dramatically painted the scenes where he placed his listeners. The spiritually poor were like people living in filthy rags compared to the righteousness of Christ. The spiritually maimed were like people with no arms, so they could not possibly earn their salvation no matter how hard they tried. He pictured Christ being scourged "till the shoulder bones are seen like white islands in the midst of a sea of blood." He told his own story of how Christ compelled him to come though he often rejected the Savior. He thought Christ would

---

38. Spurgeon, "Compel Them to Come in," para. 3.
39. Spurgeon, "Compel Them to Come in," paras. 7, 9, 11.

smack him in anger when he finally turned for help, but Jesus' arms of mercy were opened wide, and his eyes filled with tears. "He fell upon my neck and kissed me; he took off my rags and did clothe me with His righteousness and caused my soul to sing aloud for joy; while in the house of my heart . . . there was music and dancing."

One of the characteristics of Spurgeon's preaching was the fact he spoke directly to the listeners. Repeatedly he would use the pronoun "you" as he spoke. He did not speak dispassionately in the third person. He did not describe events that happened long ago and far away. He spoke to people directly and appealed to them personally. "You may have rejected a thousand invitations; don't make this the thousandth-and-one," Spurgeon pleaded. He boldly spoke from his heart to their hearts. "You have been up to the house of God, and you have only been gospel hardened. But do I not see a tear in your eye; Come my brother don't be hardened by this morning's sermon." Yet Spurgeon did not trust in his own skills to win their hearts. He pleaded with God to change them and bring them into his kingdom. He stopped in the middle of the sermon to pray for God's power to melt their hearts. "O, Spirit of the living God come and melt this heart for it has never been melted and compel him to come in," he cried out.[40]

Pathos! The sermon is filled with pathos. Spurgeon was not afraid to appeal to the raw emotions of the listeners. By today's standards, his sermon is melodramatic in its emotional appeals. Yet we can see the power of emotions in the persuasive arsenal of the preacher. No wonder the ancient Greeks considered pathos so important in rhetoric. Spurgeon spoke thusly of dying without Christ: "I cannot help thinking of you. I see you acting the suicide this morning, and I picture myself standing at your bedside and hearing your cries, and knowing that you are dying without hope, I cannot bear that." He said tears would fill his eyes when "I think I am standing by your coffin now, and looking into your clay-cold face, and saying, 'This man despised Christ and neglected the great salvation.'" Life is short, Spurgeon argued. His listeners would only have a short time to respond to his warnings. Certainly, some in the crowd that Sunday morning would not be alive in a year. He warned them, "Have you ever tried to think how frail you are? Did you ever see a body when it has been cut in pieces by the anatomist?"[41]

C. H. Spurgeon was well aware of his theological critics who would argue he was using his rhetorical skills inappropriately to win people to Christ.

---

40. Spurgeon, "Compel Them to Come in," para. 16
41. Spurgeon, "Compel Them to Come in," paras. 14–16.

However, he didn't care about the critics. He cared more about God, who would judge him for his preaching if he did not use all his abilities to reach people with the invitation of the sovereign King. Spurgeon was a Calvinist with compassion who believed in being a persuasive preacher.

> Some hyper-calvinist would tell me I am wrong in so doing. I cannot help it. I must do it. As I must stand before my Judge at last, I feel that I shall not make full proof of my ministry unless I entreat with many tears that ye would be saved, that ye would look unto Jesus Christ and receive his glorious salvation.[42]

However, Spurgeon understood the limits of human persuasion. He agreed with Paul that the real persuader was God the Holy Spirit, for only if the Spirit persuaded would the heart be regenerated. So Spurgeon concluded his sermon by trusting in God to change the hearts of his audience. He would leave the decision between his listeners and God. He would call people to the altar of the heart but leave them there with God and God alone. He would use all his abilities to bring people to the point of decision, but the choice for Christ depended on the Holy Spirit to move the heart on the altar. The altar of the heart was the place of encounter with Almighty God.

> We can now appeal to the Spirit. I know I have preached the gospel, that I have preached it earnestly, I challenge my Master to honour his own promise. He has said it shall not return unto me void, and it shall not. *It is in his hands, not mine. I cannot compel you, but thou O Spirit of God Who hast the key of the heart, thou canst compel.* Did you ever notice in that chapter of the Revelation, where it says, "Behold I stand at the door and knock," a few verses before, the same person is described, as he who hath the key of David. So that if knocking will not avail, he has the key and can and will come in. Now if the knocking of an earnest minister prevail not with you this morning, there remains still that secret opening of the heart by the Spirit, so that you shall be compelled.
>
> I thought it my duty to labour with you as though I must do it; now I throw it into my Master's hands. It cannot be his will that we should travail in birth, and yet not bring forth spiritual children. *It is with him; he is master of the heart,* and the day shall declare it, that some of you constrained by sovereign grace have become the willing captives of the all-conquering Jesus, and have bowed your hearts to him through the sermon of this morning.[43]

---

42. Spurgeon, "Compel Them to Come in," para. 16.
43. Spurgeon, "Compel Them to Come in," paras. 19–20, emphasis added.

# 5

# Influence's Arsenal

We sat on the hard, wooden benches in the little rustic chapel as the preacher finished his last message of camp. Tom, Bryant, and I had arrived two weeks earlier at Aroostook Bible Camp, a remote campground in northern Maine near the Canadian border. We lived in small, primitive cabins, slept on bunk beds, swam in the ice-cold St. John River, and played ball in the large field carved from the heavily wooded area. Our cabin had been exempted that week from the daily inspections when a skunk let loose under the floor, making all of us inhabitants identifiable by our distinctive odor! Isolated from the outside world, the setting was perfect for the preacher to reach restless fourteen-year-old boys with Christ's call. There were no distractions to contend with, and our counselors kept us focused on spiritual truths morning and night.

The public invitation began in earnest. First, we bowed our heads in silence as the preacher asked us to pray a prayer of commitment to Christ. Next, the preacher asked us to raise our hands if we had made a commitment. Finally, the preacher asked us to come forward as we sang a closing hymn to commit our lives to Christ. I responded as I had responded to numerous invitations before. Moved by the call to rededicate my life, I walked forward. Tom and Bryant soon followed me to the front of the chapel. We all knelt in prayer as the preacher talked individually with each of us about our decision to follow Jesus. After returning home, Tom and Bryant slowly drifted away from church. The pull of the world grew strong despite the emotional commitments they had made. So far as I know, they never were genuine followers of Christ. Persuaded by the social circumstances and isolated setting, they made a public choice to follow Christ, but apparently it was not motivated by the Spirit of God on the altar of their hearts.

I grew up with public invitations, vestiges of the revivalist history of American evangelicalism. I have also given numerous invitations as a preacher over the years. There are solid historical and biblical reasons for public invitations despite the critics who label them as manipulative or unbiblical. Jerry Vines and Larry Overstreet both give excellent apologetic arguments for the value of the public invitation.[1] God uses human instruments to persuade listeners to make real, spiritual decisions. I made a genuine commitment to Christ at Aroostook Bible Camp because God had moved my heart to serve him. However, there are also significant dangers inherent in public invitations. Persuasive preachers have an arsenal of weapons they can use to influence listeners, but we must beware of the misuse of influence's arsenal as well.

What are the weapons of influence? Cialdini calls them "psychological laws" that govern the process of persuasion.[2] We can see these laws at work in our lives today. They are normal experiences we face as humans living in a social world. The reality is we are not always conscious of these influences at work in our lives, and we often do not notice how we use them to influence others at home, work, or church. These influences are embedded in our human experience, so preachers naturally use them in ministry to persuade others without giving much thought to how the process of persuasion works.

## Behavioral Conditioning

Behavioral conditioning, often called compliance conditioning, observes that our positive and negative associations stimulate our responses in a human extension of Pavlov's salivating dogs. Researcher John Watson tested the hypothesis in the early 1900s with an eleven-month-old boy named Albert. Albert loved animals but exhibited a strong fear reaction whenever an iron bar was struck behind him. Every time Watson showed him a pet white rat, he struck the bar. Soon the infant associated the noise with the rat and began to cry and crawl away from the rat even after the noise stopped.[3]

---

1. Vines and Shaddix, *Progress in the Pulpit*, 155–66; Overstreet, *Persuasive Preaching*, 193–207. Both books defend the use of public invitations with warnings and instructions about their use and misuse. However, Litfin, in *Paul's Theology of Proclamation*, 340–49, critiques the use of public invitations as being manipulative.

2. Cialdini, *Pre-suasion*, 12.

3. Perloff, *Dynamics of Persuasion*, 63.

As a result of the research, educators and psychologists have advocated behavioral conditioning as a primary means of training children. Most parents use some form of behavioral conditioning in their home life by rewarding good behavior and punishing bad behavior.

Robert Cialdini argues that much influence is based upon what he calls "trigger features"[4] built into us by heredity and culture. We must make so many decisions that we learn early in life to use shortcuts, triggers that help us make decisions efficiently. Compliance professionals know how to tap into these influence reservoirs which will trigger the intended response. For example, a principle of human behavior is we are more likely to persuade someone to do us a favor if we give them a reason. Ellen Langer, a Harvard psychologist, tested this hypothesis using a library copy machine. She would go up to a line of people waiting to use the copier and say, "Excuse me, I have five pages. May I use the copy machine because I'm in a rush." Ninety-four percent allowed her to cut in line ahead of them. The success rate was different if she didn't have a reason. "Excuse me, I have five pages. May I use the copy machine" only produced a sixty percent success rate. Interestingly, the actual reason didn't matter. If she said, "Excuse me, I have five pages. May I use the copy machine because I have to make some copies," she achieved a ninety-three percent success rate. The reason was not the trigger. The word "because" was the trigger. We are conditioned to listen for the word and not to analyze the reason.[5]

Emory Griffin calls this "paired associative learning," which occurs when a persuader links something the audience already likes with something he wants the audience to like. When a person associates one with the other, he is more likely to be influenced to like the intended product. Griffin tested this idea in downtown Chicago during the Christmas season. The members of his group would take turns standing next to a woman at a stoplight. Just before the light turned green they would turn to the woman and genuinely compliment her in some way. Then they would walk the other way to demonstrate no ulterior motive. About 100 feet down the street, a Salvation Army worker was ringing a bell. Griffin predicted that the woman who received the compliment, after getting over the shock, would feel good about the compliment and would be more likely to contribute than the one who didn't receive a compliment. He was right![6]

4. Cialdini, *Influence*, 18.
5. Cialdini, *Influence*, 18; see also 15–27.
6. Griffin, *Mind Changers*, 110–13.

Attractional or "Seeker" churches use this principle all the time. Use the same formats that unchurched people like in the entertainment world to help them like the church. Music, dress, auditorium styles, lights, sound, drama, and conversational speaking, all of which are familiar formats, attract people to church. Preachers can use behavioral conditioning to influence churches to change as well. Years ago, our worship team wanted to add drums to the worship service, but our older people were against drums in our morning worship. One Sunday the worship team, unknown to me, had purchased a set of drums and installed them on the platform. I refused to let them use the drums in the service because I knew the furor it would create. We left the drums on the platform for several weeks until the Sunday that the youth group led the service. I let the young people use the drums for worship. The older people loved it because they wanted to support the young people. From that time on, we slowly integrated drums into our music. No one ever complained, not once! Why? They associated it positively with reaching our young people—something they wanted to accomplish. The influence was easy because of the paired association.

## Cognitive Dissonance

We don't like inconsistency. Watch any debate at a church business meeting or a board meeting, and you will observe people pointing out the inconsistencies in positions taken regarding a decision. Cognitive dissonance focuses on the human need to have consistency in our thinking. There are three potential relationships our thoughts might have with each other. The thoughts might be irrelevant to each other, consonant with each other, or dissonant with each other.[7] Dissonance makes us feel uncomfortable. We feel conflicted, making us vulnerable to persuasion so we can restore consonance in our thinking.

The consistency principle forms the foundation of many persuasive situations. People will work to be consistent with themselves. Cialdini calls commitment and consistency "hobgoblins of the mind" and writes:

> It is quite simply our nearly obsessive desire to be (and to appear) consistent with what we have already done. Once we have made a choice or taken a stand, we will encounter personal and interpersonal pressures to behave consistently with that commitment.

---

7. O'Keefe, *Persuasion*, 62.

Those pressures will cause us to respond in ways that justify our earlier decision.[8]

The key to persuasion is commitment. If the persuader can get the persuadee to make some level of commitment, that commitment will, in turn, work to persuade the person to make a higher level of commitment. All it takes is a minor commitment to induce greater persuasion. This process plays out in all sorts of settings, from car sales to fraternity pledges, from prison camp confessions to recruitment campaigns, and from written business goals to church testimonials. Amway, for example, found a powerful way to motivate their salespeople. They simply asked them to set sales goals by recording them on paper. Some door-to-door sales companies found that people often backed out of the sale during the cooling off period, so they devised a trick that worked effectively. Instead of the salesperson filling out the card, they had the customer fill out the commitment card and sign it. They found that people are far more likely to live up to their commitment if they filled out the card.

Public commitments retain the most power. One woman wanted to quit smoking but couldn't find the will power, so she purchased a stack of blank business cards. She wrote on each card, "I promise you that I will never smoke another cigarette." She passed out the cards to everyone important in her life. She said that quitting was the hardest thing she ever did, and many times she thought of smoking again. Yet each time she did, she considered all the commitments she had made to others, and those commitments motivated her to keep her promise.[9] Once a person has made a public stand, the person will work hard to validate that stand with future decisions even if detrimental. Cognitive dissonance is more uncomfortable than sticking with a bad decision.

We frequently use cognitive consistency as a tool for persuasion in church life. I served on the Missions Committee of a church in the 1980s that used "Faith Promise" cards to raise support for missions. We set a goal of $40,000 in faith promises. We stressed to the congregation that these were promises to God, not the church. They were made in faith that God would provide their needs. On our Faith Promise Sunday, we collected the cards in the offering plates and more than doubled our goal. Furthermore, almost all the people kept their faith promises over the next

8. Cialdini, *Influence*, 66.

9. Cialdini, *Influence*, 89–90. He gives numerous examples of the consistency principle at work in normal, everyday life (66–114).

year! Pledge cards persuade. I have also used written promises in counseling situations where I ask a suicidal person to write out a promise to seek help before doing anything harmful. The written promise becomes a persuasive commitment.

Public commitments are powerful. Going forward publicly in response to a sermon solidifies a commitment. Public testimonies reinforce decisions. Testimonies are powerful because those testimonies strengthen the resolve of the person to follow the Lord even as they encourage others in the faith. What about my friends Tom and Bryant who made a public commitment at camp and even gave a testimony to that effect? What happened to them? The public commitment was not as influential because they did so in an isolated setting where no one else they knew was present except me. They could leave that commitment behind them when they returned to the real world, which is why camp commitments are not always lasting commitments.

Even public silence in a controversial situation can be a form of assent. At a church business meeting, having the board silently stand with you is persuasive. Unfortunately, silence can also be used to persuade in less ethical ways. The assumption is that silence equals assent, so if I am silent in the face of wrongdoing, I become complicit. Silence may be co-opted by others to get their way, or by the pastor to push an agenda. Church business meetings are often places of persuasion, which is why a secret ballot is less persuasive than a public vote. The raised hands are public and, therefore, more persuasive. It is easier for a person to renege on a secret vote than a public vote, making the decision more effective long-term. However, churches sometimes opt for secret ballots as an ethical hedge against peer pressure.

## Foot in the Door

Sequential influence methods are founded on the need for cognitive consistency and skillfully use that basic human need to achieve persuasion. The persuader evaluates the situation seeking to determine the needs, values, and interests of the person being persuaded and then designs a sequenced process to persuade that person to buy what he is selling. Sequenced persuasion is commonly used in sales because of its simplicity and pragmatism. The seller gets the buyer to commit at some level and then uses that initial commitment to lead the person to the conclusion the seller seeks.[10]

---

10. Perloff, *Dynamics of Persuasion*, 291.

The process may be as simple as a sales plan which seeks an agreement regarding the needs before explaining the plan for meeting those needs. If the buyer will agree with the statement of needs ("I want a Ford sedan with two doors for less than $30,000), when the seller meets those predetermined needs, the buyer feels obligated to buy. The need for cognitive consistency makes the buyer reluctant to change his mind.[11]

"Foot in the door" or "low balling" are forms of sequenced persuasion. In this process, the persuader asks the client to agree to some lesser action than the one ultimately desired. When the client agrees to the lesser commitment, the seller "ups the ante" by increasing the commitment or cost. The client becomes uncomfortable because if he declines the new commitment, he feels inconsistent with the commitment already made. The opposite process is called "high balling." The seller presents a large request which he expects to be denied, and then he presents a small request, which is the one he planned to seek all along. The person accepts the smaller request, unaware it was the intention in the first place.[12] The sequential process is often combined with the reciprocity principle. The person feels obligated to accept the smaller request because he views it as a favor he must reciprocate.

Emory Griffin applies the foot in the door approach to witnessing.[13] If the pastor wants to help his members become better witnesses, he should not challenge them with stories of powerful evangelists because they will quickly become discouraged. Instead, the pastor would be better off to start with easy ways to witness, such as sending out Christmas cards and then work up to higher levels of witness. This is essentially the principle of sequential influence applied to Christian activity. Others have applied it in reverse to the process which unbelievers exercise in coming to faith in Christ. George Hunter sees conversion as a six-step process: "awareness, relevance, interest, trial, adoption, and reinforcement."[14] This is a sequenced process of influence that we can design and manage as church leaders, seeking low levels of commitment leading to greater commitment. If someone is not ready to trust Christ, offer to pray for them as they listen, or better yet, ask them to repeat after you a "doubter's prayer." These are preliminary steps to conversion.[15]

11. Aubuchon, *Anatomy of Persuasion*, 40–41, 70.
12. Perloff, *Dynamics of Persuasion*, 282–90.
13. Griffin, *Mind Changers*, 189–90.
14. Hunter, *How to Reach Secular People*, 76.
15. Hybels and Mittelburg, *Becoming a Contagious Christian*, 186.

The same process is used with sequenced altar calls. The preacher tells everyone to bow their heads and talk to God. It is just between them and God in the privacy of their hearts. He asks them to pray a generic prayer. Then he says, "If you prayed this prayer, raise your hands so I can pray for you. No one else is looking, but I want to pray for you. Thank you for that hand. Another one, thank you!" The invitation continues with a song while the preacher invites all who raised their hands to come forward and make a public commitment. Sometimes the process is dragged out and highly emotional. It is a classic foot in the door approach applied to persuasive preaching.

## Peer Pressure

> Some years ago, Ron Jones, a high school history teacher, conducted a week-long experiment to show how easy it is for a charismatic leader to mobilize support for his cause. Jones ordered his students to take a new seating posture, to carry paper and pencils for note-taking, and to stand at the side of their desks when asking questions. Subsequently, Jones introduced a class salute, which he called the Third Wave salute. Jones then announced, 'the Third Wave is a nationwide program to find students who are willing to fight for political change in this country.' In an effort to simulate the mass rallies that the Nazis organized during the 1930s, Jones announced that there would be a rally at noon on Friday for Third Wave members only. On the day of the rally, a feverish excitement could be felt around the school. Jones stood up to speak and gave the Third Wave salute, which was 'followed automatically by two hundred arms stabbing in reply.' Then Jones broke the news. 'There is no such thing as a national youth movement called the Third Wave,' he told the crowd. 'You have been used, manipulated, shoved by your own desires into the place you now find yourself. You are no better or worse than the German Nazi we have been studying.' The class was silent as it began to grasp the reality of what had happened.[16]

Do you think this impossible? Just look at our modern political rallies to see the power of group dynamics. It is called the social influence theory of persuasion, and it works effectively. We learn our behavior from society through a process of rewards, modeling, and observation. Humans function in social

---

16. Perloff, *Dynamics of Persuasion*, 3.

environments, which create dependencies on group approval.[17] Social approval and group conformity are methods of persuasion which are frequently used to influence people right down to special hats and T-shirts!

Cialdini calls it the "social proof" or "conformity" principle and gives numerous examples for how it works in everyday life.[18] Some call it "attribution theory" because it holds that we are influenced by the world around us—the context in which we live. People will attribute higher value to ideas they hear, see, or read from various sources, repeated over time, and through different channels.[19] The prevalence of social media in our world today has made the social influence principle even more potent than before because there are more sources and channels which can be used to advocate a message. Today people tune into a network of social media sources that function as a silo of information, repeating and reinforcing social conformity within that network. It seems like the ideas are widespread because they are so frequent and cross channels and time, but the reality is they are all part of the same social network. "Group norms" and "herd instinct" can be used for propaganda purposes. The use of "opinion leaders" to influence others in any given cultural setting is another example of social influence.[20] Cults have always used social conformity as a powerful tool of persuasion.[21]

There is a fine line here ethically for persuasive preachers because social influence does not just play out on a grand scale in our culture. Peer pressure works in local church politics as well. When Leith Anderson (and he is not alone) advocates a process for change that includes persuading the primary informal leaders of the organization so that they in turn will convince everyone else, he is implementing social influence principles in the local church.[22] The process of change he is advocating is excellent, but the persuasive process would be labeled "social proof," "attribution," or "conformity." Church boards that require unanimity instead of consensus for their board decisions end up bringing great peer pressure on the members of the board to conform. I remember one board meeting years ago where we were dealing with a controversial subject. Everyone agreed on

---

17. Woodward, *Persuasion and Influence in American Life*, 136–42; Brembeck and Howell, *Persuasion*, 78–93.
18. Cialdini, *Influence*, 115–62.
19. Griffin, *Mind Changers*, 165.
20. Jowett and O'Donnell, *Propaganda and Persuasion*, 164–66.
21. Singer, *Cults in Our Midst*, 155.
22. Anderson, *Dying for Change*, 177.

the decision except one man. He held out. We waited to decide for several months, during which time various board members tried to convince him to no avail. Finally, he gave in and voted for the proposal against his will because he didn't want to hold up the church. He was a good and honest man who felt he alone stood in the way of what everyone else wanted to do. The sad result was he and his family quietly left the church a year or two later. Peer pressure works, but is it worth it?

Evangelistic invitations often use social influence methods raising ethical questions we should consider. Charles Finney bluntly stated revival "is a purely philosophical (i.e., scientific) result of the right use of the constituted means." Finney popularized the "anxious bench," where he invited people under conviction to come forward and sit down so he could exhort them directly to believe with the crowd watching.[23] He used peer pressure to persuade the almost saved. Various evangelistic preachers "are known to seed their audience with 'ringers,' who are rehearsed to come forward at a specified time to give witness and donations."[24] Billy Graham used thousands of counselors seated throughout the stadium to stand up and come forward at the invitation, which encouraged people to respond because of the crowds moving forward together. He was using a well-established social influence method to help persuade people.

## Leveraging the Listener

In classical rhetoric, any method which focused on the audience would have been considered under the proof called pathos. Pathetic appeals were audience-centered appeals. Evangelical preachers today stress the idea we must speak to the felt needs of our audience to persuade them. For example, John Maxwell and Jim Dornan base a significant portion of their understanding of Christian influence around pathos by focusing on the audience in seven chapters of their book. According to them, the persuader "nurtures people," has "faith in people," "listens to people," "understands people," "navigates for people," "connects with people," and "empowers people."[25] Missional preaching must address the needs of people, but the danger comes when the felt needs of people distort the truth of the message.

---

23. Ahlstrom, *Religious History of the American People*, 1:557.
24. Cialdini, *Influence*, 118.
25. Maxwell and Dornan, *Becoming a Person of Influence*, 35–197.

Catering to the needs of the audience can degenerate into leveraging the listener for predetermined goals.

Preconceptions color conclusions. Sociologists call it confirmation bias. Prior knowledge does bias a person toward accepting arguments in accordance with his initial attitudes and beliefs. Even more importantly, the listener tends to polarize when confronted with additional information so he becomes even more favorable toward his initial attitudes. People simply listen more to the ideas they already agree with or appreciate. The more prior knowledge people have, the more likely they are to reject appeals that run counter to their current attitudes. Audiences become uncomfortable when they are asked to change in some way and will work to attribute value to their preconceptions.[26]

Since motivation comes from within the person being motivated, the leader persuades by appealing to those needs or ideas inside the person which will motivate him. The persuasive preacher taps into the preconceptions of the listener to use those attitudes to achieve persuasion. The special talent of leadership may well be the ability to demonstrate to others how their needs can be met by the cause the leader promotes. Perhaps the most important step in the process of persuasion is audience analysis. The leader reads the listener to interpret the felt needs that can be used to motivate the change in behavior. Developing receptivity in the mind of the listener is at the heart of real persuasion.[27] However, we must be wary of the danger of manipulation in this process. There are very real ethical limitations to pathetic appeals that I will address later in this book.

The similarity principle teaches us the more the persuader and listener are similar, the greater the probability of persuasion. A listener asks himself if the persuader thinks like him (attitude), acts like him (morality), comes from a social background like his (culture), and looks like him (appearance). So, the simplest form of persuasion is for the persuader to pattern himself after the ways of the one being persuaded. Attractional churches stress these factors in their methodology. The worship service

---

26. Bolt and Myers, *Human Connection*, 37–47; Petty and Cacioppo, *Communication and Persuasion*, 114–15; Griffin, *Mind Changers*, 150–51; Woodward, *Persuasion and Influence in American Life*, 143; Rusk, *Power of Ethical Persuasion*, 34–35; Jowett and O'Donnell, *Propaganda and Persuasion*, 109.

27. Gangel, *Team Leadership in Christian Ministry*, 223–25; Griffin, *Getting Together*, 205–9; Jowett and O'Donnell, *Propaganda and Persuasion*, 163; Kouzes and Posner, *Leadership Challenge*, 129; Aubuchon, *Anatomy of Persuasion*, 48; Nirenberg, *Breaking through to Each Other*, 200–1; Zuker, *Seven Secrets of Influence*, 15.

should reflect the attitudes, style, and appearance of the world to attract unbelievers. This concept is called "identification," "accommodation," or "entrainment,"[28] and it can easily lead to sophistry, which is precisely what Paul warns us about in 1 Corinthians 2.

The similarity principle may be the reason stories and testimonies are more persuasive than logic or facts. Stories allow the audience to self-structure the message so they can identify with the point. Everyone has their own thinking process, which acts much like the structure of their physical environment. We are comfortable within those structures, but when we get outside our normal structures either mentally or physically, we become uncomfortable and respond slowly. Persuasion is the process of structuring ideas for the audience so they can put those ideas into place for themselves. Ideas must fit together and be consistent. The persuader needs to see ideas from the perspective of the one he is seeking to persuade.[29] Such a process of adapting to the audience raises ethical questions. How far do we go in adapting to the audience? I like the way Keith Willhite answers that question. The preacher "aims to 'adjust' the audience to the biblical message without adjusting the biblical message to the audience."[30]

Listening, then, becomes a primary tool for the persuasive preacher, especially in times of conflict.[31] The pastor must become skilled at discerning the internal needs and motives of people. We must hone our abilities to read people by listening to them. Thinking out loud is a common way for the listener to order his ideas. If the pastor can get the other person to talk with him about the idea, then he can increase persuasion as the person works through the thought process. Talking ideas out is a critical component of active listening. Too often, pastors are not listening as much as they are waiting for an opening to bring up the next argument. We fear rejection, so we try to control the process with a rush of words and arguments without coming up for air. I have been in meetings where I was so intent on making my point that I ignored the ideas of others in my rush to win the debate. It doesn't work. If preachers want to be truly

---

28. Aubuchon, *Anatomy of Persuasion*, 146; Burke, *Rhetoric of Motives*, 55; Griffin, *Getting Together*, 167–71; Zuker, *Seven Secrets of Influence*, 148, 189–95.

29. Bolt and Myers, *Human Connection*, 42; Aubuchon, *Anatomy of Persuasion*, 30–32; Maxwell and Dornan, *Becoming a Person of Influence*, 102–3.

30. Willhite, "Audience Relevance in Expository Preaching," 358.

31. Gangel and Canine, *Communication and Conflict Management*, 47–59; Zuker, *Seven Secrets of Influence*, 142–77; Maxwell and Dornan, *Becoming a Person of Influence*, 85.

persuasive, we need to let the listeners talk. They will feel validated and often will talk themselves through the process to a good result. Listening is a powerful weapon in the arsenal of the preacher.

The expectations which a pastor has for others are also powerful forms of persuasion as people seek to live up to those expectations.[32] This is sometimes called the Pygmalion Effect. The name comes from the Greek myth about Pygmalion, a sculptor who falls in love with the statue he has created. It is also known as the Rosenthal Effect, after a researcher who demonstrated that teacher expectations have a profound influence on student performance. Positive expectations are powerful persuaders. The opposite, known as the Golem Effect, is also true—low expectations lead to poor performance. Influencers have a profound effect on people through the "phenomenon of self-fulfilling prophecies."[33] Stress an expectation long enough, and the prediction becomes fact. Rhetorically, this process is known as attribution theory. The persuader attributes to another person the behavior which he wants the person to perform or the attitude which he wants the person to adopt. "Rather than telling it like it is, you tell it like you want it to be."[34] Pastors use this method often in sermons as we hold up ideals that we expect Christians to fulfill. The repetition of these ideals is powerfully persuasive over time.

Many people assume an idealistic viewpoint of persuasion. Essentially, people think if the idea is true, it will be irresistible. All the persuader has to do is present the information so the audience understands it and listeners will accept it. Unfortunately, this is rarely the case, given the predispositions of people. Another audience-oriented tool of persuasion is to show listeners the value of an idea in a way that makes implementation worth the cost. People tend to view the goals we advocate as preachers in terms of what it will cost them to implement those goals. Honestly, preachers do the same with our time and energy! Persuasive preachers show people how the result is worth the price. Jesus challenged the crowds to count the cost if they wanted to be his disciples (Luke 14:28). The reward for following Jesus is worth the cost (Matt 16:24–26; 19:27–30; Luke 12:33–34). Emory Griffin coined the term "minimax" to describe the principle that "humans act so as to maximize their benefits and minimize

---

32. Griffin, *Getting Together*, 199–200; Maxwell and Dornan, *Becoming a Person of Influence*, 53.

33. Kouzes and Posner, *Leadership Challenge*, 271.

34. Griffin, *Mind Changers*, 184–85.

their costs."[35] It may be a selfish orientation, but we cannot ignore human nature in our persuasive process. Jesus didn't!

## Source Credibility

Emory Griffin illustrated the principle of source credibility to his speech students at Wheaton College by presenting a series of famous quotations and attaching the names of famous people to those quotations. He gave each member of the class the same list of quotes but changed the names of the sources, mixing them up with good and bad quotations. Then he asked each student to rate the quotes based upon how strongly they agreed with what was said. Even though most students thought the source of the quote would have no bearing on their choices, the end result was there was always more agreement with Martin Luther than Mao Tse-tung or Joseph Stalin no matter what quote was attached to their names.[36] The exercise proved the power of source credibility in persuasion.

Source credibility refers to what Aristotle labeled "ethos."[37] Virtually everyone who studies rhetoric, particularly from a Christian perspective, identifies source credibility as a matter of primary importance in persuasion.[38] Kouzes and Posner, in their classic study of leadership, call it, "The First Law of Leadership: If we don't believe the messenger, we won't believe the message."[39] Joseph Stowell writes that "respect" is the foundational "platform" for pastoral leadership. He tells the story of his first board meeting at Highland Park Baptist Church. He spoke to the staff about the need for mutual respect and one staff member brutally, but accurately, pointed out, "respect is something that has to be earned."[40] The Blackaby brothers identify three illegitimate sources of influence as position, power, and personality. Spiritual leaders influence people in two ways, by who they are and what they do.[41]

---

35. Griffin, *Mind Changers*, 100.
36. Griffin, *Mind Changers*, 117.
37. Aristotle, *Art of Rhetoric*, II. Vi. 7–13. Cunningham, *Faithful Persuasion*, 112–15.
38. To cite just a few sources: O'Keefe, *Persuasion*, 132–41; Jowett and O'Donnell, *Propaganda and Persuasion*, 164; Woodward, *Persuasion and Influence in American Life*, 160–65; Gangel, *Team Leadership in Christian Ministry*, 247–48; Stowell, *Shepherding the Church*, 147–76; Maxwell and Dornan, *Becoming a Person of Influence*, 15–33.
39. Kouzes and Posner, *Leadership Challenge*, 26.
40. Stowell, *Shepherding the Church*, 102–5.
41. Blackaby and Blackaby, *Spiritual Leadership*, 154.

What determines the credibility of a source? When people use the term, they often have very different ideas about credibility. Some consider credibility a matter of good, moral character; others consider a speaker credible if they are competent and objective; while others consider credibility a matter of believability.[42] Perloff identifies four key dimensions of credibility: "expertise, trustworthiness, similarity and physical attractiveness."[43] Griffin considers three factors in his view of credibility: "enthusiasm or dynamism," "trustworthiness or integrity," and "competency or authority."[44] Kouzes and Posner did two surveys in 1987 and 1995 regarding the characteristics which were most admired in leaders. The top four characteristics in both surveys by a wide margin were "honest, forward-looking, inspiring and competent."[45]

I think there are three factors in source credibility: 1) integrity or trustworthiness, 2) competency or expertise, and 3) likability or similarity. The highest-rated character trait from the surveys by Kouzes and Posner was honesty. Honesty is more than just speaking the truth. Honesty is living the truth.[46] It is integrity. Trustworthiness is a major factor in determining source credibility. Trustworthiness certainly means the leader will follow the prescription "DWYSYWD—Do What You Say You Will Do."[47] Pastors are in the character business. People expect us to live what we preach, to be authentic. However, trustworthiness is more than merely telling the truth. Listeners are evaluating our intentions. One critical factor listeners use in evaluating our integrity is our perceived motives. If the preacher is perceived as being manipulative, trust is greatly reduced because trustworthy people do not use and abuse other people for their ends.[48] Selfish motives kill our trustworthiness. Peter stresses pastors must shepherd the church with integrity, not using people for our gain or bullying people to get our way (1 Pet 5:2–3). God reserved his fierce anger for the false shepherds who were feeding themselves rather than feeding the flock, abusing the flock instead of caring for the sheep (Ezek 34:1–10).

---

42. Woodward, *Persuasion and Influence in American Life*, 150, 164.
43. Perloff, *Dynamics of Persuasion*, 141–53.
44. Griffin, *Mind Changers*, 120–21.
45. Kouzes and Posner, *Leadership Challenge*, 21.
46. Stowell, *Shepherding the Church*, 106–7.
47. Kouzes and Posner, *Leadership Challenge*, 211.
48. Woodward, *Persuasion and Influence in American Life*, 162.

Competence received the fourth-highest rating in the surveys behind "forward-looking" and "inspiring." I consider the visionary and inspiring traits of leadership as elements of competency. Audiences use many factors in determining the competency of a leader, but skill in oral communication is highly important for determining competency in our society. Listeners consistently rate an articulate speaker's competency much higher than one who cannot speak well. Some of the factors of competent communicators in our culture include inspiring ideas, compelling language, moderately fast rate of speech, speaking loudly, varying pitch, conversational style, and the use of common, mainstream vocabulary.[49] People like leaders who speak their language. Competent preachers inspire listeners with a familiar speaking style that exudes confidence, enthusiasm, and passion.

Leaders demonstrate competency by their expertise in a given field. Listeners will not follow the vision of a leader they don't think has the necessary knowledge. For pastors, expertise in the Bible and theology are important, but so is expertise in family needs, programming, and outreach to the community, among other factors. One of the reasons pastoring is so hard is people are evaluating the expertise of a pastor in so many areas. Credentialing is a powerful tool for establishing the perception of academic competency. Life experience is another factor in determining competency. Hard work builds respect from people. Our image-conscious and affluent society uses the perception of quality to determine competency. Quality programs, services, and buildings have a way of "rubbing off" on the persuader.[50] People are attracted to success, so the trappings of success are persuasive. This is one reason why people gravitate toward churches with great campuses, modern facilities, and excellent programs. They consider the pastor highly competent if the facilities are impressive.

Robert Cialdini extensively documents the "liking principle" as a powerful tool of persuasion, but so do many others.[51] The liking principle says people are more likely to be persuaded by those they like than by those they don't like. This is one reason why friends are more persuasive than salespeople, as the success of various businesses built on friendship sales in the home attests. Friendship evangelism illustrates the power of liking in church

---

49. Perloff, *Dynamics of Persuasion*, 178.

50. Kouzes and Posner, *Leadership Challenge*, 21; O'Keefe, *Persuasion*, 132–33; Woodward, *Persuasion and Influence in American Life*, 154; Perloff, *Dynamics of Persuasion*, 3–4; Stowell, *Shepherding the Church*, 107–8; Griffin, *Mind Changers*, 113.

51. Cialdini, *Influence*, 163–202; O'Keefe, *Persuasion*, 148–49; Perloff, *Dynamics of Persuasion*, 155; Bolt and Myers, *Human Connection*, 121–32.

ministry. Liking a persuader can even influence the audience's evaluations of source trustworthiness. We tend to believe a source based on how well we like that source. Persuaders know if they can get a person to agree with them on one or two points, they start to build up the liking principle, which in turn can be used to further persuade the person.[52] Pastors use the liking principle frequently in leading their congregations. We build up bank accounts with people through relational deposits, which encourage them to like us. When people like us, they tend to trust us. Pastoring is a people business, and healthy relationships are vital to persuasion.

The liking principle is a corollary of the similarity principle, which says people are more influenced by people they like and are like. Similarity does not guarantee acceptance of a position, but it does give the persuader a significant platform from which to influence, and it can affect the trustworthiness of the pastor.[53] One pastor I know moved to Maine from another region of the country. He struggled to fit in with the rural Maine community because he was not like them, and they didn't trust him. He broke through the barriers when he started getting up at 3:00 AM to join the loggers for a day trucking lumber from the woods to the pulp mills. His willingness to become like them helped them like and respect him and opened doors for ministry. Another example of the liking principle at work is the use of testimonies in evangelism. Sociologists call the use of testimonies the "convert communicator" method.[54] New converts are effective persuaders because they are like the world to whom we witness. The early church used eyewitness accounts powerfully in evangelism, and Christians are called witnesses for the same reason.

Credibility is in the eye of the beholder. Two people can listen to the same speaker and interpret the same message very differently because they perceive the credibility of the speaker differently. Credibility is not intrinsic to the communicator in every context but in terms of the value judgments made by a particular audience in question. In many ways, ethos is determined by the audience as they make judgments about the speaker.[55] Our listeners are making judgments about us as well as the message we preach.

---

52. O'Keefe, *Persuasion*, 139; Jowett and O'Donnell, *Propaganda and Persuasion*, 117.

53. Cialdini, *Influence*, 163–202; O'Keefe, *Persuasion*, 148–51; Woodward, *Persuasion and Influence in American Life*, 162.

54. Perloff, *Dynamics of Persuasion*, 154–55.

55. Woodward, *Persuasion and Influence in American Life*, 159–60; Cunningham, *Faithful Persuasion*, 119.

They make those judgments, many times, based on peripheral factors such as dress, style, charisma, and personality, along with collateral information about us drawn from our relationships and associations. Church members have long memories, and those memories can color the judgments they make about our credibility in specific situations.

Credibility is variable and expendable. We should think of our credibility as preachers like a bank account. We make deposits into that account through our relationships with people.[56] Every hospital visit or time we help in a crisis are deposits in our credibility account. I was amazed, upon retiring from pastoral ministry, how many testimonies focused on those personal moments of ministry rather than public events like preaching. We also make deposits through doing what we say, leading with integrity, handling conflict in love, avoiding selfish manipulation, treating people fairly, and managing money carefully. However, we make withdrawals when we persuade people to take action in some way that costs them. Our persuasion may be for a budget decision, church vision, or ministry expansion. We withdraw from our credibility bank account when we counsel people to change their behavior or invest their time and energy in ministry. Trust is expendable. If we keep making withdrawals without new deposits we will eventually bankrupt our persuasive abilities with the congregation we lead.

## The Chameleon Effect

The danger is persuasive preachers can become chameleons who cater to and reflect the audience instead of preaching biblical truth. We can tell people what they want to hear under the pretense of being relevant. Persuasive preachers can begin to look at people as projects in our quest to win them over to our objectives. Even evangelism can become manipulative if we shape the message to cater to our targets (2 Tim 4:3–4). Persuasive preachers can become pragmatists who evaluate the methods we use solely on whether those methods are appealing.

Elaina Zuker developed her theory of persuasion from the simple principle that "like likes like." She developed a self-assessment instrument which she calls "the influence styles inventory" to assist persuaders in determining their natural style of persuasion. Her formula for success is, "Influence = Attentiveness + Flexibility (altering your habits to match

---

56. Griffin, *Mind Changers*, 126.

or mirror what you've seen or heard the other person say or do)."[57] The persuader learns the style of the other person, the target audience, by careful listening (attentiveness) and then alters his own style (flexibility) to influence the other person.

Joel Osteen grew Lakewood Church to over 30,000 members by preaching a prosperity gospel. People want to hear a positive message, so he preaches that we dishonor God with a mindset of poverty. "What would you think if I introduced our two children to you and they had holes in their clothes, uncombed hair, no shoes, and dirt under their fingernails? . . . God is not pleased when we drag through life, defeated, depressed, perpetually discouraged by our circumstances. No, God is pleased when we develop a prosperous mindset." It is the good news of success that many flock to hear as he reflects the desires of the audience to gain followers.[58]

Persuasive skills can produce a chameleon effect in preachers. We conform to our audience to win their approval. The experts tell us how to target a specific audience, so we shape our message to reflect the demographic target. Effectiveness becomes the highest priority, and when effectiveness is the highest priority in persuasion, sophistry is not far behind. The danger is that preachers give people what they want to get what they want.

---

57. Zuker, *Seven Secrets of Influence*, 191.
58. Leblanc, "Thou Shalt Not Be Negative," para. 7.

# 6

# Logos: The Central Route

*In the beginning was the word,
and the word was with God,
and the word was God.*

(The Apostle John)

New Testament preaching was word-saturated, gospel-centered, and Christ-exalting. Too much modern preaching is word-simplified, gospel-relativized, and Christ-minimizing. Jesus is the "creative Word" (John 1:3) who existed in eternity past and came to explain God to man (John 1:18).[1] Logos, the word, is central to Christianity. "The Gospel is a Gospel about the word."[2] Logos is the message, the word we preach as Christians. In the quest for relevancy and results, modern preachers sadly neglect the centrality of Logos to the persuasiveness of preaching. There are many routes to persuade people, but there is only one central route for Christian persuasion. Logos is the central route to all Christian influence. Christianity is message-centric; the message is a revelation God calls preachers to proclaim. We did not invent, and we cannot improve, the message given to us by the Spirit of God.

The elements that ancient orators used to argue their case were known as proofs, the same word the New Testament writers use for faith (*pistis*). There were two categories of proofs: 1) artificial or technical means of persuasion and 2) inartificial or nontechnical means of persuasion. Artificial or technical proofs referred to proofs the orator invented. They depended on the skill or technique of the orator. Aristotle devoted most of his attention to the techniques or methods that the orator invented. Inartificial or

---

1. Bernard, *Gospel According to St. John*, 1:3, see cxxxviii–cxlvii for a full discussion of the *Logos* in Jewish and early Christian theology.
2. Morris, *Gospel According to John*, 72.

nontechnical proofs referred to proofs that were not invented by the orator. They were not dependent on the skill of the speaker to create. Factual data, objective evidence, witnesses, documents, and legal precedents are all nontechnical proofs which the speaker could use to prove his case.[3] Theologically, as Christian preachers, we must consider Logos, our message, to be inartificial or nontechnical because Logos was the revelation of God. The speaker did not invent or create the message. God revealed his word to be proclaimed to this world.

## ELM

The "Elaboration Likelihood Model" of persuasion (ELM) proposes there are two routes to changing the attitudes, beliefs, and behaviors of people. The central route seeks to stimulate the audience to think seriously about the core issue or message being debated. The peripheral routes use social and cultural "cues" or "triggers" to help people decide the issue according to the objective of the persuader.[4] The degree to which the audience is likely to elaborate mentally on the issue and process the relevant information determines the degree to which the central route will be persuasive. If the recipient has the ability and is motivated to process the core issue, then cognitive processing will lead to attitude change. If the recipient is unable or not motivated to process the central issue, then the persuader must use peripheral routes to induce the person to process the issue prior to persuasion.

Social psychologists John Cacioppo from the University of Iowa and Richard Petty from the University of Missouri-Columbia developed the model based upon extensive research in the field of social persuasion. Their groundbreaking book became foundational for modern research in the field of social psychology. I have adapted and summarized the process with the following diagram:

---

3. Campbell, "Rhetorical Design in 1 Timothy 4," 193; Rapp, "Aristotle's Rhetoric," 5. Artificial proofs (*entechnoi pisteis*) and inartificial proofs (*atechnoi pisteis*) were carefully distinguished from each other, see Christensen, "Healthy Pastoral Persuasion," 64, 96.

4. Petty and Cacioppo, *Communication and Persuasion*, vii–viii, 173.

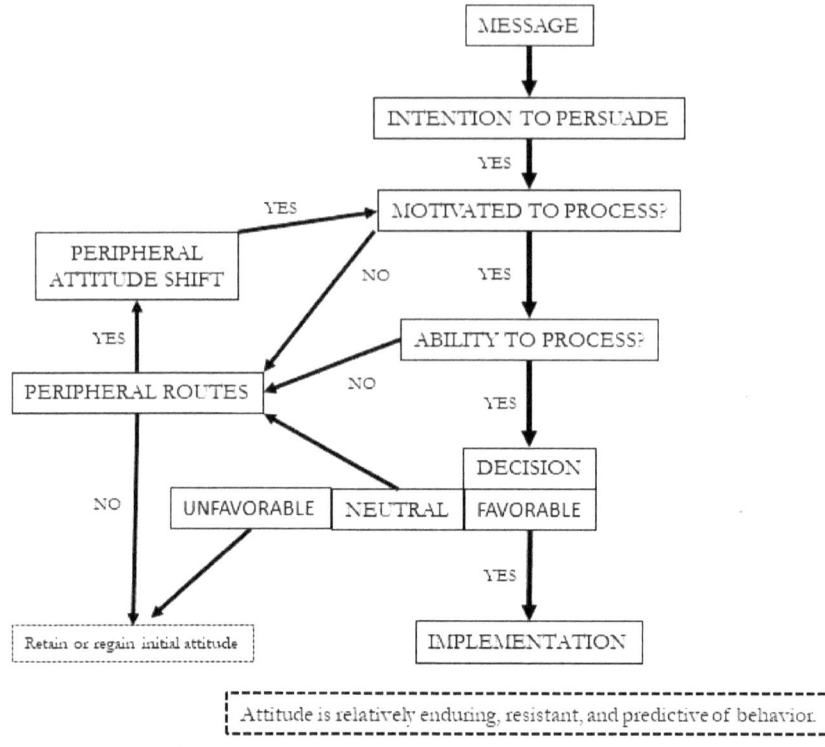

(Adapted from Petty and Cacioppo, *Communication and Persuasion*, p.4)

ELM is very helpful for pastoral persuasion. The model is based on five postulates which help us understand how persuasion works. First, the motivation and ability of the listener to elaborate on information are variable. People are inundated with messages today, so they use shortcuts to make decisions rather than engaging in a serious examination of the central issues. Second, these shortcuts function as peripheral cues to help in decision-making. Third, as the motivation and ability to process the central issues decrease, peripheral cues become more important to persuasion. Fourth, as the motivation and ability to process the central issues increase, peripheral cues become less important to persuasion. Finally, persuasion that results from the central route is more permanent and predictive of behavior than persuasion that results from peripheral routes.[5]

## How Can We Help People Process the Central Message?

One of the best ways to form attitudes is to elaborate the information upon which the attitude is based. Elaboration means the person carefully examines the core arguments of the message. Since people process information differently, they may be persuaded by different approaches while still focusing on the central issues. We are to "preach the word," the central message, but we help people process that information by always being prepared to demonstrate, convince, and exhort them "with great patience and instruction" (2 Tim 4:2). Often the person will add his/her prior knowledge to the information being presented, generating a form of self-persuasion which is highly effective. This self-generation of information is one of the major reasons why the central route of elaboration will produce results that are longer-lasting than persuasion via peripheral routes which must be constantly reinforced.[6]

ELM explains the primary reason why the "sleeper effect" is true. The sleeper effect refers to the proven fact that the effects of persuasive communication increase over time.[7] The longer a person attends church and listens to the messages, the more likely the person is to change beliefs and behaviors. Source credibility and peripheral cues may produce a short-lived result, but researchers have demonstrated that often long-term persuasion runs directly counter to the initial credibility of the source. Low credibility sources proposing certain persuasive arguments often have better long-term results. Credibility is a force over time only when the message and the messenger are inseparably linked in the mind of the hearer. The amount of mental exercise used to listen to the message explains the phenomenon. It takes more mental energy to listen to a noncredible source than it does to listen to a credible source. Over time that increased attention can result in greater influence. Even though the initial attention was negative—the hearer is listening for

---

5. Petty and Cacioppo, *Communication and Persuasion*, 5. Petty and Cacioppo list seven postulates which I have summarized here. For a complete explanation, see 6–24.

6. Petty and Cacioppo, *Communication and Persuasion*, 7–23.

7. Perloff, *Dynamics of Persuasion*, 180–83.

reasons to disagree—the greater attention causes greater retention. Long after the source is forgotten the influence persists.[8]

Elaboration, as the central route of persuasion, is based upon the well-established principle that repetitive exposure (modern terminology), or "amplification" (classical terminology), is foundational to long-term persuasion.[9] One of the principles of communication is that the speaker needs to help the listener "overlearn" the main point of the speech through repetition. Preachers must keep "the main the main thing" if they want to have any lasting influence.[10] The principle of repetition is also the reason why stories are often so powerful in helping the listener retain the information being communicated.[11] Stories humanize truth and provide another way to say the same thing. Preachers need to use multiple ways to help listeners elaborate on the truth. Paul centered his message on the Scriptures but used reason, explanation, evidence, and proclamation to persuade his listeners to trust Christ (Acts 17:2–4).

When elaboration likelihood is high, then cognitive resources are devoted to the issue. The listener will devote mental and emotional resources to examine the message closely. What about distractions? Do distractions hinder the listener from processing the message? Repeatedly, researchers have discovered mild distractions enhance rather than inhibit persuasion, but major distractions reduce persuasion significantly. If people are opposed to the idea, a mild distraction can reduce the development of counterarguments, which allows peripheral persuasion to take place. It should be noted the central and peripheral routes to persuasion are not mutually exclusive but exist on a continuum so both are taking place at the same time as people listen to our messages.[12]

When elaboration likelihood is low, then the decision is usually based on peripheral cues or triggers and not an examination of the central issues. The listener will decide based upon the shortcut techniques available in the setting. When people decide based upon peripheral cues, the persuasion is usually short-lived. For this reason, initial resistance to a proposed idea is a

---

8. Griffin, *Mind Changers*, 123–25; Petty and Cacioppo, *Communication and Persuasion*, 21–23.

9. Petty and Cacioppo, *Communication and Persuasion*, 131; Perloff, *Dynamics of Persuasion*, 57–60; Kennedy, *New Testament Interpretation through Rhetorical Criticism*, 21–22.

10. Griffin, *Mind Changers*, 136.

11. Kouzes and Posner, *Leadership Challenge*, 222–26.

12. O'Keefe, *Persuasion*, 98–103; Perloff, *Dynamics of Persuasion*, 114–15.

necessary part of real, long-term persuasion. As preachers, we tend to think resistance to our proposals is bad, but resistance increases the person's attention to the matter. Casual agreement can be the enemy of true persuasion. If people agree too quickly with what we are saying, we often find the results of the persuasion to be merely temporary. A preacher should not fear resistance and, in the absence of resistance, should push for further commitment or action as a test to determine if the agreement is weak. If people are willing to take the next steps, then they are likely focused on the central issue more than the peripheral cues.[13]

I think ELM helps us as preachers understand the process of persuasion for five reasons. First, ELM allows for a full understanding of rhetorical theory while giving high priority to the centrality of the message itself. Second, the model defines effective persuasion as permanent. True persuasion results in a persistent and permanent decision, not a temporary and expedient decision. This must be our goal as persuasive preachers. Third, the model respects both the person and the process, providing a strong ethical foundation. Fourth, ELM acknowledges what we know to be true to life. We often choose based upon certain cues important to us (shortcuts) without examining in detail all the factors important to an issue, so the theory passes the test of real life. Fifth, this model sets up a theoretical grid for evaluating ethics. The ethical persuader can focus first on the central route while allowing for the fact that some will decide via peripheral routes.

The goal of the persuasive preacher is to avoid using the peripheral routes for essential matters of persuasion while retaining the use of peripheral routes for peripheral matters. The more important the decision, the more critical it is the choice be the result of examining the core issues in the message. Such an approach is much more difficult, but the results over the long-term are much more desirable. We should not be surprised if many preachers refuse to adopt the more difficult approach, preferring to cut corners to achieve rapid results. The fact is churches can grow numerically through peripheral routes of persuasion. People do respond to shortcuts. However, when that happens, we should be wary that manipulative and unethical persuasion may be taking place.

---

13. Nirenberg, *Breaking through to Each Other*, 124–28.

## The Convergence of Spirit and Word

God is the great persuader, but he uses the word spoken by preachers to lead people to salvation (Rom 10:8–9). Persuasive preaching is necessary because God chooses to use the spoken word to save people (Rom 10:14). God could surely use any method he chooses, but he chooses the spoken word. The Spirit of God convinces the world of sin, righteousness, and judgment (John 16:8–11). How does the Spirit convict the world? He works through us. Jesus is addressing the disciples in these verses by using the second-person pronoun twice (John 16:7, 10). The Spirit alone convicts, but he uses us as his conduits to the world, simultaneously relieving the pressure on us to produce converts while encouraging us with his power. The Spirit invests our words with his convicting power.[14] We see the same dynamic earlier in the upper room discourse when Jesus tells his disciples the Spirit "will testify and you must testify" (John 15:26–27). The Spirit is the primary witness, and we are the secondary witnesses. There is no "must" to the Spirit's testimony, but there is a "must" to our testimony.[15] Our witness, as preachers, is persuasive to the extent that we accurately and winsomely express the word of God to the world around us.

Logos is the central route to persuasion for biblical preachers. Paul wrote "the word (*logos*) of the cross is foolishness to those who are perishing, but to us who are being saved it is the power of God" (1 Cor 1:18). Paul launches into a contrast between the wisdom of the world and the foolishness of the preached word in the following verses. He uses a word for preaching (*kērygma*) which means what is preached, the proclamation of the preacher (1 Cor 1:21). It comes from the word for preaching which means heralding the message. Paul returns to these twin themes when he writes, "and my word (*logos*) and my preaching (*kērygma*) were not in persuasive words of wisdom, but in demonstration of the Spirit and of power, so that your faith would not rest on the wisdom of men, but on the power of God" (1 Cor 2:4–5).

My father, Jack Christensen, was my first and foremost mentor in ministry. The word of God was always central to his preaching, but the world of men was always the focus of his message. He poured his heart into passionate preaching in a way I seldom have, if ever, seen. Many times I watched him appeal for people to come to Christ with tears streaming

---

14. Christensen, *Friends with Jesus*, 218–19.

15. Christensen, *Friends with Jesus*, 195–96. The verb can be either a present indicative or imperative, but I think it is best taken with an imperatival force.

down his cheeks, so winsome was his witness. Yet he always knew his winsomeness for Christ could not win anyone to Christ. The Spirit of God alone could change the hearts of humans. My parents began their ministry to reach Muslims in Pakistan. They loved the Muslims passionately, but the ministry was hard, and the converts few. One day a mullah came to his office to speak with him. The mullah was angry that he was boldly preaching Christ in the city. My father asked him what he thought about Christianity. The mullah replied with one word, "foolishness." My father replied that the Bible predicted he would call it foolishness, to which the man asked where the Bible said that. He took him to Paul's words in 1 Corinthians 1:18 and asked him to read those words in the Urdu New Testament. The mullah stormed out of the office without saying another word. The message is foolishness unless the Spirit moves (1 Cor 2:14).

How does the Holy Spirit of God use the preaching of the word of God to persuade people to believe the truth of God? Paul gives us a clue in 1 Corinthians 2:12–13. We have received the Spirit of God "so that we may know the things freely given to us by God, which things we also speak, not in words taught by human wisdom, but in those taught by the Spirit, combining spiritual thoughts with spiritual words." The Spirit joins what we know from God with what we speak for God in the persuasion process. A spiritual convergence takes place between the spoken word and the spiritual truth the Spirit empowers persuasively in the moment of preaching. Let's carefully unpack this verse to understand better that spiritual dynamic.

Writers debate the meaning of the last clause of the verse. The verb can have three meanings: 1) to combine, 2) to compare, and 3) to explain.[16] Furthermore, the "spiritual with spiritual" phrase is somewhat ambiguous. Consequently, writers have translated the clause in different ways. Witherington suggests we interpret or explain spiritual matters to spiritual people.[17] Overstreet understands Paul to be saying the Spirit compared spiritual truths with spiritual words. The Spirit judged whether Paul's words matched the Spirit's truths, and when there was an exact match, the Spirit directed Paul to write those words.[18] However, I agree with Litfin that we should understand the clause to mean combining spiritual ideas with

---

16. Arndt and Gingrich, *Greek-English Lexicon*, 774.
17. Witherington, *Conflict and Community in Corinth*, 128.
18. Overstreet, *Persuasive Preaching*, 174–75.

spiritual words. Form and content should converge so both method and message are Spirit-directed.[19]

Paul is talking about speaking the truths God has freely given to us. We speak those truths in "words" (*logois*) which are taught to us by the Spirit, so the best and simplest way to translate the clause is "combining spiritual ideas with spiritual words." Paul connects things that are like, not unlike, in nature so both the spiritual truth and the spiritual speech are taught by the Spirit.[20] When God aligns the preparation of the preacher with the word of God (*Logos*), the message becomes spiritually persuasive. Paul is concluding his explanation of preaching, which he began in 1 Corinthians 2:1–4, by telling us how this spiritual dynamic takes place in preaching so the resulting faith rests on the power of God and not the wisdom of the world. The Holy Spirit combines God's revelation with our speech so our preaching is Spirit-directed and Spirit-empowered. Without that spiritual convergence, our message is foolishness and unpersuasive to the natural man (1 Cor 2:14).

D. Martyn Lloyd-Jones understood this convergence between the preparation of the preacher and the unction of the Holy Spirit. They are two sides of the same coin. On the one side, the preacher preaches to persuade.

> He (the preacher) is there—and I want to emphasize this—to do something to those people; he is there to produce results of various kinds, he is there to influence people. He is not there merely to influence part of them; he is not only to influence their minds, or only their emotions, or merely bring pressure to bear upon their wills and to induce them to some kind of activity. He is there to deal with the whole person; and his preaching is meant to affect the whole person at the very centre of life. Preaching should make such a difference to a man who is listening that he is never the same again.[21]

The other side of the coin is the unction of the Holy Spirit. Preachers depend on the Spirit of God to anoint their efforts with the power of God. God's enabling power "lifts up the efforts and endeavors of man" to the point the preacher becomes "the channel through whom the Holy Spirit works." Lloyd-Jones writes:

---

19. Litfin, *Paul's Theology of Preaching*, 240–242.

20. Meyer, *Epistles to the Corinthians*, 55. Robertson, *Grammar of the Greek New Testament*, 654.

21. Lloyd-Jones, *Preaching and Preachers*, 53.

> Careful preparation, and the unction of the Holy Spirit, must never be regarded as alternatives but as complementary to each other. We all tend to go to extremes; some rely only on their own preparation and look for nothing more; others, as I say, tend to despise preparation and trust to the unction, the anointing and the inspiration of the Spirit alone. But there must be no 'either/or' here; it is always 'both/and.' These two things must go together.[22]

Many years ago, as a Bible college student, I served as part of a five-man singing team called "The Crusader Men," which represented Philadelphia College of Bible, now called Cairn University. We traveled the Mideastern states one summer performing concerts in different churches each night. As part of the concert, one of us would preach a short sermon and give an invitation to respond. The invitation was twofold. We invited people to trust Christ as Savior, and we invited Christians to rededicate their lives to serve Christ. Greg Aikens and I alternated the preaching responsibilities. Greg later went on to serve as a missionary to Iceland for many years, and I became a Bible college professor and pastor in New England.

Night after night, we took turns preaching, and night after night we called people to raise their hands in response to the preaching. It soon became apparent that God was bringing fruit when Greg preached, but nobody responded when I preached. Many would raise their hands and make commitments on the nights that he preached, but no hands were raised when I preached. I became frustrated and discouraged. I told the members of the team I was going to quit as a preacher. Greg could handle it. The other men tried to encourage me, but they knew I was going through a time of soul searching, so all they could do was to pray for me. We arrived in a small town in Ohio that afternoon. We were early, so we had time to relax after we set up our equipment in the church. It was stifling hot that summer afternoon as I went for a walk. I was mad at God, frustrated with myself, and ready to quit. If I'd had a way home, I would have gone. The others all could see my spiritual struggle but could do little to help me.

The oppressive sun bore down on me, so I found the only shade I could find. It was a small tree on the edge of a large field. I sat down under the tree and pouted. The thought crossed my mind that I was not much different than Jonah in my anger and frustration. God surely had the right to work as he sovereignly chose to work. I wrestled with God that afternoon, and God humbled my heart. I broke down and surrendered to his control. The results

---

22. Lloyd-Jones, *Preaching and Preachers*, 305.

were not mine to determine. I would leave them to him. I walked back to the little church building. The men were setting up for the concert, and people were starting to arrive. I told them, "I'm preaching tonight." They knew God had won the victory in my heart. I preached my heart out that night. I knew something was different. The unction of the Spirit was upon me. It was the same sermon I had preached many times before, but, then again, it was not. I said all the same words, but they were imbued with new power. I gave the invitation, and hands went up all over the room. I was overwhelmed by the response. I turned to the other men on the platform and saw each of them had raised their hands too. My eyes filled with tears for I knew I had just experienced the anointing power of the Holy Spirit. Lives were changed by God—not me—in that little country church. I saw that night in a little town in Ohio the convergence of my words with the Spirit's power that transforms lives. It is a humbling and exhilarating experience to see God work so powerfully through his word.

## The Sawdust Trail

I grew up with public invitations at the end of sermons, and I've given my share of invitations in years past. The public invitation to walk the aisle to the altar at the front of the church has been a staple of evangelical revivalism since the 1800s. Revivalists like Billy Sunday covered the floors of their large tents with sawdust so that the crowds called forward would not kick up too much dust. I graduated from seminary in the Billy Sunday tabernacle in Winona Lake, Indiana, where we literally walked the sawdust trail to get our diplomas. Altar calls to walk the sawdust trail and be converted swept across middle America in the early 1900s. Revivalists like Rodney "Gipsy" Smith advertised they could produce converts for $4.92 apiece. The team of Billy Sunday and Homer Rodeheaver reduced conversion costs to $2 per person.[23] Soul-winning had become a business!

Social manipulation and psychological coercion are very real dangers in altar calls.[24] Persuasive preachers must beware of techniques that induce decisions while reducing the centrality of logos to the choice. Long, drawn-out invitations filled with many verses of "Just as I am" wear down the resistance of the listener. Seeding the audience with people who come forward stimulates others to walk the aisle for the wrong reasons. Overly dramatic, intense,

---

23. Ahlstrom, *Religious History of the American People*, 2:205.
24. Litfin, *Paul's Theology of Preaching*, 348–49.

fever-pitched preaching excites the audience while reducing the mental engagement of the listener with the gospel message. Emotional sermons filled with heart-tugging human interest stories can obscure the centrality of Christ in the choice. Sequencing the appeal is manipulative. Asking for a show of hands while all heads are bowed followed by asking those who raised their hands to come forward at the end manipulates people psychologically. Telling people that no one is looking as all eyes are closed while having counselors watching for people who respond is unethical. Preaching about a topic like a healthy marriage followed by an invitation to accept Christ as Savior is a mixed message to the listener, especially if the preacher advertised the meeting as a marriage seminar. The listener feels manipulated. They came under false pretenses, so the invitation seems contrived.

When I was in high school, a rock band came to do a concert in our gymnasium. The concert was to take place at night, but they performed a preview before an assembly at school during the day. Many of us knew what it was secretly about since the performers had forewarned us they were Christians. They had contacted local churches in advance to be prepared to follow up on the evangelistic invitation to be given. However, none of my peers knew what was happening. The concert was billed as a rock concert featuring all the best songs of the day. A large crowd of young people came to the concert that night. The band performed all the popular songs of the day without any indication there would be a Christian message. At the end of the concert, the lead singer talked about his faith in Christ. He made the gospel clear in a few short minutes and invited young people to ask Christ to save them. He then asked that they fill out response cards and give them to the ushers. Two of my friends made professions of faith that night. I know because I received their response cards. I tried to follow up with them to no avail. One of them later joined the Unification Church and became a follower of Sun Myung Moon. We called them "Moonies" in the 1970s as they flocked after a man who claimed to be Jesus Christ. Manipulative invitations may achieve human results that inoculate the person against the truth.

However, extending an invitation for people to respond can be an effective tool in the persuasive preacher's toolbox. God certainly uses public invitations to achieve eternal results. There is a biblical basis for God calling people to respond publicly in response to a message.[25] Moses called for all who were for the Lord to come to him after the sin of the golden calf (Exod 32:25–26). Joshua called for the nation of Israel to

---

25. For a fuller explanation, see Overstreet, *Persuasive Preaching*, 195–99.

make a public commitment to God at the end of his life (Josh 24:14–15). King Josiah asked all the people to stand up with him in covenent renewal (2 Chr 34:31–32). Elijah called the people gathered on Mount Carmel to stand with him and the Lord against Baal and the false prophets (1 Kgs 18:20–35). Ezra called for tangible actions by the people in rededicating their lives to follow the ways of God (Ezra 9–10). Jesus called his disciples to make a public commitment by leaving their nets and following him (Matt 4:18–20). He called crowds to come to him to find rest for their souls (Matt 11:28–30). Peter preached his powerful sermon on the day of Pentecost, and the crowds asked what they should do. They understood his sermon to be a call to action. Peter told them to repent and be baptized. The people responded, and 3,000 souls were baptized in the many mikvehs near the temple complex that day (Acts 2:37–41).

The altar call can be both effective and ethical if we follow healthy guidelines. First and foremost, focus on Logos, the central route to persuasion. As the saying goes, "keep the main thing the main thing." People need to choose for the right reasons. Make sure the audience stays focused on the message, not the messenger. As James Denney said, "No man can give the impression that he himself is clever and that Christ is mighty to save."[26] We cannot call attention to ourselves while we simultaneously focus attention on Christ. Give short, clear invitations that call people to a specific response. Be urgent in appeal but authentic in character. Be loving in word and winsome in spirit. Avoid Christian clichés that might confuse the listener. Help them think carefully about the truth of God's word and God's call to respond. Leave the decision between the listener and God. We preachers do not win souls. God is the soul winner. Trust God for the results.[27]

There are many ways to give an invitation without walking the "sawdust trail" to the front of the church. Often invitations ask for a show of hands. Other times the listener is invited to stay afterward to talk with one of the leaders. Some preachers use a separate room where people can talk privately with a counselor. Billy Graham used both the call to come forward with a private room for counsel in his crusades. Often, I have invited people to respond in their hearts and share it with someone later. I have seen people make profound commitments privately at the close of a service, which they later shared with me.

---

26. Cited by Piper, *Expository Exultation*, 148.

27. For some good advice on how to give an ethical invitation, see Overstreet, *Persuasive Preaching*, 201–7.

Communion can be an effective time to invite people to trust Christ because, as Paul writes, we preach Christ in communion (1 Cor 11:26). I have often explained communion to people and warned them not to partake if they were not Christians but called them to examine their hearts in that moment of worship (1 Cor 11:27–31). I remember one young couple attending our church. She was a Christian, and he was not. One Sunday, as we prepared for communion, God convicted her that he should not participate, so she told him they had to leave. He wanted to stay. He had never seen this ritual before, but she insisted, so they left. Outside the church, he confronted her about it. She took the opportunity to explain to him that she was a Christian, and he was not. She explained the gospel to him for the first time and why communion was so important. He listened to her authentic witness but made no decision. They continued to date, and he regularly came with her to church. On the first Sunday of each month, we practiced communion. She would partake, and he would not out of respect for her. He listened to the messages. Finally, one communion Sunday, the bread was passed down the aisle, and he picked up a piece. Their eyes met, and she knew that he had become a Christian. It was his first public commitment. I know this story because I later led them through premarital counseling and performed their wedding.

Calvin Miller writes, "A sermon that loses its godly summons is at best a current event and at worst a morality monologue."[28] All good preaching has an altar call, but not necessarily in the way we might think. The issue of a call is not the place or the form but the heart. Many people walk an aisle in a building who remain obstinate in the heart. The altar of the heart is the only altar that matters. Altars are places where man meets God in Scripture. Therefore, all good preaching should call people to the place where they meet God person to person and heart to heart. We must call people to a fresh encounter with God every time we preach.

Calling people to a fresh encounter with God is a mystery of the Holy Spirit. We must always remember it is not our persuasion that changes hearts (1 Cor 2:4–5). Only the power of the Holy Spirit can transform lives. Faith is dependent on the power of God, both in preaching and responding. We can fail miserably in our preparation to preach, and the Holy Spirit can still use our words powerfully in the lives of people. We can excel in our skill as preachers, but if we do not have the Holy Spirit at work in the sermon, it will be powerless. We must be filled with the Holy Spirit, as Paul

---

28. Miller, *Marketplace Preaching*, 25.

tells us in Ephesians 5:18. We must have a fresh encounter with God if we would call our people to a fresh encounter with God.

## Green Tomatoes

Early in ministry, I was out on visitation for our church in New Jersey, and I talked to this one young man in his kitchen for three or four hours. It was one of the most frustrating experiences in evangelism I have ever had. The man was very interested. He wanted to know more. He asked lots of questions. He acknowledged his sin, but he just couldn't come to the point of making a decision. I felt obligated to persuade him and tried every argument I could muster, but it was all without fruit. Why? I was trying to pick a green tomato. It was not the Holy Spirit's time. I have no idea what happened to that man, but I wouldn't be surprised if two years later he is talking to a friend for five minutes who says, "you know you need Jesus," and he believes. Someone will walk away saying, "Wow! Who said evangelism is hard? This man just believed in five minutes, and I didn't do a thing." Why? It is the work of the Holy Spirit to open blind eyes and set the captives free. We can't do it. All too often, we are trying to drag people by the scruff of the neck, kicking and screaming, into the kingdom, but God is always patient because he knows the heart better than we do. We do so much damage when we try to pick green tomatoes instead of waiting until they ripen in the hands of the Holy Spirit.

Bill (Mac) MacDougall had been coming to our church for a year or two with his wife Margie. His son was an active member of our fellowship and told me that while his mother was a believer his father was not. Still, he came. He asked me if I would ride with him to see his brother who was dying of cancer in a town an hour away because he was wanted his brother to talk with a pastor. I joined Mac and Margie for the drive. We arrived, and I soon discovered his brother had recently come to Christ through a local pastor. Mac's brother shared openly about his new faith, and I could see his unexpected witness moved Mac. We headed home with Mac driving. Margie and I were conversing when Mac suddenly broke in to share that he didn't know where he would go if he were to die. I began talking to him about faith in Christ. He became quite emotional. The car began to weave on the country road as he tried to focus on my words while driving through his tears. I suggested perhaps we should wait until we got home to finish our talk. I was ready to meet God, but perhaps not that night! He agreed. Soon we sat together in his kitchen, and Mac put his faith in Jesus as his Savior and Lord. He was later baptized and has continued as a faithful member of our church even after Margie went to be with the Lord. I asked Mac why he kept coming to church for so long before he was a Christian. He told me he came because I explained the Bible to him. He was tired of people always trying to "get him saved," but I just explained what the Bible said. The Holy Spirit worked over time to draw Mac to Jesus.[29]

---

29. Christensen, *Friends with Jesus*, 195–96.

## 7

## Shortcuts: Peripheral Routes

Pope Gregory XV coined the term "propaganda" on June 22, 1622, when he established an organization designed to propagate the doctrine of the Roman Catholic Church. The term originally referred to the methods used to spread or promote theological ideas, and the modern concept of propaganda evolved from that point. Some advocate a neutral use of the term and classify propaganda as white, gray, or black, depending on the degree of false information contained in the messaging. Propaganda, in this view, may be positive and healthy, so some describe Christianity as a propaganda organization. In this view, the rise of Christianity in the first four centuries is a classic example of the power of propaganda.[1]

Martin Luther was a master propagandist in this view because he used popular dissatisfaction with clerical practices such as indulgences and papal corruption as a foundation for shaping public opinion and promoted his views through the printing press. Luther exploited the German political instability of his time to his own ends. He used dramatic symbolic gestures such as nailing the 95 theses to the door and the artistic engravings of Lucas Cranach to promote the reformation of the church along with the vigorous and entertaining style of his speaking and writing.[2] Televangelists, celebrity pastors of megachurches, popular Christian writers, and singers

---

1. "It is from Latin—'congregation de propaganda fide'—meaning congregation for propagating the faith of the Roman Catholic Church" (Jowett and O'Donnell, *Propaganda and Persuasion*, 15, 17–18, 42, 49, 158).

2. Jowett and O'Donnell, *Propaganda and Persuasion*, 44–48. The authors also cite as examples of great American propagandists such figures as Thomas Paine, Samuel Adams, Benjamin Franklin, Thomas Jefferson, and George Washington. They point to the Declaration of Independence as one of the great propaganda documents of all time. Benjamin Franklin understood the psychology behind the modern propaganda movement today according to the authors (51–57).

would all be considered propagandists for their promotional skills under the neutral definition of propaganda.

However, propaganda is normally considered a pejorative term because it is most often connected with manipulation, distortion, and deceit. Propaganda is a form of unethical influence because it restricts a listener's freedom of choice by intentionally avoiding a fair presentation of all the facts necessary for an informed decision. A propagandist contrives the conditions for persuasion in a manner that coerces compliance through half-truths and emotional appeals. Propaganda works by using motivational devices that trigger acquiescence from the audience without an examination of all the evidence. It usually involves one-sided and simplistic methods of influence. Propaganda uses methods like name-calling, slogans, misleading generalizations, straw man arguments, bullying, and red-flag words to trigger emotional responses from listeners. Therefore, neither Martin Luther nor the early Christians were propagandists in the normal usage of the term today.[3]

There are five characteristics of propaganda the persuasive preacher should avoid. First, propaganda controls the flow of information to maintain consistency in messaging. Second, it deliberately misuses or misrepresents the facts via outright lies or half-truths. Third, it serves the interests of the propagandist at the expense of the one receiving the information. Fourth, it utilizes rhetorical devices, which make it very difficult for the recipient to exercise any significant freedom of choice in the matter. Fifth, it exploits people and symbols to accomplish the objectives of the propagandist.

Marketing, like propaganda, is a term that can be used in a neutral sense but often slides into negative connotations associated with peddling a product to unwary consumers. George Barna, one of the foremost Christian marketers, popularized the term for evangelical ministries. As a result, marketing methods have shaped the church growth movement to the point where evangelism is commonly viewed as a form of marketing. When we lead another person to accept Christ as Savior, "a marketing transaction has occurred."[4] Barna is quick to point out conversion is ultimately the work of the Holy Spirit, and we merely function as middlemen in the process. Furthermore, ministry must function fairly and honestly,

---

3. Jowett and O'Donnell, *Propaganda and Persuasion*, 15; Henry, *Baker's Dictionary of Christian Ethics*, 541; Macquarrie, *Dictionary of Christian Ethics*, 278; Harrison, *Encyclopedia of Biblical and Christian Ethics*, 333.

4. Barna, *Step-by-Step Guide to Church Marketing*, 20–21.

and we must not compromise the truth. These are excellent modifiers for the marketing methods of evangelical ministries. However, the bottom line is ministry is marketing, and preachers are marketers in the view of many evangelical leaders today.

If marketing is strictly a neutral concept, then, like propaganda, we all market the message in one form or another. Every church advertises and promotes its events, and we present the gospel using styles of dress and music that will communicate to the world. We want our witness to be winsome, so we adjust the way we speak to the needs of the people without compromising the message. Unfortunately, the danger of marketing, like propaganda, is marketing methods become more important than the message. As pastors become obsessed with the latest and greatest gadgets promoted by the marketing gurus, the methods bury the message.[5] If evangelism becomes merely a transactional event, then we are nothing more than modern sophists guilty of the very failures Paul warned us about in the first century (1 Cor 1:18—2:5). Marketing, like propaganda, degenerates quickly into unethical influence, turning preachers into peddlers, and ministries into merchants.

Paul warned we are not to be like many preachers in the first century who "peddled the word of God" to the world (2 Cor 2:17). The word translated "peddling" meant to merchandise God's word, and carried a distinctly negative connotation in Paul's day. The noun referred to a retailer and was used in the Septuagint for wine merchants who watered down the wine for greater profits (Isa 1:22). Philosophers, like Plato, described the sophists who marketed their teaching for money with this word. It became synonymous with deceitful hawking of merchandise for unfair profits—profiteering. The prophet Zechariah foresaw the day when "there will be no Canaanite" in the temple (Zech 14:21). The word "Canaanite" referred to the traders or merchants from Phoenicia who sold their wares in the Fish Gate and controlled the financial exchanges at the temple.[6] Jesus undoubtedly saw the same huckstering in the temple in his day, which led to his cleansing of the "robber's den" (Matt 21:12–13). There is no room for mercenaries in the ministry.

---

5. Hull, "Is the Church Growth Movement Really Working?," 141–42.
6. Windisch, "kapēleuō" 3:603–5; Rienecker, *Linguistic Key*, 458.

## Branding the Gospel

Crowds streamed into downtown Atlanta in 2005 for the second annual MegaFest, an event created by T. D. Jakes's "Potter's House" ministry. Since then, MegaFest has become a major evangelical event, drawing hundreds of thousands of people to places like the Kay Bailey Hutchison Convention Center in Dallas. Popular entertainment figures like Oprah Winfrey and Steve Harvey have regularly dotted the program along with Christian singers and speakers. The four-day events mixed spiritual messages and prayer services with gospel aerobics classes, self-help workshops, food, entertainment, and commercial opportunities. Spawned by the growing number of megachurches across America that are skilled at marketing, MegaFest seamlessly meshed spiritual and commercial brands together into one event. Young evangelicals increasingly enjoy the easy syncretism that exists between commercialism and religion because it makes them feel part of the American mainstream.

Corporate brands like Coca-Cola, Ford, American Airlines, Bank of America, and Bank of the West sponsored the events in exchange for logos, ads, and promotional brochures both at the event and in the churches promoting it. Branding experts consider the evangelical brand worth courting for commercial reasons. The product of the evangelical brand is Jesus Christ and linking to that brand name is desirable for corporate sponsors seeking to sell their products to evangelicals who are considered highly brand loyal. David Melancon observed brands "tap into people's need to belong," but warned "when you are using people's core beliefs to sell a product, you are tapping precious emotions."[7] So, the gospel has become a brand that sells everything from t-shirts to coffee mugs! Branding the gospel is big business.

Branding is "the marketing practice of creating a name, symbol, or design that identifies and differentiates a product from other products."[8] Branding has become essential for growing ministries, according to experts in Christian marketing. A church brands itself to communicate who they are and distinguish themselves from other churches in the area. Branding sets the church apart from other church brands. A logo is not just a symbol; it promotes the perception the church wants to communicate about itself to those it is trying to reach.[9] The age of mass marketing is over. Today is

---

7. J.v., "Preaching the Brand Gospel," lines 163–64. See also Kuo, "MegaFest."

8. Koepke, "Branding the Gospel," lines 5–6, citing a definition from *Entrepreneur* magazine without further documentation.

9. Reising, *Church Marketing 101*, 155–74.

the day of niche marketing. The goal is to create a niche market and then target the specific people in that niche market. Ministries try to segment the market and appeal to a target audience to be successful as a church. The assumption, the theory, is other churches will target other audiences so that the net effect is to reach the whole world for Christ through segmented ministries. Each church specializes their ministry in order to achieve excellence and reach their target audience effectively.[10]

What happens when all the churches in each geographical region target the same audience? Does branding to reach a niche market reflect the intended scope of the Great Commission (Acts 1:8)? Are churches merely different retailers offering different products to consumers, a virtual religious shopping mall? Do churches grow because they have better marketing methods than other churches? These questions and many others raise concerns about our influence as preachers. The reality is most churches are targeting the same or similar niche markets, so the best marketers pull people from other churches in the region. More importantly, what does an emphasis on marketing our ministries do to the way we influence others? Do we place our emphasis more on our marketing budgets than we do on the Christian message? Will we flavor our message with popular themes like love, acceptance, and grace, and avoid doctrines like sin, repentance, and self-denial? Do we put our faith in our methods more than God's truth? Does our self-promotion obscure the centrality of the cross?

Marketing is "all the business activity involved in the moving of goods from the producer to the consumer, including selling, advertising, packaging."[11] The emphasis in marketing is on the "moving of goods," not the goods themselves. The emphasis in marketing the gospel is on our methods, not our message. The subtle, seductive danger of marketing the gospel is the message loses its centrality in our ministries. Marketing methods may get the attention of people, but it should be so they will look closely at the message. The message is vital. If people come to our church because of the methods but never engage with the central message of Christianity, then we have failed to be persuasive preachers. Marketing is not the central route to Christian persuasion. Marketing is a peripheral route to help people engage with the gospel. The goal is the gospel, not the methods. We can use peripheral routes to help people consider the message, but they must engage with the central message—the Logos—to become Christians.

10. Barna, *Step-by-Step Guide to Church Marketing*, 28–30.
11. *Webster's New World College Dictionary*, s.v. "marketing."

Richard Reising has a helpful definition of marketing that points us in the right direction. He defines marketing as "the management of perception."[12] In other words, marketing gets people's attention like a good introduction to a sermon. It makes people receptive. I would say the purpose of marketing is to prepare people to focus on the message. After that, marketing has no value. Marketing is not evangelism. Marketing is preevangelism. It sets the stage or gives us a platform to point to the message, but the message alone is of primary importance. Logos is the central route of Christian persuasion. To the degree people are ready to elaborate on the central message, we do not need to use marketing or any other peripheral routes. To the degree they are not ready to elaborate on the central message, we use peripheral routes to draw people to the message. We do not want anyone to believe because of our marketing; we want them to believe because they examined and accepted the Logos, the central message of the Christian faith.

## Other Peripheral Routes of Persuasion

People are bombarded with often-conflicting information today, so they make many decisions based on triggers or cues that are shortcuts to examining the message in detail. Peripheral routes of persuasion are shortcuts designed to help people make choices with minimal investments of time and thought. The result is many decisions, even spiritual decisions, are often made without careful analysis or thorough investigation. Marketing, like propaganda, works for that reason. However, choices based on peripheral cues are temporary and malleable. For this reason, a child growing up in a Christian home can make a decision for Christ that she easily rejects in college. She made a choice based on peripheral routes of persuasion. Many people choose to follow Christ for social, cultural, and economic reasons. Missiologists long ago identified "rice Christians" as people who made professions of faith because the missionaries gave them rice to eat. Such conversions are not real conversions even though they appear real. Peripheral routes of persuasion are shortcuts leading to temporary commitments.

The central route of persuasion engages the listener with the message. To the degree the listener is prepared to elaborate on the message, the listener is ready to be persuaded to make a decision. He will devote mental and emotional resources to examine the message carefully (See diagram).

12. Reising, *Church Marketing 101*, 23.

## THE CENTRAL ROUTE OF PERSUASION

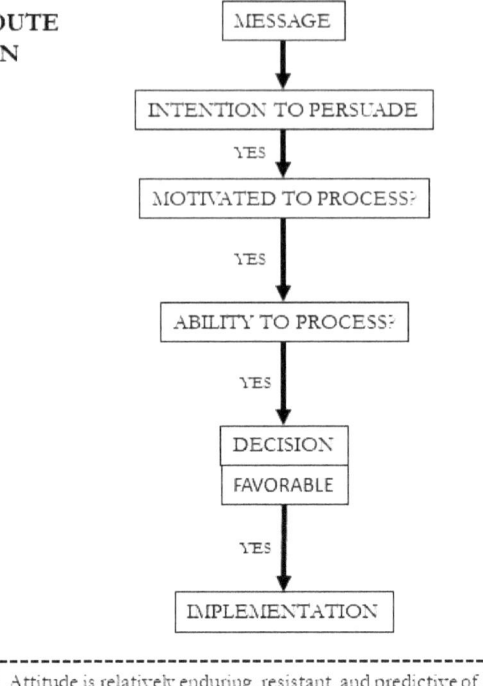

(Adapted from Petty and Cacioppo, *Communication and Persuasion*, p.4)

The persuasive preacher begins with the message and intends to persuade the listener to accept that message. The recipient is ready to elaborate on the message, so time is spent helping the person grasp the core issues in as winsome and effective a way as possible. The persuasive preacher urges the recipient to make a well-informed decision without coercion. Once the listener decides, the persuasive preacher helps the recipient implement the implications of that decision in his/her life.

Peripheral routes of persuasion change the perception of the recipient and prepare the recipient to think about the message. To the degree the recipient is unwilling to examine the message carefully, peripheral routes of persuasion help move the recipient to process the information. The central and peripheral routes of persuasion are not mutually exclusive. Often, they are used simultaneously and in concert with one another in the persuasion process. There are many peripheral routes of persuasion, but I will highlight six common routes used by persuasive preachers.

## Reciprocity

The principle of reciprocation is embedded in human nature and established by human culture. The rule of reciprocity says, "that we should try to repay, in kind, what another person has provided us." The reciprocity principle is so powerful and universal every society down through human history has employed and reinforced it in some form.[13] There was a strong reciprocity system in the Hellenistic culture in which Paul functioned in the first century.[14] The principle is applied in almost every avenue of life, from politics to religion, from sales to friendship.[15] Bill Hybels invoked the principle for evangelism.[16] A powerful corollary to the principle is we not only feel obligated to repay favors, but we feel obligated to repay a concession made to us by granting a concession in return. The principle is so powerful that a person who violates the principle is generally disliked by the group or society.[17] The principle of reciprocity can be easily exploited by compliance professionals who understand it well. Politicians give us what we want in exchange for our support. Marketers and propagandists know how to use reciprocity to their advantage in achieving their goals.

Why do Christian organizations start fundraising promotions with a request for a five-hundred-dollar donation only to lower the request to five dollars before the end of the call? It is because offering a concession makes us feel obligated to give something. Free books, cards, or key chains are effective tools for getting us to give to the organization. Once we accept the gift, they know we will be more likely to give a gift in return. For many years, I sent out birthday cards to everyone in our church. I had my secretary purchase cards in bulk and then address them for the month. I would spend an hour or two signing cards at the beginning of each month, and she would mail them out each week. People were touched by this simple gesture and surprised I would remember their birthdays! One church I know has a team of people bake loaves of bread each week. Every new visitor to the

---

13. Cialdini, *Influence*, 29–31.
14. Danker, "Paul's Debt," 263; Watson, "Rhetorical Analysis of 3 John," 483.
15. Cialdini, *Influence*, 29–65; Zuker, *Seven Secrets of Influence*, 17.
16. Hybels and Mittelberg, *Becoming a Contagious Christian*, 146–47.
17. Cialdini, *Influence*, 45–47.

church receives a brief visit that week and is given a loaf of homemade bread as a thank you for attending the church. Hospital visits and telephone calls are gifts of service we make to people. They are normal parts of every pastoral ministry, and there is nothing wrong with these gifts. We must beware, though, not to exploit the gifts we give to people when it comes time to persuade them to make a decision. We must give without strings, or we are guilty of unethical influence.

I know a man who suffered a horrific snowmobile accident one winter in Maine. He almost died from loss of blood after a collision on the trail and ended up permanently disabled. The man was unable to go back to work at the mill, and the family was struggling to pay their bills. A small local church in the town did what rural churches often do. They reached out to help the family with food and money. At first, the man protested. "I don't go to your church, so why would you want to help me?" The pastor responded, "We would do this for anyone. You don't have to come to our church for us to love you and care about your needs." As time passed, the man and his family eventually came to church. They listened to the messages the preacher taught them and felt the love of the people. They paid attention to the gospel, and eventually the entire family came to Christ and became active members in that church. The reciprocity principle is effective when used to point people to the central message of Christ. Genuine love given to others leads them to consider the message of love contained in the gospel. However, we must never use reciprocity to manipulate people to decide because it is a peripheral route to persuasion.

## Scarcity

Social psychologists experimented in the 1970s using chocolate chip cookies and a cookie jar. Researchers gave half of the participants in an experiment a jar of ten cookies while they gave the other half a jar of two cookies. The participants were asked to taste and rate the cookies. Tasters rated the cookie much higher when it was one of two than when it was one of ten cookies. A second experiment offered the participants a jar of ten cookies and then took it away, replacing it with a jar of two cookies. The response was even stronger than before. Do we want something more when it is continuously scarce or when it has recently become scarce? The answer is clear. Newly experienced scarcity—the loss of something we once had—makes us want it even more.[18]

The scarcity principle, otherwise known as psychological reactance, trades on another one of our human weaknesses for shortcuts to elaboration. FOMO, the fear of missing out, persuasively stirs the emotions of people. Robert Cialdini calls psychological reactance "the rule of the few" and defines it this way: "opportunities seem more valuable to us when their availability is limited."[19] People are attracted to lost options and will work to regain their right to those opportunities. The loss does not even have to be real to evoke emotions. The mere threat of taking something away makes it more attractive, producing an emotional reaction.[20] We want more what we can't have, and we want it even more when it is taken away from us.

Emory Griffin, at that time a professor at Wheaton College, tells the story of his reaction to the possibility of loss. Faculty members at the Christian college were given two free meals a week in the dining hall and encouraged to spend time with students at lunch. He rarely took advantage of the free meals and chose to work in his office throughout the lunch period. The business manager sent out a warning that the free lunch program might be cut because of a lack of funding. Griffin reacted against the potential loss of lunch even though he rarely used the opportunity. He quickly re-established his right to the free lunches by eating with the students and objecting to the threatened loss.[21]

When we feel that an opportunity is scarce, it seems to trigger an emotional reaction, a sense of loss, all out of proportion to the true value of the opportunity. Banned books become bestsellers. Prohibiting a romance between teenagers produces what has been called the Romeo and Juliet effect wherein the romantic feelings grow stronger because of the ban. This is not to say parents should avoid exercising parental control, especially with young teens. It is only to recognize that heavy-handed prohibitions sometimes produce the opposite effect as teens get older. Godly wisdom is needed to guide our young people through the process.

Marketers often use deadlines as a persuasive tool to induce a decision. Deadlines are another form of the scarcity principle. The recipient only has a certain time period before the opportunity is gone. Persuasive preachers use

18. Cialdini, *Influence*, 247–48.
19. Cialdini, *Influence*, 230.
20. Griffin, *Mind Changers*, 50.
21. Griffin, *Mind Changers*, 50.

the scarcity principle when we stress today is the day of salvation. You never know how much time you have. You may walk out of here tonight and never get another opportunity to follow Jesus. The message is true. The warning is real. Many years ago, the famous Billy Graham movie, *Thief in the Night*, was a popular evangelistic tool. I remember serving as a counselor at one of the showings. The theme was clear. Christ could return at any moment, and you might be left behind. Jesus would come like a thief in the night, and if you weren't ready, you were lost. The scarcity principle made the message powerful, but the danger of manipulation was inherent in the method. Someone could choose to follow Christ out of fear, not faith.

## Authority

The authority principle operates on established and valid foundations but may be misused to produce excessive obedience and slavish respect for authority. Every culture faces a dilemma because respect for authority is a core value of an ordered society, and yet respect can go too far, resulting in "authoritarianism."[22] In any group setting, there are usually only a few leaders whose prestige or position can legitimize or delegitimize organizational decisions. These leaders can wield their power ethically for the good of all, or they can abuse their power to control and dominate people in the group. Leaders who demand loyalty to themselves above all other relationships produce an authoritarian structure in the organization that corrupts the mission and the people. Sadly, we have seen many examples of pastors who slowly degenerate into authoritarian models of leadership, damaging the churches they lead.[23]

God vests biblical authority in pastors as shepherds of his people (1 Thess 5:12–13; 1 Tim 5:17; Heb 13:17). However, God also warns authority must not be misused and pastors should model for their people the humility of the chief Shepherd, Jesus Christ (1 Pet 5:1–5). Pastors must always maintain a balanced biblical authority as they lead their churches. We will answer to our Lord for the way we lead his people in the church (1 Pet 5:4; 1 Cor 4:1–5), and we must recognize God expects the people we

22. Woodward, *Persuasion and Influence in American Life*, 165–66, 174–77; Cialdini, *Influence*, 203–28.

23. Stetzer, "Power and Pastors," para. 3; Shellnut, "Acts 29 CEO Removed," paras. 1, 4, 32; Shellnutt and Lee, "Mark Driscoll Resigns from Mars Hill," para. 4; Shellnutt, "Darrin Patrick Removed," para. 2; Shellnutt, "Willow Creek Investigation," para. 6; Ross, "Sex, Money . . . Pride?," para. 3; Enroth, *Churches that Abuse*.

lead to hold us accountable as leaders (1 Tim 5:17–22; 3:1–13). Influence is power, and the way we wield our influence must temper leadership with love and humility.

There are many ways pastors invoke their authority in church settings. Positional authority can lead us to throw our weight around to get what we want done. Titles are one of the easiest markers of authority we can use. Titles like "Pastor," "Reverend," and "Doctor," can subtly establish our authority over others in the church. Credentialing is a symbol of power, so our academic degrees become tools of influence in some churches. We display our diplomas on our office walls and accept the titles in public settings. I remember a big debate in our church when I became the pastor was about my title. My wife and I had been part of the church before I became the pastor since I was the academic dean at the local Bible college. We were just "Dave and Janie" until I became the pastor. Many insisted I could no longer be "Just Dave." They wanted to call me "Pastor Christensen," but my father would forever be "Pastor Christensen" in my mind, so we settled on "Pastor Dave" or "PD" for short. When I retired after 28 years, I told them I was now "JD," "Just Dave" again!

Church attendance is a primary marker of success and is often used to credential our authority as pastors. Our culture is so success-oriented that greater attendance validates our authority as preachers in the perspective of our listeners. The larger the church, the greater our influence. Language can become a way to establish authority. Theological jargon or technical language is known as "mystification"[24] when used to pull rank on the less knowledgeable in our churches. People are not as likely to challenge our authority when we use such language to make our point. God-talk in particular is a powerful persuader, especially when we invoke God's will to validate our plans. The use of Greek or Hebrew words in our sermons reinforces our superiority, as do specialized theological terms. These methods of enhancing our authority are peripheral modes of persuasion, which by themselves have temporal limitations.

Pastor Wes was on the line. I picked up the phone and, after the preliminaries, he asked to see the confidential file on one of our students at the Bible college who was a member of his church. I told him I couldn't give him that information because it was protected by law, and it was unethical for me to violate the confidentiality of the student. I had seen some red flags about Pastor Wes for a while, but this event led me to express my concerns directly

---

24. Woodward, *Persuasion and Influence in American Life*, 166.

to him about his growing authoritarianism. Unfortunately, he did not agree with my advice, and we never spoke again until shortly before his death.

Pastor Wes was a soft-spoken man and gifted Bible teacher. At first, his ministry was excellent, and the church had an effective ministry. He seemed to be the epitome of a humble, biblical, and effective pastor, but over time he slowly grew more controlling in his ministry. Only certain preachers were qualified to teach in his church. I was one of the few who enjoyed his approval, but that changed when I disagreed with him about the student from his church. He dismissed the members of the Board of Deacons because they were unqualified as spiritual leaders. People began to leave the church as he grew more controlling. He removed from membership all who were no longer attending and any who disagreed with his leadership. All decisions, no matter how small, required his approval. It was best for the church, he said, because he was protecting them from theological error. Next, the few remaining members voted to put the church property in his name, and he had absolute control of all church finances.

Pastor Wes became involved with theophostic prayer and delved deeply into repressed memories, particularly of women in the church. His repressed memory therapy led to the breakup of at least one marriage as the husband left the church while his wife remained loyal to Pastor Wes. The family was torn apart by the accusations of one daughter under the control of Pastor Wes who accused her father of sexual abuse. He was eventually exonerated and reunited with his children after a long, hard legal battle. Frontpage headlines told the story of the authoritarian ways of Pastor Wes.[25] I was part of a large group of evangelical pastors who met and published a statement condemning his pastoral methods. Slowly the church declined until it eventually disbanded due to his poor health and eventual death.

Ron Enroth, in his book *Churches that Abuse*, writes "the desire to control others and to exercise power over people" is part of our human nature. Pastors are hardly exempt from that temptation. Abusive authority in churches develops slowly as pastors put control mechanisms in place. Benign leadership turns authoritarian as pastors become aware of how to use their influential power in ever-increasing ways.[26] The result is unethical influence. The story is not always as dramatic as that of Pastor Wes, but the temptation toward heavy-handed pastoral control is very damaging to a

---

25. "Baptist Pastor's Therapy," *Bangor Daily News*, May 14, 2002.
26. Enroth, *Churches that Abuse*, 216–17.

church. Biblical and limited pastoral authority is effective, but authoritarianism is unbiblical and a destructive influence.

## Fear

Fear is a legitimate and powerful persuader. It is also biblical. "The fear of the Lord is the beginning of wisdom," Solomon wrote (Prov 1:7; Ps 111:10; Job 28:28). Paul, after talking about the fact we will all appear before the judgment seat of Christ, wrote: "Therefore, knowing the fear of the Lord, we persuade men" (2 Cor 5:11). Research has demonstrated fear works to persuade people. However, research has also demonstrated a curious and surprising side effect of fear motivation. Medium or low fear works effectively, but high or excessive fear is counterproductive. Up to a point, fear works to persuade people, but after that point, fear becomes ineffective as a tool of persuasion.

How do we know when we reach the point where fear no longer works? Some people argue any use of fear as a motivating method is wrong. I disagree. Fear is a legitimate if peripheral, route to persuasion. However, there are limits to our use of fear we must remember. Emory Griffin identifies three reasons for resistance to high fear motivation that should limit our use of the method.[27]

First, high fear brings avoidance because people no longer want to think about what makes them afraid. When a person says, "I was scared out of my mind," it leads them to avoid considering anything related to what scared them. It is too terrifying to think about, so they avoid the subject. As preachers, we must be sensitive to the body language of people and realize the person is going to be too scared to elaborate mentally on the message. They will turn us off or tune us out. Fear is a peripheral route designed to move people to consider the central message, but if they are too afraid to consider it then we have failed in our persuasion.

Second, high fear depends upon probability. Low fear works to get people to consider the message because it seems probable or likely to happen. High fear often seems improbable. The worse the threat, the less likely it seems to us. The listener thinks, "It will never happen to me." The threat of hell seems remote to most people, so they ignore the message. The thought their marriage might break up is more realistic, so it is more effective at leading them to consider their need for Christ. The effectiveness of an appeal

---

27. Griffin, *Mind Changers*, 67–77.

to fear increases as the probability of what is feared becomes more likely. A person who is facing death is more likely to want to get things right with God and so more willing to consider the message of Christianity.

Third, high fear demands a solution. Fear boomerangs when fright outweighs the credibility of the solution being offered. If people say, "I don't think it will do any good," when they hear our solution, then the message will not be very persuasive. The fear principle involves two steps in the process. We must show people what they should fear, and then we must help them consider the solution to their fears. If the solution does not reasonably address the fear, then they will not listen. We can overcome the resistance as we establish our credibility with the person. Our relationship with the person helps them trust us so they will listen to our message. The solution is more reasonable because the preacher is credible. Fear works as a peripheral route to persuasion intended to draw the listener to consider the message itself.

## Guilt

Guilt is a powerful, persuasive tool and is probably the most common tactic used by preachers to motivate their listeners.[28] Certainly there is a legitimate use of guilt in the church when it comes to behavior that violates God's revealed standards (Lev 5:17; Jas 2:10). Jesus stressed guilt to challenge his listeners in the Sermon on the Mount (Matt 5:21–22). Paul laid a heavy guilt trip on the Christians in Corinth to judge the sexually immoral man in their church (1 Cor 5:1–13) and spoke of being guilty of the body and blood of the Lord to call them to self-examination (1 Cor 11:27–28). The goal of guilt is to lead us to grace (Rom 6:23; Gal 6:1). Guilt is good when it draws us to Jesus. It is a peripheral route of persuasion to lead a person to consider God's offer of grace.

However, guilt can be misused and abused by persuasive preachers to control others in the church. God's laws are clear, but we can extend those laws to stress obligations we place on people through our preaching.[29] Sometimes preachers fail to distinguish between the oughts of God and the oughts of man, the thou shalt nots of God and the thou shalt nots of the preacher. We can elevate our human convictions to the level of divine obligation. Guilt trips are one of the easiest weapons of manipulation in the arsenal of a preacher.

28. Griffin, *Mind Changers*, 36–37.
29. Backus, *Telling Each Other the Truth*, 57.

Guilt works, in the short term, producing immediate persuasive benefits. The listeners do what the preacher wants done. This quick result is the attraction of guilt as a peripheral route of persuasion.

The long-term effects of guilt motivation are dangerous in three ways. First, guilt, like fear, brings avoidance. Research demonstrates guilt will cause people to avoid whatever makes them feel guilty. As a pastor, I have observed this process time and again. People feel guilty, so they pull away from the church because it makes them feel worse. They stop attending church, which exacerbates the guilt even more as they spiral downward spiritually. Second, guilt leads to antagonism. People who feel manipulated by guilt tend to dislike the person or place that made them feel guilty. The pastor guilts someone to serve in the children's ministry. They do it for a time but resent the pastor for manipulating them into doing a job they didn't want to do. Third, guilt brings outward compliance, but there is little inward commitment. Next time the person refuses to serve in the children's ministry because he/she was never committed to it in the first place. Those who are guilty of sin return to their old habits as soon as no one is monitoring their compliance.[30]

The church in Corinth had a problem. They were tolerating a horrible sin in their midst. A man was carrying on an immoral sexual relationship that was being ignored by the church out of pride that they were so loving. We can easily anesthetize guilt through denial and rationalization. Paul challenges them to exercise church discipline and remove the man from their fellowship (1 Cor 5). The church descends into conflict as factions develop both for and against Paul, whose heart is broken by the infighting. Later, Paul gets word from Titus they did address the sin, and the man repented of his sin. However, the church was still embroiled in their church fight over the matter. Some self-righteous members felt victorious and were intent on making the man pay for his sinfulness. Paul challenges the church to forgive and comfort the man so he will not be "overwhelmed by excessive sorrow" (2 Cor 2:7). They need to reaffirm their love for him and restore him to fellowship so guilt does not destroy him.

Sin may swamp us with sorrow if motivated by legalism or perfectionism. Paul goes on to warn that God's guilt leads to repentance, while false guilt destroys the soul (2 Cor 7:10). Guilt needs grace, or it becomes destructive, consuming the soul. Perfectionism is guilt without grace. It leaves no way out for the guilty soul. David Seamands, in his book *Healing*

---

30. Griffin, *Mind Changers*, 61–66.

*for Damaged Emotions*, writes: "Perfectionism is the most disturbing emotional problem among evangelical Christians. It walks into my office more often than any other single Christian hang-up."[31] False guilt leaves no way out. No way out breeds hopelessness. Hopelessness leads to helplessness, which leads to despair. Biblical guilt shows people how they can find release from their past through the redeeming grace of Jesus Christ. Biblical guilt points to repentance, which is freeing not controlling, liberating not imprisoning. Guilt as a peripheral route of persuasion must always lead back to the central message of God's grace.

## Conformity

The conformity or social proof principle is a powerful but peripheral tool of persuasion that has been well established by research testing and observation in a wide variety of settings.[32] Social proof is certainly valid in many situations where corporate decisions must be made in a timely manner. Church business meetings often involve elements of the conformity principle as the congregation struggles to make a corporate decision. After four years of work, planning, and open discussions, our church was finally ready to vote on a building proposal from a local firm. We gathered for a time of prayer and discussion, seeking to come to a consensus. Our building committee had presented all the information to the church both in person and in print the month before. Now it was time to vote. Two of our older women were the first to speak after our time of prayer. Both women were highly respected by others in the church for their spiritual wisdom. They both said they believed God was leading our small church to take this step of faith and build the new worship center. One by one, others followed their lead until it was obvious there was consensus in our church. No one spoke against it. We called for the vote, but it was superfluous at that point. The decision had already been made. Social proof is a unifying principle in a community of faith.

However, conformity, as a peripheral tool in persuasion, applies group pressure on individuals to conform to the group consensus. One family in our church remained silent during the meeting, but I later found out they were leaving our church because they disagreed with the flat roof structure being proposed for the building. They didn't say anything in opposition

---

31. Seamands, *Healing for Damaged Emotions*, 78.
32. Cialdini, *Influence*, 115–62; Griffin, *Mind Changers*, 193–212.

because they felt pressured by the group. Our decision-making process had been sound. We offered multiple opportunities for dissent throughout the process and listened to the ideas of many so that by the time the decision was made there was a strong consensus in the church. Even so, one felt silenced in the process.

Social psychologists call it "groupthink," the process where individual members of a group accept the decision of the group because they are conforming to the group consensus. While it can be a positive process, groupthink is often negative when alternatives are ignored, and dissent is discouraged.[33] Groupthink can lead to poor decisions if the church body fails to gather and examine all the information needed to make a wise decision and give full opportunity for all ideas to be discussed. Groupthink can also be used to bring subtle social pressure on individuals making personal decisions. Evangelists who "salt" the audience with "ringers" who leave their seats scattered around the auditorium and come forward at the altar call to encourage people to decide to follow Christ are using a form of social proof in decision making.[34] The conformity principle is a peripheral tool and should not be used to apply direct pressure to the will of the person being persuaded. There is no internal commitment regarding the issue, and the person is likely to return to his previous viewpoint as soon as the pressure is removed.

Does crowding a room facilitate persuasion? Yes. Emory Griffin tested this hypothesis using multiple groups in a classroom. He found a crowded room resulted in the individual members of the audience being persuaded much more effectively by the speech as measured by their responses on a survey. But why? He tested the matter more carefully and found the primary reason was the greater level of excitement produced by a crowded room. Crowds produce persuasive excitement. They used this information in the church. The average attendance was 250 in each of two services in the large auditorium which seated 400. The chapel seated 200 people, so they decided to switch the early service to the chapel and see what would happen. The effect was immediate. The greater excitement led to increased attendance until the average attendance in the early service was 300. Crowding a room was an effective influencer.[35]

---

33. Schmidt, "Groupthink," lines 1–4; Bolt and Myers, *Human Connection*, 84–107.
34. Cialdini, *Influence*, 118.
35. Griffin, *Mind Changers*, 57–60.

We noticed a similar phenomenon in reverse. We had been crowded in two services in our multipurpose room while we built our new worship center. Our multipurpose room seated 150, and we were 80 percent full at both services. Our new worship center seated 300. After settling into the new worship center, we noticed a loss of excitement in the service. The singing was not the same, and the emotional dynamic of the service was bland. The people felt scattered in the larger space, so I temporarily took out seats to draw people together, and it helped. However, any time we joined together back in our multipurpose room for a smaller gathering, people always noted the greater excitement of being crowded together in a smaller space.

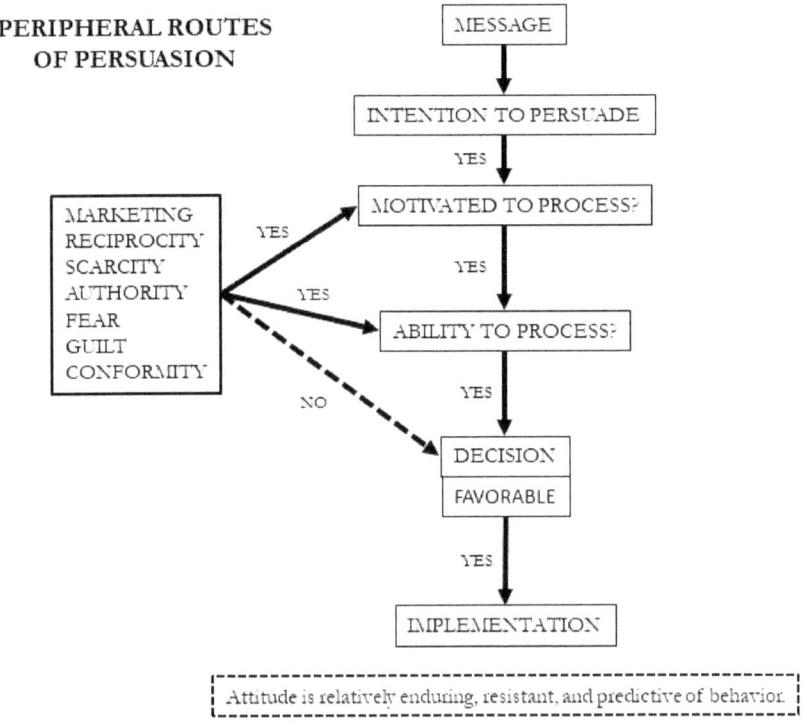

(Adapted from Petty and Cacioppo, *Communication and Persuasion*, p.4)

## SHORTCUTS: PERIPHERAL ROUTES

The persuasive preacher uses peripheral routes to influence listeners to process the message (See diagram). If the listeners are unwilling or unable to process the message, then the preacher uses the peripheral triggers to engage them. Ethical persuasion avoids using peripheral routes to apply direct pressure on the decision since the listener would then be persuaded for the wrong reasons, and the decision would be temporary at best. We use peripheral routes of persuasion to draw the recipient back to the central message, the core issue, we advocate. We want our listeners to elaborate and internalize the message before making a decision. Only then will we see changed attitudes that are enduring and predictive of changed behavior.

# 8

# Ethical Controls: Process

THERE IS SOME OF the manipulator in every person, Everett Shostrum argued in his seminal study of influence.[1] He divided his eight types of manipulators into two broad categories. There are "top dog" and "under dog" kinds of manipulators. Top dog manipulators are aggressive, controlling, and dictatorial. Under dog manipulators are sensitive, warm, and supportive, but all manipulators exhibit certain fundamental characteristics. Manipulators are deceptive, using hidden agendas to influence others. Manipulators control others to get them to do what the manipulator wants them to do. Manipulators view relationships through the lens of two alternatives: to control or be controlled. Some manipulators control others through weakness and need. Other manipulators bully people, coercing them to follow the manipulator. Each of us has the potential for manipulation as we participate in group settings. However, all manipulators can become healthy leaders by transforming their natural tendencies into leadership styles that motivate others to share common aspirations and mutual goals. The objective of all effective leaders is to turn their manipulative methods into healthy persuasion that leads to enduring change and mutual commitment.

All effective leaders know where they are going, why they are going there, how to get others to join them in the journey, and what are the ethical methods that will influence others to want to go where they are leading them. Kouzes and Posner, in their classic book on leadership, define it "as the art of mobilizing others *to want* to struggle for shared aspirations."[2] The wanting is the key to ethical influence. They discuss the difference between a calculating style of leadership and a committing style of leadership, which

---

1. Shostrum, *Man the Manipulator*, 36–55.
2. Kouzes and Posner, *Leadership Challenge*, 30 (emphasis added).

they call "transformational leadership."[3] A calculating style of leadership calculates where the leader wants the group to go and what it will take to get there with no concern for how the process will affect the individuals in the group. A transformational style of leadership seeks to move the group toward shared aspirations so both the individual members and the leader are transformed in the process. Transformational leadership is leadership that truly, effectively, and ethically persuades others.

Persuasive preachers will have the greatest influence on people when we are the least manipulative because the influence will last, and lives will be transformed by God's Spirit.[4] We need an ethical model to guide our persuasive process. The ethical model should establish verifiable norms by which we can measure our influence. Second, the model should possess a flexibility of application to a variety of situations. Third, the model should possess the ability to balance conflicting tensions. And fourth, the model should promote a grid for processing Christian influence (See diagram).

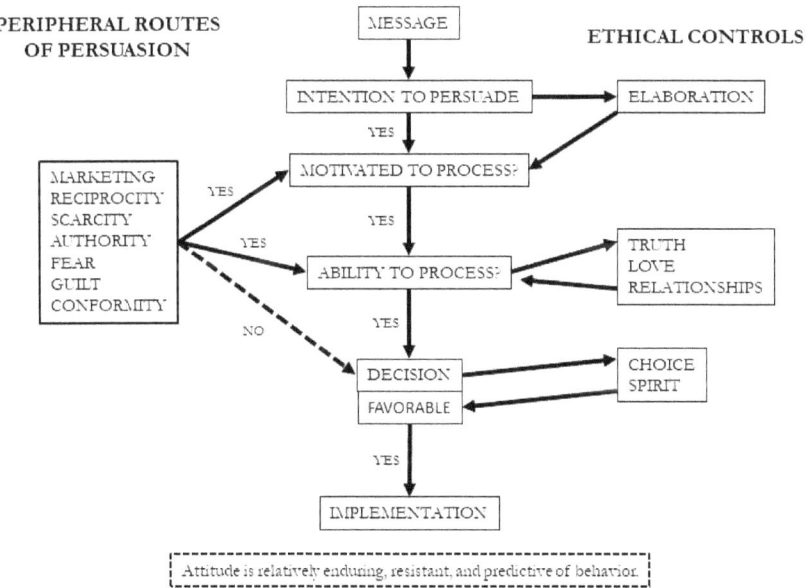

(Adapted from Petty and Cacioppo, *Communication and Persuasion*, p.4)

3. Kouzes and Posner, *Leadership Challenge*, 133.
4. Griffin, *Mind Changers*, 6; Overstreet, *Persuasive Preaching*, 163–69.

## Elaboration: Influence's Intention

"The end never justifies the means," is one of those trite clichés we should scrap. The line is inadequate at best. Purpose can be a sound justification for the means of persuasion and is at least a partial basis for ethical influence.[5] If purpose (end) does not justify means, what does? Our intention, our objective, is a primary factor in deciding whether our persuasion is appropriate at all. This is not to say a good end justifies every means of persuasion. Shady methods are not justified by a good end. It is to say, however, that the first ethical consideration in evaluating any persuasion must be the purpose of that persuasion. What is the intent of the persuader? Is it a good intention or an evil intention? Influence's intention is the first check on the ethics of any persuasive attempt.[6]

Elaboration is the goal of Christian persuasion. The persuasive preacher should not "wrangle about words" but should focus on the "word of truth" avoiding "empty chatter" that leads to "further ungodliness," Paul argued (2 Tim 2:14–16). Placing our emphasis on "Logos," understood as facts and reason, is a significant factor in Christian ethics.[7] D. Martyn Lloyd-Jones argued preachers should appeal to the mind as the central focus and not put direct pressure on the will.[8] Duane Litfin believed the intention of the Christian communicator should not go beyond comprehension of the message.[9] Others have properly pointed out such an exclusive emphasis on the mind creates a "cult of reason." Reason is not the only method of making a decision, even reason directed by the Holy Spirit. Other factors, including emotions, may trigger the decision quite apart from pure reason if there is such a thing.[10]

The critical issue in Christian persuasion is less about comprehension than it is about elaboration. The persuader intends to seek elaboration, not merely comprehension. The persuasive preacher wants the listener to process the information by devoting his mental, emotional, and perhaps even physical resources to examine the message being presented by the persuader.

---

5. Brembeck and Howell, *Persuasion*, 452–53.
6. Johannesen, *Ethics and Persuasion*, 14.
7. McLaughlin, *Ethics of Persuasive Preaching*, 130–33.
8. Lloyd-Jones, *Preaching and Preachers*, 271.
9. Litfin, *St. Paul's Theology of Proclamation*, 261.
10. Johannesen, *Ethics and Persuasion*, 10, 35–38, 87.

Results-oriented preaching is not sophistry.[11] All persuaders intend that the listener assimilate the message (Logos). Assimilation, however, is much more than comprehension. Emory Griffin calls it "internalization."[12] Petty and Cacioppo call it "elaboration."[13] The apostle Paul avoided attempts to impress his audience with sophistry, but he wanted the audience to elaborate on the "word of the cross" (1 Cor 1:18).

The issue of long-term persuasion centers around the likelihood that the listener will elaborate on the information by processing or internalizing it. If the person is motivated to process the information, then the next step is to find out if they have the ability to process the information. If at any of these stages the answer is "No" then peripheral triggers must be used to stimulate the person to make a peripheral attitude change. The result of this peripheral attitude change is not yielding, but processing. The person is now ready and able to process the information being presented. Only at this point can attitude change (yielding) begin to take place, and new beliefs/behavior take shape (see diagram).

The objective of elaboration is to encourage responsiveness so the listener processes the information before arriving at the point of decision. Elaboration focuses on changing attitudes that are predictive of behavior. There is a direct correlation between attitude and conduct, belief and behavior. The ethical persuader focuses first on attitude change rather than behavior change, and the result is lasting change. Ben Patterson considers this to be a critical distinction. He writes, "in selling, you change a person's behavior without changing beliefs. In persuasion, you change a person's beliefs and, therefore, behavior."[14]

Social psychology has promoted the concept that actions and attitudes are involved in a reciprocal relationship whereby actions produce attitude change. The result is marketers seek to induce a change in action, knowing it will bring about a change in attitude. A lesser action leads to greater commitment. The seller pushes for a minor agreement, knowing it will pressure the recipient into a major decision. However, changed behaviors do not last unless there is a corresponding change in belief. Methods that stress taking some action (public invitations) are persuasive, but

---

11. McLaughlin, *Ethics of Persuasive Preaching*, 129–30.
12. Griffin, *Getting Together*, 175–80.
13. Petty and Cacioppo, *Communication and Persuasion*, 4.
14. Patterson, "Preacher as Pitchman," 73.

if such actions do not result in further elaboration of the message, then the belief change will be short-lived.

Healthy persuasion stresses a thorough examination of the information to produce a willingness to implement the desired actions in life. Abuses of persuasion fall under two categories. There are "abuses of the ends served" and "abuses of the means employed."[15] If the ends are selfish, the persuasion is abusive. If the means employed trigger responses designed to gain compliance without understanding, the persuasion is abusive. In both cases, if the persuader keeps elaboration as the goal, then the persuasion will be more ethical. Abusive preachers reject outside feedback, discourage questions, and do not tolerate criticism. All of these controls are markers of unethical persuasion. Propaganda restricts the flow of information so the recipient is discouraged from asking questions outside the restricted area determined by the persuader. No deviation from the party line and no critical thinking are allowed.[16] These methods of persuasion intentionally avoid any possibility of elaboration on the part of the listener.

Cult leaders use a variety of methods to avoid elaboration. The leader will speak in a manner that seems logical but is not. Such a speaker intends to produce a sense of detachment in the listener. The cultic speaker will ramble and contradict himself, but the speech sounds logical while being filled with paradoxical ideas. The listeners, mesmerized by the words and emotions, enter a state of mental detachment, which, in the worst cases, becomes trancelike.[17] Politicians (and preachers) can often resort to a method known as "inoculation" or "immunization" to avoid elaboration. The speaker will give the subject a weak dose of information he does not want the audience to accept, and he easily refutes it. The recipients become inoculated against it, thus preempting them from elaboration when the subject is introduced later.[18] "Silencers" are unethical because the persuader seeks to silence his opponent through an appeal to authority, tradition, technical language, ridicule, or counter-charges. "Diversions" are unethical because they seek to divert attention away from the issue being debated to some questionable aspect of the author's argument by using emotional appeals

---

15. Ehninger, *Influence, Belief, and Argument*, 3–5.

16. Enroth, *Churches that Abuse*, 147, 162; Jowett and O'Donnell, *Propaganda and Persuasion*, 15–16.

17. Singer, *Cults in Our Midst*, 155.

18. Jowett and O'Donnell, *Propaganda and Persuasion*, 109.

or shifting the basis for the claim being presented.[19] All of these methods are unethical because they eliminate elaboration and thus avoid lasting influence. These methods replace elaboration with some form of pressure designed to induce yielding without internalization.

Therefore, influence's intention is to bring about elaboration of the central message or core issues involved in the decision. Once the recipient is ready to elaborate, meaning ready and able to process the message, then the persuader should run three ethical checks on the process. These checks are 1) truth, 2) love, and 3) relationships. These tests form the boundaries of ethical persuasion during the processing phase. The elaboration process should be evaluated before proceeding to the decision phase of the persuasion process.

## Truth: Influence's Foundation

Truth has long been recognized as a critical test of ethical influence.[20] Dishonesty undermines our credibility as persuasive preachers. Misleading people is a primary mark of manipulation. Two diagnostic questions help us identify manipulators. First, are the intentions conscious or unconscious? Is the persuader self-aware enough to recognize what his intentions are, or does he unconsciously manipulate people? Second, are the intentions honest or dishonest? Does the persuader have hidden motives distinct from the arguments presented to the recipient?[21] Intentionality in our communication is the first test of truth for the persuader. Good intentions should be open and transparent. Ethical intentions are honest and truthful.

Intentionality alone is not enough to test the truthfulness of our persuasion. The test for a Christian must include the test of Scripture. Ethical persuaders have an obligation to subject all ideas to the scrutiny of their own analysis to make sure they are truthful, but Christian persuaders also must submit all ideas to the authority of Scripture. We must avoid any persuasion which violates Scripture or is even questionable in the light of Scripture. Biblical truth is the foundation for ethical persuasion.

---

19. Ehninger, *Influence, Belief, and Argument*, 117–21.

20. Pogoloff, "Isocrates and Contemporary Hermeneutics," 345; Cunningham, *Faithful Persuasion*, 40–41; Packard, *Hidden Persuaders*, 154–55; McLaughlin, *Communication for the Church*, 29; Hughes, *Christian Ethics in a Secular Society*, 61–65; Geisler, *Ethics*, 13–20; Davis, *Evangelical Ethics*, 15–16; Zuker, *Seven Secrets of Influence*, 11.

21. Gordon, *Theory and Practice of Manipulative Communication*, 46.

Preachers who tickle the ears of listeners who do not want truth are unethical persuaders (2 Tim 4:3–4).

God's truth is not open to debate. Truth is absolute and given by revelation for us to proclaim. Unfortunately, many preachers today seek to placate the modern audience by making the message more popular. Speaking to please the felt needs of our world, preachers strive for relevancy at the expense of God's truth. If the needs of our world become more important than the truth of God's word, our sermons will become misleading and manipulative. Any preacher who seeks to persuade people at the expense of biblical truth is a manipulator of modern minds. We dare not shape the message according to the results we want to achieve. The message is not a variable in the persuasive process.[22] We are not free to enhance or adapt our message to make it more popular or appealing. These tactics may be successful at attracting crowds to our churches, but we are guilty of sophistry when we build our ministries on human wisdom and not the power of God (1 Cor 2:4–5).

We must apply the truth test to our actions as well as our words. The relationship between knowing the truth and doing the truth is stressed in Scripture, so character (ethos) is foundational to ethical persuasion.[23] Who the persuader is makes a significant difference to the persuasion process. Being true is more important than being truthful, but being truthful is the foundation for being true. One of the subtle temptations that can seduce any preacher is the tendency to imply to others that we agree with them when we don't. Silence can be a form of acquiescence. It may not be lying, but it is deceptive and leads inevitably to the accusation of being two-faced. Misrepresenting information or distorting the evidence is unethical. Preachers are in the character business. Therefore, it is imperative a pastor be true in his relationships with the people he seeks to persuade.[24]

Once we mislead or deceive others in the church, we break trust with them. We will find it very difficult to influence them effectively. Pastors can become so focused on achieving their objectives that they begin to frame the message to accomplish their goals. We spin the vision while casting the vision. It is short-sighted. When trust is breached even once, the people begin

---

22. Litfin, *St. Paul's Theology of Proclamation*, 207–8, 194–96.

23. Hughes, *Christian Ethics in a Secular Society*, 18; McLaughlin, *Ethics of Persuasive Preaching*, 125–26.

24. Backus, *Telling Each Other the Truth*, 16–17; Stowell, *Shepherding the Church*, 152–67; McLaughlin, *Ethics of Persuasive Preaching*, 141–42.

to question future attempts. Lead pastors with hidden agendas damage their credibility when the truth comes out. Associate pastors who undermine the leadership of the church breed a spirit of mistrust on the board. Expressing agreement at a board meeting only to question the decision of the board in small groups or with individuals leads to a loss of leadership. Once we break the bond of trust, our influence becomes minimal.

There is general agreement among compliance professionals that the following means of persuasion are unethical. 1) It is unethical for the speaker to distort or falsify information. 2) It is unethical for the speaker to make a piece of evidence communicate something it was not intended to communicate. 3) It is unethical for the speaker to conceal his intentions and to misrepresent himself as being without bias when he has a clear purpose in his speech. 4) It is unethical for the speaker to distract the audience away from his weak arguments by use of emotional appeals or specious attacks on the opposition.[25]

How a speaker uses language can be a counterfeit form of influence. The use of ambiguity is unethical. In this case, a sentence is framed to allow for two different interpretations, or a statement lacks precision of meaning, leading people to read their meanings into it. Equivocation, in which the same word is used to mean two very different things, is another counterfeit proof. One common counterfeit proof preachers use is emotionally loaded language. Loaded words have powerful connotations because they stimulate emotions. "Liberal" and "conservative" are emotionally loaded words that can be used to influence people unethically.[26] Extending a claim beyond the evidence is unethical. Such proofs include overstatement, transfer of meaning, and reducing a counterclaim to absurdity. Preachers who make dogmatic assertions beyond what the Bible says are extending the claim beyond the evidence. Forcing a false dichotomy (either/or decision) when there are other possible solutions is unethical. So is emphasizing a trivial point as the main point because it causes people to choose for the wrong reasons. Pastors can become deceivers when we lead people to believe truth for untrue reasons.[27]

---

25. Johannesen, *Ethics and Persuasion*, 9, 36.

26. Ehninger, *Influence, Belief, and Argument*, 113–15; Brembeck and Howell, *Persuasion*, 116–17. They cite eighty words which are considered "loaded."

27. Ehninger, *Influence, Belief, and Argument*, 116–17, 121–23.

The Institute for Propaganda Analysis (1937–1942) listed some "devices" which are commonly considered unethical.[28] Among these devices are "name calling" (using labels to influence), and "glittering generalities" (associating someone or something with a word which is not open to verification). Unfortunately, we preachers often like to label people and positions in ways that influence others inappropriately. The institute considered "card stacking," a method of selecting information to present based upon whether it supports the idea and avoiding evidence that might detract from the idea, as unethical. The "plain folks" technique seeks to paint the persuader as one of the ordinary people he is seeking to influence. Finally, the "bandwagon" method influences people through peer pressure. All these methods are intended to produce results without any thoughtful analysis of the subject matter.

Esau famously chose to sell his birthright for a pot of stew (Gen 25:27–34). We can succumb to the seduction of Esau's choice whenever we trade the eternal gospel for political success. Winning political battles or attracting large crowds to come to church are examples of short-term success. If we achieve our goals at the expense of truth, we fail Christ and destroy our witness. We sell our eternal birthright for temporal success. The gospel must not be peddled by propaganda tools. One of the easiest ways to sell our integrity is on the altar of influence.

I would summarize the tests of truthfulness in persuasion in five areas.[29] 1) The preacher must meet the standard of knowledge. He should know his subject and encourage others to examine the subject carefully. 2) The preacher must present his material fairly and accurately. 3) The preacher must reveal his sources of information and must not conceal his motives. 4) The preacher must respect and admit opposing arguments and opinions. 5) The preacher should exert a level of influence proportional to the degree of certainty which he possesses regarding the truth of the claim. These tests will help us avoid undue influence for dubious claims.

## Love: Influence's Dynamic

> Do nothing from selfishness or empty conceit, but with humility of mind regard one another as more important than yourselves.

---

28. Jowett and O'Donnell, *Propaganda and Persuasion*, 136; Brembeck and Howell, *Persuasion*, 48; Johannesen, *Ethics and Persuasion*, 8, 33–34.

29. Adapted and expanded from Johannesen, *Ethics and Persuasion*, 51–55.

> Do not merely look out for your own personal interests, but also for the interests of others. (Phil 2:4–5)

Emory Griffin suggests the ethical persuader has two foundational responsibilities—love and justice. Love seeks the good of the person being persuaded. Love cares about what happens to the recipient in the persuasive process. Justice cares about whether the attempts to influence another are right or wrong.[30] Margaret Singer argues one of the primary characteristics of a cult leader is a highly self-centered approach to influence.[31] Persuasion is selfish, not caring whether the result is good for the recipient or not. Spiritually abusive influence uses guilt, fear, and intimidation to control members in an authoritarian environment. Discipline involving public shaming or humiliation is a common attribute of highly authoritarian groups.[32] Propaganda is self-serving influence. One of the quickest ways to identify a propagandist is to ask: Who has the most to gain from this proposal?[33] Is it best for the persuader or the persuadee?

Everett Shostrum wrote, "a manipulator may be defined as a person who exploits, uses, and/or controls himself and others *as things* in certain self-defeating ways."[34] Manipulation objectifies people. It places a higher value on the result than it does on the person and treats the person as a tool to achieve the goal. Sometimes we need to step back and realize the person is not a thing to be used but a friend to be loved even if the result is not what we wanted to achieve. Manipulation in the pastorate is destructive because using people to do a task without caring about them erodes respect. Furthermore, using our position as a pastor for personal advantage undermines the effectiveness of our ministry in the long-term.[35] Fred Smith aptly defined the difference between motivation and manipulation:

> Motivation is getting people to do something out of mutual advantage. Manipulation is getting people to do what we want them to do, primarily for our advantage. Manipulation carries a hidden agenda. Motivation carries an open agenda, allowing for honesty.[36]

---

30. Griffin, *Getting Together*, 160; Griffin, *Mind Changers*, 31.
31. Singer, *Cults in Our Midst*, 8.
32. Enroth, *Churches that Abuse*, 103, 152.
33. Jowett and O'Donnell, *Propaganda and Persuasion*, 156–57.
34. Shostrum, *Man the Manipulator*, 15 (emphasis added).
35. Stowell, *Shepherding the Church*, 108–9.
36. Smith, "Motivation Versus Manipulation," 3:280.

When the persuasive preacher treats a person as an object or a means to an end, he treats that person selfishly, and his influence is unethical. Power corrupts us even as it destroys others. When we disregard the needs of others because we have the right to do what we want to do, we become destructive influencers. Our power seduces us to want more power. Chuck Colson, no stranger to the corrupting influence of political power, wrote, "Power is like saltwater; the more you drink, the thirstier you get."[37]

Love leashes power. It is the antidote to the destructive nature of power. Many have pointed out the foundation for Christian ethics is found in the great commandment to love God and one's neighbor (Matt 22:37–40).[38] By loving God, we give power into his hands. When we love others, we limit our use of power to what will meet their needs. Influence is power. Love harnesses the power of influence so it can be truly effective. Limiting the power of our influence to stay within God's boundaries keeps us from dishonoring God. Limiting the power of our influence to what is best for our listeners protects us from spiritual abuse.

Emory Griffin helpfully clarifies how persuaders love inappropriately. He summarizes his findings under six types of false love, which he labels: "the nonlover, the legalistic lover, the flirt, the seducer, the rapist, and the smother lover."[39] These are all forms of false love. The nonlover does not lead at all but remains distant and aloof. The legalistic lover is passionate about his goals but has predetermined the standards by which he measures people in highly personal ways. The flirt has no deep commitments to the group and moves on to new conquests when the opportunities arise. The seducer uses any and all methods to get his way. As long as he achieves his goals, any method will do. The rapist relies on force to make things happen. The smother lover never takes no for an answer but insists on inducing compliance through a persistent emphasis on incentives.

Learning to listen well is one of the most important, and often neglected, aspects of ethical influence.[40] Listening well is an act of love. We are exploring the other person's viewpoint, which is essential to effective influence. The persuasive preacher takes the time to ask good questions,

---

37. Colson, "Power of Illusion," 27.

38. Geisler, *Christian Ethic of Love*, 26–33; McLaughlin, *Ethics of Persuasive Preaching*, 107; Hughes, *Christian Ethics in a Secular Society*, 12.

39. Griffin, *Getting Together*, 160–65.

40. Zuker, *Seven Secrets of Influence*, 142–77; Backus, *Telling Each Other the Truth*, 138–55; Rusk, *Power of Ethical Persuasion*, 70–81.

which validates the person and leads to permanent persuasion. Listening well requires the preacher to accept, respect, and take a genuine interest in the other person, even if the preacher does not agree with the other person. When we listen to another person, we demonstrate an honest desire to understand that person and see their perspective. Such a viewpoint demonstrates love because the preacher gives respect to that person even though that person may oppose the position being advocated. Listening well is also risky and requires a sense of security for the preacher because his own position might be changed in the process of loving listening.

Love is essential to leadership. Effective leaders provide a place where people matter. They validate people by caring about them first as individuals, regardless of whether they perform the tasks the leader wanted them to perform.[41] Effective leaders invest time in the lives of people and refuse to exploit people as a means to an end. Ken Gangel wrote, "motivation arises from what leaders give, not from what they take."[42]

## Relationships: Influence's Framework

Griffin's dictum, "communication = content + relationships,"[43] is a good place to begin to understand the importance of community with respect to ethical influence. Paul's ethical focus in his Epistles was grounded in the assembly (*ekklesia*), the local community of faith. Paul's letter to Philemon demonstrates the physical family or household structure needs to be transformed by the spiritual relationships in the church.[44] An excellent check on the potential abuse of pastoral persuasion is to recognize the priesthood of all believers and to recover the reformation emphasis that the pastor's ministry "is conditional upon the support of the people of God."[45] There must be a sense of accountability that pervades all influential relationships in the church.

---

41. Stowell, *Shepherding the Church*, 177–203; Kouzes and Posner, *Leadership Challenge*, 305; Spader and Mayes, *Growing a Healthy Church*, 73.

42. Gangel, *Team Leadership in Christian Ministry*, 230. He goes on to list a variety of ways in which leaders invest in people, thereby producing genuine motivation on the part of the followers.

43. Griffin, *Getting Together*, 91.

44. Witherington, *Paul Quest*, 263, 267–68.

45. McGrath, "Better Way," 310.

Influence is set in the framework of relationships. Since persuasion involves the rearranging of people's lives, one important test of ethical persuasion is community value. The pastor should use a process of "end inspection," which views the persuasion from the vantage point of the common good.[46] What is in the best interest of the church as a whole—the assembly? "Leadership isn't about imposing the leader's solo dream; it's about developing a shared sense of destiny."[47] Pastors motivate and mobilize people in the church by helping them see how their aspirations align with the vision of the church. Members of the local church commit their gifts and resources to a shared vision because they can see the common good in the vision. People buy into the vision because they can see the value for the whole community.

Power plays hinder ethical influence. Charles Kelley, in his seminal work on the "destructive achiever," points out that most leadership begins with a "problem-solving process," which later devolves into a "power process." He writes, "the natural tendency of leadership is constantly to progress in the direction of power."[48] The destructive achiever, according to Kelley's study of corporate America, uses power in ways that destroy trust, commitment, and innovation by authoritarian models of leadership and self-promoting behavior. He makes sure it is unhealthy to disagree with him. The destructive achiever may encourage disagreement on minor issues but not on anything that matters to him. He is an absolutist who sees things only in black and white, and on those issues accepts no disagreement. The destructive achiever may take credit for work done by others, undercuts them, promotes himself at their expense, and values his own objectives over the objectives of the company.[49]

The same destructive forms of influence can occur in the context of a local church. In 2019, Harvest Bible Chapel fired their founding pastor, James MacDonald, a gifted Bible preacher, for his destructive, authoritarian leadership. Lina Abujamra served under his leadership for many years as the women's ministry director. She had left the church six years earlier because of his intimidating style of leadership. Lina shared the hurt she felt with these words:

---

46. Brembeck and Howell, *Persuasion*, 455–56, 460.
47. Kouzes and Posner, *Leadership Challenge*, 124.
48. Kelley, *Destructive Achiever*, 24.
49. Kelley, *Destructive Achiever*, 6–9.

> My story is messy. And it still hurts. . . . It's been six years. Six years since I first walked out of a church I loved. . . . Six years since I last trusted a church leader. Six years since I've been able to shake that feeling of guardedness that now surfaces every time I step into church. . . . Six years since I felt safe among God's people.[50]

Abusive pastors intimidate and control others with their powerful voices of authority, thus damaging relationships and destroying people. Presumptive authority based on position or personality is a weak foundation for pastoral influence. Absolutist tendencies do not produce long-term effectiveness in church ministry. Popularity and self-promotion are also weak foundations for pastoral influence, yet are all too often used in the local church. A critical spirit is debilitating to the long-term success of pastoral influence. When we value the strengths of others in the church people come to respect and admire us as leaders. Our influence multiplies as we celebrate the contributions of our people.[51]

There are three kinds of power that have the potential to be abused: "position power, expertise power and charismatic power."[52] Position power deals with the control of decisions and information by virtue of the pastoral position. Expertise power is the power of knowledge. The pastor is recognized to be the authority in certain areas of knowledge, such as theology, and this expertise is used to control the decisions by the church. Charismatic power has to do with interpersonal communication skills and the power of personality. The strong personality who is skilled in public speaking can influence the process in destructive ways. There is a strong relationship between power and dependence. "The power or influence one person has over another person is equal to the dependence the latter has on the first."[53] The more people become dependent on the pastor, the greater the temptation for the pastor to abuse his power.

Power is important for leadership and is not necessarily unethical. We should not fear the use of power in ministry simply because the potential exists for the abuse of power. I remember a time when I pulled back emotionally from leading the church because of the sting I felt from the barbs

---

50. Roys, "RESTORE Chicago Video," paras. 11–14; Perry, "Willow Creek and Harvest Struggle," paras. 23–24.

51. Stowell, *Shepherding the Church*, 97–102.

52. Kelley, *Destructive Achiever*, 27–31; Gangel and Canine identify five kinds of power—"reward power, coercive power, legitimate power, referent power and expert power" (Gangel and Canine, *Communication and Conflict Management*, 203–6).

53. Gangel and Canine, *Communication and Conflict Management*, 202–3.

of one critic in the church. One of the board members spoke privately with me. He said, "Pastor, we need you to lead us. You can't be afraid to lead." Pastors can use the power of their influence to meet people's needs or to call them to serve the greater good. Persuasive power can mobilize a church into action and be the conduit for God's transforming grace in the lives of people. However, we use this power to influence in the context of community. Relationships are the framework for ethical influence.

How is influence exercised in a community of faith so it is both effective and ethical? Two theories of leadership in the corporate world shed light on our pastoral influence. "Theory X Leadership" is leadership that compels or coerces others to implement what the leader wants to be implemented based on his authority. It is a "win-lose" or "zero-sum" leadership style. Every decision has a winner and a loser creating a climate of constant conflict. The leader pushes an agenda, and others try to sabotage the agenda. The long-term effects of "Theory X Leadership" are negative for the health of the people and the organization.[54]

"Theory Y Leadership" is "win-win" in its orientation. It begins with the idea people want to accomplish organizational goals that are mutually beneficial. The leader wins when others adopt the idea he advocates. Others win because they now agree with the idea too. They share in the plan together, so both leader and follower are winners. Theory Y Leadership is team leadership which inspires a shared vision between leader and followers. The long-term effects of "Theory Y Leadership" are transformative for both the people and the organization.[55]

The law firm of Wagenmaker and Oberly researched and prepared a legal evaluation report for Harvest Bible Chapel as part of the termination process of James MacDonald. They concluded MacDonald exhibited a "pattern of aggressive and adversarial tactics against church leaders who opposed him." They wrote that "MacDonald's powerful and subversive leadership style" and "his development of an inner-circle leadership group through which he could control" the church led to an "unhealthy power structure." The result was they accused MacDonald of misusing financial resources for his own benefit. He used a "heavy-fisted exclusionary

---

54. Nielsen, *Politics of Ethics*, 93, 39–46.

55. Nielsen, *Politics of Ethics*, 60; Kouzes and Posner, *Leadership Challenge*, 18; Gangel, *Team Leadership in Christian Ministry*, 12.

leadership" style and a close inner-circle of leaders to help him control church decisions without accountability.[56]

Sharing power and honest accountability are essential for long-term effectiveness in the church.[57] Healthy persuasive preachers strive to establish relationships of mutual dependence. We need each other in the community of faith. We work together to accomplish a shared vision for ministry. Healthy persuasive preachers know the more they try to control others, the less the people will trust them in the future. "Leaders don't command and control; they serve and support."[58] The relational framework for ethical influence is shared service. Servant leadership is critical to long-term effectiveness as a pastor. Emory Griffin states it bluntly: "he who meets needs, leads."[59]

A healthy persuasive preacher taps into the deep yearnings of the people he leads. He listens to their hearts shared in small groups and private meetings. He watches people react in church and is good at reading the body language of his people. He asks probing questions as he develops healthy relationships. He builds trust through honestly shared feelings. A healthy persuasive preacher loves his people enough to listen empathetically to their hurts and fears. He is both true and truthful in all his dealings with his people so they come to trust him and his words. He weaves the threads of their individual needs into a tapestry of the shared vision. Out of this framework of relationships, the healthy persuasive preacher calls people to higher goals and challenges people to live like Christ in an antichrist world.

---

56. Wagenmaker, "Harvest Bible Chapel," paras. 2, 4–5, 20.

57. Gangel and Canine, *Communication and Conflict Management*, 208–9.

58. Kouzes and Posner, *Leadership Challenge*, 16; Jowett and O'Donnell, *Propaganda and Persuasion*, 25; Zuker, *Seven Secrets of Influence*, 15.

59. Griffin, *Getting Together*, 59.

# 9

# Ethical Controls: Decision

DECISION TIME. THE PROCESS had been time-consuming. We had spent three years preparing for this moment. Now the church would vote on a new constitution, a new way of operating which was radically different from the past. The church formed a constitution committee that regularly reported to the official board of the church. We started with the mission statement, refocusing the mission of the church around the Great Commission (Matt 28:17–20). The church would be restructured around the Great Commission. The past organization had been a hodgepodge of boards and committees that functioned as a giant wheel with the pastor at the hub. I was an *ex-officio* member of every committee. Over fifty people had to be elected every year to fill the offices of a church averaging less than 200 in attendance. The church held regular business meetings to vote on almost all decisions, no matter how minor. Now we would elect elders and deacons/deaconesses to lead the church. We had transformed into an elder-led congregation. Each elder would be responsible for leading one of the five segments of the Great Commission or the two support workgroups. All decisions within the limitations of the annual budget would be made by the Board of Elders. For a Baptist church, this was a radical change from congregational government to an elder-led church.

Many meetings preceded the final vote. The constitution went through dozens of iterations as the officers of the church suggested minor changes. We rolled out the draft of the constitution to the members of the church far in advance of the vote. I preached sermons explaining how multiple elders and shared leadership followed the biblical model for church government. I held an open forum with the congregation where they could ask any question they wanted to ask. Small group meetings discussed the plans. Finally, the time had come to decide. We took a vote. It was unanimous. The church ratified the new constitution. Healthy persuasion leads to unified decisions.

Assuming the pastor has stimulated elaboration by the ones being persuaded, and he has put that elaboration process through the grid of truth, love, and relationships, the next stage is the decision stage. The person (or group) being persuaded is being asked to decide. He (or they) knows the information necessary to make the decision and has been properly brought to the point of decision. There are two critical steps the pastor should think through before calling for a decision. They are the issues of choice and the Holy Spirit. Choice is an ethical limitation the persuasive preacher places on himself, and the Spirit is the preacher's confidence no matter what the result. The pastor can confidently limit his influence because he is trusting in God to superintend the process. The result is freedom for both the persuader and the persuaded.

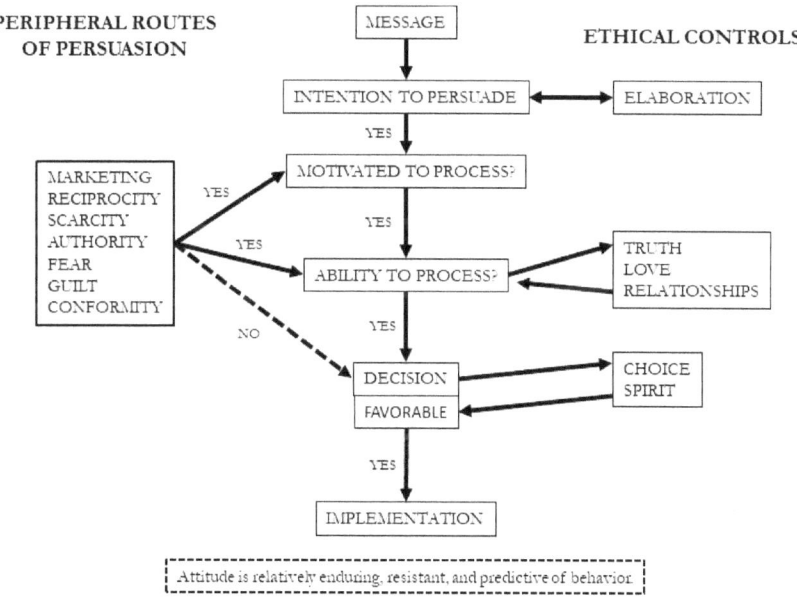

(Adapted from Petty and Cacioppo, *Communication and Persuasion*, p.4)

## Choice: Influence's Limitation

The manipulator seeks to understand others for one purpose—control. The purpose of propaganda is to get people to accept the viewpoint of the propagandist by controlling the flow of information, which increases the influence of the message. Control is the mark of spiritual abuse in the church because it denies freedom in Christ to individuals who are under the pastor's authority. Abusive churches control any exits and make it emotionally painful for a person to leave the group, thus controlling the choices of the group. The biggest difference between persuasion and coercion is choice. Cults are effective at forcing the individual to surrender his or her mental process and yield to the will of the cult leader to receive the benefits of the group.[1]

"If Steve (Timmis) is challenged in any way, which he always takes as a threat, then the tables are turned and the challenger is made out to be the one at fault," said fellow British pastor, Melvin Tinker. "This is classic manipulation." Timmis was the founding pastor of The Crowded House, a well-known church in Sheffield, England, before becoming the CEO of Acts 29. He was removed from leadership for spiritual abuse. "People were and are afraid of Steve Timmis," said a former elder who worked with him in the church. If anyone rejected his correction, he would publicly declare that the person was "a law unto himself," one of his favorite expressions drawn from Romans 2:14. People were intimidated. They could follow his decisions or leave.[2]

Choice is the key difference between coercion and persuasion. If the person sees no choice, then the process is coercive no matter what form the influence takes. As long as the person perceives a choice to accept or reject, then the influence is not coercive. A call to change tied to an explicit or implicit threat is coercive. "You ought to change or else." The call may be open or hidden, but if the recipient sees his choice with an "or else" attached to it, then the influence is degenerating into some form of pressure on the will.[3] There is, of course, a place for reward systems in Christian ethics, but such methods should be carefully monitored to ensure the reward does not put direct pressure on the will.[4]

---

1. Shostrum, *Man the Manipulator*, 25–32; Jowett and O'Donnell, *Propaganda and Persuasion*, 154–55, 162–66; Enroth, *Churches that Abuse*, 169–86, 216–17; Perloff, *Dynamics of Persuasion*, 20; Singer, *Cults in Our Midst*, 20.

2. Shellnutt, "Acts 29 CEO Removed," paras. 4, 12, 16.

3. Perloff, *Dynamics of Persuasion*, 12–13; McLaughlin, *Ethics of Persuasive Preaching*, 18; Lifton, *Thought Reform and the Psychology of Totalism*, 438.

4. Lloyd-Jones, *Preaching and Preachers*, 271.

## ETHICAL CONTROLS: DECISION

Leith Anderson distinguishes between power and authority based upon the issue of choice.

> Power forces others to obey, even against their wills. Authority is earned. Authority is freely given. Authority is people listening to and acting on the words of a leader because they choose to and want to. Authority is trust and confidence. Not understanding the difference and assuming authority that has not been given is a certain route to disaster in a church or an organization.[5]

This distinction between power and authority is helpful for pastors. As pastors, we have a certain amount of biblical authority, but it does not give us the right to be authoritarian. Authoritarianism is coercive power which controls the thinking and conduct of Christians in the church.[6] Power plays by the pastor are destructive to the church.

Paul's use of rhetoric demonstrates his respect for the "independence" of his listeners and his desire to found the Christian community on principles of persuasion rather than simple commandment.[7] Freedom to choose is a significant ethical limitation placed on persuasion. Persuasion seeks voluntary change on the part of the one being persuaded. Ethical influence grants the receiver the freedom to say "No."[8] God alone has the right to invade the privacy of the heart, not human persuaders. There are times when persuasive preachers must back off and allow the listener the freedom to decide. Faith cannot be coerced. Eternal decisions are between the person and God.

Faith is both the process and product of persuasion. There is a strong linguistic and conceptual relationship between persuasion and faith in the New Testament.[9] Persuasion is both the cause of the change of mind and the effect, result, or state of conviction arising from the change of mind. Faith, in the same way, can be defined as "persuasion of a thing, confidence, assurance" or "that which gives persuasion or confidence."

---

5. Anderson, *Dying for Change*, 191.

6. Gangel, *Team Leadership in Christian Ministry*, 71.

7. Witherington, *Conflict and Community in Corinth*, 45–46.

8. Jowett and O'Donnell, *Propaganda and Persuasion*, 28; Burke, *Rhetoric of Motives*, 50; Johannesen, *Ethics and Persuasion*, 63; Kouzes and Posner, *Leadership Challenge*, 252; Backus, *Telling Each Other the Truth*, 81–99; Cialdini, *Influence*, 61–65, 108–14, 155–62, 200–2, 223–28, 256–60.

9. Christensen, "Healthy Pastoral Persuasion," 205–18. Faith (*pistis*) meant both a belief and a persuasion.

Persuasion sometimes refers to the process of persuading, and sometimes it refers to the product of being persuaded. Faith has the same dual meaning. Faith can be the product of being persuaded or the process of believing. The word for faith is also the word for proofs, which are the means of persuasion in Greek rhetoric.[10] Faith is both the product of God's persuasion and the process by which he persuades. God is the great persuader, but he chooses to use human *pisteis* (persuadings or proofs) to accomplish his persuasion to *pistis* (faith).

There is a strong etymological and semantic connection between the terms "believe" and "persuade" in the New Testament.[11] The word "persuade" is used to describe the process of persuasion as employed by Paul and others in the New Testament.[12] However, the same verb is also used in the sense of "product" and translated by terms like "trust" and "confidence."[13] We see this interplay between persuasion and faith in Acts 28:23–24. Paul was preaching to large groups of people about the kingdom of God and "trying to persuade them concerning Jesus." Luke goes on to say "some were being persuaded," but "others would not believe." The process of "trying to persuade" results in one of two products. The first product is "being persuaded," and the words spoken are the means of persuasion. The second product is the opposite. Some would "not believe." Not believing is the opposite of being persuaded, making being persuaded equivalent to believing. Persuasion is used here as both a process and a product. Persuasion as a product is equivalent to faith.

Faith, therefore, is being persuaded. Ultimately, God does the persuading, but he uses human persuaders in the process. The temptation is for human persuaders to coerce faith through the persuasion process by not trusting God to persuade. The result is not faith for faith is being truly persuaded, and the person is not truly convinced. True persuasion is an inner conviction that what God says is true. Being truly persuaded means the

---

10. Kinneavy, *Greek Rhetorical Origins of Christian Faith*, 33, 22; Liddell and Scott, *Greek-English Lexicon*, 1186.

11. Christensen, "Healthy Pastoral Persuasion," 208; Burke, *Rhetoric of Motives*, 51–52; Kinneavy, *Greek Rhetorical Origins of Christian Faith*, 101–6; The words *pisteuo* and *peitho* are grouped together under the headings of Michel, "Faith, Persuade, Belief, Unbelief," 1:587–606.

12. 2 Cor 5:11; Acts 19:8, 26; 28:23; The term is also used in the sense of process regarding the means by which others persuaded (Acts 12:20; 14:19; 21:14); Clapp et al., *Analytical Concordance of the Greek New Testament*, 1:2081.

13. Luke 18:9; 2 Cor 1:9; 2:3; Phil 1:6, 14, 25; Phlm 21; Heb 2:13.

person internalizes the message so they not only mentally agree but they emotionally commit to the gospel. That is God's work, so we must leave the results with God lest we manipulate people into false faith.

Freedom to choose then is the essence of ethical Christian persuasion. Emory Griffin properly writes "any persuasive effort which restricts another's freedom to choose for or against Jesus Christ is wrong."[14] The freedom to choose is the best method to produce a decision based on elaboration. The recipient internalizes the decision by devoting mental and emotional resources to examining the gospel, so the most ethical process is also the most effective process for true persuasion. Duane Litfin wrote:

> The preacher cannot, must not, take the weight of decision-making from the shoulders of his hearers by employing persuasive techniques in such a way that he induces the listener to yield; but he can and must do everything in his power to induce comprehension of the reality of God's claims upon the listener.[15]

If we substitute elaboration for comprehension, this is an excellent expression of the principle. The objective of the persuasive preacher is to produce elaboration, not mere comprehension. Elaboration, as we have seen, is more than a mental understanding of the gospel. Elaboration involves devoting all the elements of being human toward internalizing the gospel in such a way that the will becomes engaged in the process. At the point where the will is engaged, and a decision is faced, the persuasive preacher places an ethical limitation on his efforts to persuade.

I may be deeply engaged in the persuasive process with a person. I may have invested significant time and effort to convince the person he or she should do what I think they should do, but at that point I must set the person free to choose for themselves. I risk the rejection to avoid any taint of manipulation. I value the person over the decision, recognizing the person must willingly choose, lest the choice be false. There comes a point when the persuasive preacher must release the person to make a choice.

This point of release frequently happens in pastoral ministry. I argue strongly to convince a good friend not to quit the leadership of an important ministry in our church because we need him. The ministry would fail without his gifts. However, in the end, I tell him the choice is his, and he

---

14. Griffin, *Mind Changers*, 28, 41, 165, 180.
15. Litfin, "Perils of Persuasive Preaching," 17.

will still be my friend even if he chooses not to do what I ask. Playing the friend card would be coercive.

The board is preparing to vote on spending money to upgrade the facility. I don't think it is a wise use of our resources even though many on the board are excited about it. I try to convince them not to do it, but ultimately I must release the decision to the board. I will support what they decide.

She is a gifted musician who would enhance our worship ministry significantly, but she is struggling with some family matters. I try to convince her to join our worship team, but I also must respect her decision if she decides not to join.

Forewarning is another helpful check against manipulative influence. Forewarning the subject induces a cognitive response toward rejection because it allows the subject to develop counterarguments ahead of time. Petty and Cacioppo did significant research in support of their Elaboration Likelihood Model of influence, which demonstrates that forewarning the subject produces greater resistance, particularly on any issues which the subject considers important.[16] For this reason, unethical persuaders try to avoid giving people information in advance for fear they will become resistant. However, the resistance bias produced by forewarning can be used as an effective ethical guard rail against coercive influence.

When issues are important, it would be highly ethical for the persuasive preacher to give forewarning so the one being persuaded can truly elaborate on the issues. The forewarning will increase the difficulty of the persuasion process but will also increase the freedom of choice for the recipient. The net effect is the influence will be more ethical, and the choices made will have more permanency. The danger of manipulative influence is greatest when the persuader seeks to influence the person without the person knowing all the information.

The church must decide about a major new ministry initiative and the funding needed to accomplish the task. The persuasive preacher will make sure the agenda is posted for all to see well in advance of the meeting. We should make sure our people have all the information they need to make an informed decision even if some of the information conflicts with the recommendation. They should know in advance so there are no surprises. I remember one business meeting we had scheduled to vote on a new building proposal. The week before we were to vote, we came across

---

16. Petty and Cacioppo, *Communication and Persuasion*, 116–30; Perloff, *Dynamics of Persuasion*, 114–15.

some questions the architect could not answer, so I canceled the meeting until we had enough information to make a healthy decision. When the time came to hold the meeting, our congregation trusted our recommendations because they knew we had been careful with the decision-making process. Healthy influence that values the people more than our goals breeds trust in our leadership.

## The Holy Spirit: Influence's Confidence

Tears welled up in his eyes. I had just asked Mark to prayerfully consider joining our pastoral staff at the church. Mark and Sara were part of our church. I had the privilege of performing their wedding, and both had been students at the Bible college where I taught. Now I was inviting him to start as an intern with the plan that he would eventually become a pastor. "Why didn't you tell me this before?" he asked. "I just went through a process with another local church who invited me to become a candidate for the pastorate. You knew we were praying and talking about moving to serve in that church, but you didn't tell me you were thinking about asking me to stay here." Mark had just told me they had decided God didn't want them to move to a new ministry, but they were frustrated because they didn't know what they were going to do now. Health concerns had ended their dream to serve as missionaries, and now they seemed to be at another dead end for ministry. I responded, "Mark, I have been praying about your decision and thinking about asking you for many months now, but I wanted to make sure God was not leading you elsewhere. I didn't want to muddy the waters. I trusted God to lead us both through this process." Mark accepted the call and, after serving as a pastoral intern and later one of our pastors; he became the lead pastor of the church when I retired seven years later. The Holy Spirit directed them, our church, and me through the entire process from start to finish. Today, Mark is my pastor!

We often claim to trust in God's Spirit to work in our ministries, but our frantic efforts to convince others to follow our plans puts the lie to our lip service. Do we trust the Holy Spirit enough to surrender our influence to his control? Can we trust God to persuade others to do what he wants when he wants? The Bible encourages us to wait on the Lord for his will and his timing, but we chafe under the charge to wait (Pss 27:14; 37:7–11; 130:5–6; Prov 20:22). God tells us to trust in the Lord and not our own plans, and God will direct our steps (Prov 3:5–6). As pastors, we are good at applying this truth to the lives of others, but when it comes to the church, we sometimes slip into unhealthy patterns of influence, rationalizing our persuasive efforts as leadership. We need to spend more of our ministry waiting on the Lord and less time manipulating others to achieve our goals. If we believe God is sovereign, we should put our faith into practice by trusting the Spirit of God to influence others to join us as we follow the Lord together. Coercive leadership is a mark of unbelief—a lack of faith in the Holy Spirit.

The Stoics viewed rhetoric (persuasion) as a tool to teach moral truth, but if the rhetor (persuader) tried to use rhetoric as more than an instrument, it became a trap.[17] The same danger exists for the modern pastor. Paul's example in 1 Corinthians 2:1–5 places an ethical boundary on persuasion by emphasizing our dependence on the power of the Spirit working in and through the message to change the lives of the listeners. Ethically, Paul—and modern preachers—must trust the Spirit for the results.[18] Trusting the Spirit does not mean the preacher refuses to seek results in his preaching. Results-oriented preaching is not sophistry. Trusting the Spirit means the spiritual leader refuses to seek results at all costs and by all means. It means the persuasive preacher does not put his confidence in human methods or techniques. He may use those methods, but he will not place his confidence in his methodology. Trusting the Spirit means the spiritual leader understands he is limited and must allow the recipient the freedom to choose without threat or pressure.

Trusting the Spirit frees the persuasive preacher from the tyranny of results. Our confidence as preachers rests in the work of God the Holy Spirit to produce lasting change. We can step back from the brink of manipulation and respect the process and the person, while remaining confident of the results. J. Oswald Sanders, in his classic book on leadership, expressed it this way:

> The spiritual leader, however, influences others not by the power of his own personality alone but by that personality irradiated and interpenetrated and empowered by the Holy Spirit. Because he permits the Holy Spirit undisputed control of his life, the Spirit's power can flow through him unhindered.
>
> Spiritual leadership is a matter of superior spiritual power, and that can never be self-generated. There is no such thing as a

---

17. Pogoloff, "Isocrates and Contemporary Hermeneutics," 346.
18. Litfin, *St. Paul's Theology of Proclamation*, 207, 250.

## ETHICAL CONTROLS: DECISION

self-made spiritual leader. He is able to influence others spiritually only because the Spirit is able to work in and through him to a greater degree than in those whom he leads.

> It is a general principle that we can influence and lead others only so far as we ourselves have gone. The person most likely to be successful is one who leads not by merely pointing the way but by having trodden it himself. We are leaders to the extent that we inspire others to follow us.[19]

The temptation for church leaders today is that we become impatient. Waiting on the Spirit to woo and work can be frustrating, so we begin to implement the latest marketing methods that draw crowds. The modern church growth emphasis on being relevant and touching felt needs may lead us away from the Pauline emphasis on the cross. It can be parallel to the sophistry which Paul was attacking in Corinth with its super-apostles who stressed marketing and methodology over the cross and sacrifice.[20] Church growth methodologies, structures, and strategies may become idolized as the pathway to spiritual leadership. There are, of course, many excellent ideas advocated by the church growth movement which can help us in our ministries if we make certain the ideas serve, not supplant, the Spirit. We can move the hearts of people with our eloquence and attract large crowds with our methods, but only the Spirit of God can produce faith. Only the Spirit can change hearts. The preacher can bring listeners to tears, but only the Spirit can make listeners new. Our best methods will never make people Christians. Faith is more than an apprehension of the gospel. Faith is a persuasion of the gospel, which can only happen by the power of the Spirit.[21]

Faith is both a process and a product. John Calvin defined faith as "a knowledge of the divine benevolence toward us and a sure persuasion of its truth."[22] Faith is the product of God's work of grace in the human heart, but faith is also a process by which we understand the work of God. Calvin wrote:

> When we call faith 'knowledge' we do not mean comprehension of the sort that is commonly concerned with those things which fall

---

19. Sanders, *Spiritual Leadership*, 19–20; See his discussion of the filling of the Spirit as the "indispensable requirement" for spiritual leadership (70–74).
20. Horton, "Subject of Contemporary Relevance," 327–353.
21. Christensen, "Healthy Pastoral Persuasion," 212.
22. Calvin, *Institutes*, 3.2.12, see 2.3.6.

under human sense perception. For faith is so far above sense that man's mind has to go beyond and rise above itself in order to attain it. Even where the mind has attained, it does not comprehend what it feels. But while it is persuaded of what it does not grasp, by the very certainty of its persuasion it understands more than if it perceived anything human by its own capacity.[23]

Faith is both the product of the Spirit's influence and the process by which we understand spiritual truth. Spiritual conviction cannot be produced by human methods but by the Spirit of God alone (John 16:5–15). Augustine taught that God's grace operates on the human will by making the unwilling person willing to believe.[24] Martin Luther argued our will is changed under the "sweet influence" of God's Spirit so we act by our own desire.[25]

Perhaps Jonathan Edwards understood this dynamic relationship between the product and the process of faith as well as anyone. He argued the will cannot determine the will without being an uncaused cause, so no decision of the will is free in the sense of being uncaused. There are causes that act upon the will to produce the motive behind the choice. Humans never choose to do something contrary to their greatest desire but always act in accord with their strongest motive. The choice of the will is always determined by the strongest motive in that situation and inducing or exciting the will produces the strongest motive.[26] We always choose to do what we most want to do, given the circumstances. The choice to believe—faith—is the product of persuasion by the strongest influence, the Spirit of God. Faith is also the process of understanding spiritual truth because it acts as the greater influence in the lives of those who believe.

The watershed issue regarding faith, the human will, and divine sovereignty revolves around the moral persuasion of God. Is this moral persuasion resistible or irresistible?[27] Faith is a dynamic, not a static, process. God initiates the process of faith. Faith is a gift of God's grace. However, faith is not a gift in the sense of being a static, self-contained entity. The gift of God's grace is the persuasive work of the Holy Spirit who moves man's will so man chooses to believe based upon man's own strongest motive. Since God is sovereign, and his power is infinite, the wooing work of God is irresistible.

23. Calvin, *Institutes*, 3.2.14.
24. Sproul, *Willing to Believe*, 65–66.
25. Luther, *Bondage of the Will*, 102–3.
26. Edwards, *Freedom of the Will*, 172–73, 142; Sproul, *Willing to Believe*, 155–62.
27. Edwards, *Freedom of the Will*, 120–21.

God orchestrates the circumstances and molds the secondary causes so either something internal or external to the will influences the will to believe. God's saving call is efficacious as a result of the persuasive process of God's Spirit, but man's choice remains free. God does not coerce faith. He persuades the will to believe. Millard Erickson puts it this way:

> God works in such a suasive way with the will of the individual that the person freely makes the choice God intends. With respect to the offer of salvation, this means that God does not begin by regenerating those he has chosen, transforming their souls so that they believe; rather, he works in an appealing, persuading fashion so that they freely choose to believe, and then he regenerates them. . . . There were, to be sure, times when God compelled persons to obey him. Most of the time, however, the picture is more like God making his will so persuasive and attractive that persons willingly and even joyfully accept it and carry it out.[28]

The Spirit's influence motivates spiritual choices. The only way for faith to rest on the power of God and not the wisdom of man is for the message to come by the proofs which the Spirit delivers to human minds (1 Cor 2:4–5). Persuasive preachers depend on the Spirit's power to influence human wills and change human hearts. What about the heart, mind, and will of the preacher? How can we be effective conduits through which the Spirit of God can work? Overstreet has an excellent explanation of the preacher's responsibility for keeping the channels unclogged.[29] Persuasive preachers are conduits for the spiritual words taught by the Spirit of God to flow to the minds of the people who are listening (1 Cor 2:12–13). Our job as preachers is to keep the conduits clear of debris like pride, laziness, ingratitude, prayerlessness, bitterness, envy, and unforgiveness that would hinder the work of the Spirit in our preaching.

## 1. Don't quench the Spirit (1 Thess 5:19)

The word translated "quench" meant to put out a fire. Here the word is used figuratively to stifle or suppress the work of the Holy Spirit. No human has the power to extinguish God the Holy Spirit, but we can hinder the flow of his ministry in our lives. The Spirit brings to our lives and the life of the

---

28. Erickson, *Christian Theology*, 330–31. This view is sometimes called congruism, compatibilism, or soft determinism.

29. Overstreet, *Persuasive Preaching*, 171–92.

church a passion that burns like fire. But an individual can be like a bucket of water poured out on the fire that the Holy Spirit kindles in the church. Each of us can be a wet blanket on the enthusiasm the Spirit kindles in others by how we respond to them in our fellowship. Paul is telling us to stop being a wet blanket on the work of the Holy Spirit.

The immediate context helps us understand how even preachers can become wet blankets on the Spirit's fire. Leaders can quench the Spirit by maintaining tight control over what happens in the church so there is little freedom for the Spirit to work (1 Thess 5:20). Spiritual leaders need to exercise control in the church (1 Thess 5:21; 1 Cor 14:20–40) without inhibiting the work of the Spirit. I think we sometimes have been guilty of underemphasizing the ministry of the Spirit because we fear the excesses we have observed in others. The passion of people in the church suffers when spiritual leaders become too controlling. We should examine everything through the grid of Scripture, but be careful not to suppress the Spirit.

We can quench the Spirit when we are critical, divisive, or argumentative (1 Thess 5:12–14). Spiritual leaders must be patient, encouraging, and helpful to those under their charge, even as the people must live in peace with one another. A vengeful spirit is sinful (1 Thess 5:15). Sadly, persuasive preachers all too often hold grudges that become a wet blanket on the work of the Spirit in the church when we put down or reject the contributions of those we dislike. Persuasive preachers must always be motivated by what is good for all people and not play favorites in the church (1 Thess 5:15). Joy, prayer, and a grateful spirit should characterize the ministry of effective pastors if we want to instill those values in our people (1 Thess 5:16–18). Prayer should become like an "incessant cough" throughout our daily lives so we do not stifle the Spirit in our ministries.[30] When we practice these principles, we will keep the conduits of our hearts clear for the Spirit to influence the hearts and minds of our people.

## 2. Don't grieve the Spirit (Eph 4:30)

The word translated "grieve" means to experience sorrow like one feels at the death of a loved one. The Greek construction indicates we are to stop continuously and habitually grieving the Holy Spirit. Paul implies we often grieve the Spirit. The Holy Spirit is a person, and he has feelings like any person. The command to stop grieving the Spirit is sandwiched between verses that

---

30. Overstreet, *Persuasive Preaching*, 186.

stress the importance of what we say to others. Words matter. The admonition is particularly important for preachers who make a living by talking. Our speech must be wholesome and edifying so that we give grace to our listeners (Eph 4:29). Grace is the wobble room we extend even to those who don't deserve it. We are to avoid all bitter, angry, divisive, and slanderous talk (Eph 4:31). When we attack others from the pulpit or insult people in private, we hurt the feelings of the Holy Spirit. Preachers who live by the words they say must take these instructions very seriously. God does (Jas 3:1)!

We can hurt the Spirit deeply by how we talk to one another. We tend to excuse our harsh and angry words as insignificant sins. Some preachers today even take pride in the coarse language they use in the pulpit by saying it helps them be relevant to their audience. Others defend crude and angry talk by claiming they are being real with people. They are not afraid to be politically incorrect because they are telling it like it is, they say. Coarse talk is almost fashionable today, a crude badge of honor with some. God says, "Stop hurting me." God cries when a husband says nasty things to his wife in the bedroom. God cries when a wife tears down her husband in the living room. God cries when preachers use nasty language and spout angry rants in their sermons. We are polluting the spiritual environment with our crude words. They stink. God smells our rotten words and cries.

Why? Because it is the Holy Spirit who seals us for the day of redemption. The Holy Spirit stamps us with his presence when we become Christians. He takes up residence inside us. The Spirit is God's guarantee we will live forever with him, a pledge of our future inheritance on the day of redemption (Eph 1:13–14). Since we are sealed with the Holy Spirit and he lives in us, then every experience we have, he has. When we say unholy words, God is there experiencing those unholy words with us. In between our day of sealing, which takes place when we become Christians, and our day of redemption, which takes place when we go to heaven, is the day we live—today. Why would we want to do anything today which is inconsistent with our day of sealing and our day of redemption?

The Spirit uses our words to meet the needs of people where they are at that moment. We should regularly ask God to make our speech holy. I picked up a practical tip many years ago I try to implement daily. Speak five uplifting words for each critical word because we remember negative words so easily it takes five positive words to outweigh one negative word. The Spirit of God will use our words to meet the needs of others when we keep the conduits of our mouths clean. Holy speech is productive, not destructive.

Holy speech builds people up. It doesn't tear them down. Holy speech is gracious, not vindictive. Holy speech enriches others, it doesn't degrade or spoil them. We must not sadden the Spirit by what we say.

### 3. Be filled with the Spirit (Eph 5:18)

Paul gives two commands which are set in contrast with each other. Don't get drunk, and be filled with the Spirit. Paul is not saying to be filled with the Spirit is like getting drunk; Paul is saying the opposite. Getting drunk means losing control of our faculties. Don't seek to lose control. Seek to gain control—the control of the Holy Spirit, who is a God of order. The results of the Spirit's filling are not wild, out-of-control actions. The filling of the Spirit produces wise conduct which makes the most of each day by following the will of God (Eph 5:15–17). The filling of the Spirit guards our speech with one another in worship and calls us to subject ourselves to one another in the fear of Christ (Eph 5:19–21). God is a God of order, not confusion (1 Cor 14:33), so being filled with the Spirit leads us to live in orderly ways with one another, including God's orders for marriage (Eph 5:22–33).

What does it mean to be filled with the Spirit? The filling of the Spirit means we allow the Spirit to control our lives so we produce the results he wants to produce in our lives. The filling of the Spirit is not about a special experience, but a fruitful life. Paul has just drawn a contrast between the fruits of light and the deeds of darkness (Eph 5:6–14) when he commands us to be filled with the Spirit (Eph 5:18). The Spirit produces the fruit of light, which is "goodness, righteousness, and truth trying to learn what is pleasing to the Lord" (Eph 5:9–10). When we are obedient to the Spirit's control, we will produce the fruit of the Spirit in our lives.

The command is passive. We are to allow ourselves to be filled with the Spirit. He fills us. We open our lives to him and invite him to fill us with all his fullness as we are obedient to his control. The command is also plural, not singular. The filling will always relate to our relationships in the body of Christ. The context of this command is relational in nature. We exhibit the filling of the Spirit in the context of our Christian communities. If we can't get along with others in the church, then we aren't filled with the Spirit of God. The command is also a present, continuous command. We do not get filled once and for all, and forevermore we are filled with the Spirit. The filling of the Spirit is a moment by moment, everyday experience. The filling of the Spirit is a repeated and repeatable experience of obedience to and control by the Holy Spirit. How do we know when we are filled with the Spirit? When we exhibit the marks of the Spirit in our relationships with others. It is not about a mystical experience, but the fruit of the Spirit.

I have prayed two requests to God early each Sunday morning throughout my years of ministry as I prepared to preach. First, I tell God this sermon is my offering of worship to him. I have prepared the best I have this week so I can give it as my sacrifice of praise. I ask God to take the words I say and use them for his glory. Second, I ask God to fill me with his Spirit. Take control not only of my lips but my attitudes and actions. I ask that the Holy Spirit control all I am and have as I seek to be obedient to him. Please demonstrate the fruit of the Spirit in my ministry today. I want no clogs in the conduit so the Spirit's life can flow through his word to the hearts of his people.

## Diagnosing Ethical Influence

The model for evaluating ethical persuasion can be summarized with some diagnostic questions we can ask ourselves as preachers. The persuasive preacher can use the following questions as he evaluates the ethics of any specific persuasive encounter in the ministry.

1. Am I focused on stimulating people to elaborate on the central issue to be decided? Does the person have enough time to think through the issues before making a decision?

2. Am I encouraging a decision based upon peripheral triggers? Have I given the person enough information to internalize the choice?

3. Am I misrepresenting the truth by life or by word? Have I given the person accurate information on which to make an informed decision? Am I genuine in my presentation?

4. Am I certain the desired response is in the best interest of the other person, or does it serve my own interest more?

5. Am I treating the person as a project or a means to an end? Is the person more important than his/her decision?

6. Am I respecting the relationship structure in which we both function? Is the person free to seek answers outside my control?

7. Am I misrepresenting the choice? Are there hidden intentions or agendas behind my initial invitation?

8. Am I violating the person's responsibility to choose? Will I accept a "No" answer without threat, recrimination, or abandonment?

9. Am I trusting the Holy Spirit to produce the results God wants more than the results I want? Do I trust God's timing for the decision, or will I push an answer on my timetable? Am I willing to wait for the Spirit to produce his results in his time?

# 10

# Paul and Philemon: A Case Study in Pastoral Influence

*Leadership is influence, the ability of
one person to influence others.*[1]

PASTOR JOE WAS FRUSTRATED. He felt strongly that Ken, a gifted young man in his church, was ready to take the next step into spiritual leadership. Pastor Joe had been meeting regularly with him for several years now, and Ken had grown rapidly both in his knowledge of the Bible and his commitment to Christ. Ken could help the church grow. However, Bob was unconvinced. Bob was a key leader in the church. What he said often carried the day at business meetings because he was highly respected. Bob was a successful businessman whose donations were critical to the financial health of the church. What was more, Bob was a man of integrity. He loved and served the Lord with his whole heart, which is what made his reluctance to accept Ken all the harder for Pastor Joe to handle.

It was true, Bob had gone out on a limb some years earlier and given Ken a job. Ken quit abruptly, leaving Bob holding the bag. Bob felt Ken was unreliable, but Ken had changed. He was a new man. Pastor Joe was worried Ken would leave the church and use his gifts elsewhere if Bob could not accept Ken in leadership. How could Pastor Joe convince Bob to support Ken in his desire to serve as a leader in the church without manipulating or pressuring Bob? After all, President Harry Truman famously said, "A leader is a man who has the ability to get other people to do what they don't want to do, and like it."[2] Maybe that meant he wasn't a leader if he couldn't get Bob to change his mind!

---

1. Sanders, *Spiritual Leadership*, 31
2. Cited by Blackaby and Blackaby, *Spiritual Leadership*, 33.

The apostle Paul's letter to Philemon is closer to a business or personal letter than any of Paul's Epistles. Business letters developed apart from the formal rhetorical handbooks on style so prevalent in the Greco-Roman world,[3] yet we see from this letter how Paul exercised persuasive rhetoric to influence Philemon to accept his young slave Onesimus back. Therefore, this letter becomes an excellent case study in pastoral influence. Pastor Joe can follow the model set for him by the apostle Paul to exercise healthy spiritual influence with Bob in the matter of Ken.

## Rhetorical Framework

We must first speak the language of the recipient to influence his decisions. Businessmen like Philemon understood the rhetorical styles of their day, so Paul conforms his writing to the structure of the first-century world of Philemon. The letter can be classified as deliberative rhetoric following examples such as Quintilian. There are five elements of a speech in classical rhetoric, and we can see three of them in Paul's letter to Philemon.[4] Paul chooses to write in the style Philemon would understand.

### Exordium or Beginning (4–7)

The purpose of the exordium is to gain the goodwill of the reader by evoking a warm response and establishing a positive foundation for the appeal. Paul is about to ask Philemon for a favor, and so he begins by establishing the loving generosity of Philemon to set the stage for his later request (7). Philemon's generosity was a rich source of comfort and joy for Paul, who commends him for refreshing the hearts of the saints. Words like "joy," "comfort," "love," and especially "hearts" are highly emotive words designed to establish a personal connection between Paul and Philemon. A man who brings such love, joy, and refreshment to many could hardly refuse the coming request.[5]

---

3. Betz, *2 Corinthians 8 and 9*, 136.
4. Martin, "Rhetorical Function of Commercial Language," 322–23. Church, "Rhetorical Structure and Design," 21–22.
5. Lohse, *Colossians and Philemon*, 195.

## Confirmatio or Proof (8–16)

Paul begins his proof by waiving his right to exercise authority over Philemon (8). Paul could have chosen to command Philemon, but instead he appeals to him in love. One of the mistakes we often make in pastoral persuasion is we seek compliance by exercising our authority. Such an approach rarely works for true change. As the saying goes, "a person convinced against his will is of the same opinion still." Persuasion by authority yields short-term results. Long-term change never comes by coercion. The bully pulpit is not a biblical pulpit.

Paul throws in a highly personal, and openly emotional appeal (pathos), based upon his chains in Christ (9). Such appeals were designed to evoke powerful emotions as a means of gaining the goodwill of the audience.[6] Paul was not against such methods and appears to have viewed his chains to be his credentials (ethos), which open the door to bold requests.[7] He follows this statement of his credentials with another appeal (10). In this way, Paul beautifully balances ethos, character, and credentials with pathos, the emotional appeals intended to tug at the heart of Philemon.[8] Paul communicates all of this before he even introduces the request. Real pastoral persuasion cannot be rushed. We must set the stage for our appeals if we want real change to happen.

Deliberative rhetoric dealt with two primary motives for change. The first motive was honor (*honestas*), and the second motive was benefit (*utilitas*).[9] Paul's use of the well-known pun regarding the name Onesimus (useful), along with his affirmation regarding his usefulness establishes the second motive (10–11). Then Paul appeals to Philemon's honor when he refuses to do anything without Philemon's consent so his goodness would not be under constraint (14).[10] Paul is using common commercial language and style to reach Philemon, the businessman, without making him feel like he is being forced to do anything. Throughout his letter, Paul uses the very touching term "inward parts" (heart) three times (7, 12, 20) to establish a warm relationship with Philemon. Paul masterfully weaves together ethos and pathos as motives for his appeal. He is very careful to stress Philemon

---

6. Watson, "Rhetorical Analysis of 3 John, 487.
7. Smillie, "Ephesians 6:19–20," 212–13.
8. Church, "Rhetorical Structure and Design," 25.
9. Church, "Rhetorical Structure and Design," 19.
10. Martin, "Rhetorical Function of Commercial Language," 327.

is free to make his own decision. Still, as yet, Paul has not made his actual request. He implies the request, but he does not state the request until he has fully paved the way for it.

## Peroration or Conclusion (17–22)

Finally, Paul makes his request to Philemon (17). "Welcome him as you would me." Paul bases his request on his partnership with Philemon by saying, "if you have me as a partner." Our relationships in Christ are the foundation for all true influence in Christ's church. Fellowship, partnership in Christ, is like a bank account. We make deposits and withdrawals in our relationships, so if we want to make a withdrawal, we better have a relational account to draw upon. No partnership means no influence.

We can see all the elements of Aristotle's explanation of persuasion in Paul's conclusion. Paul asks Philemon to welcome Onesimus as he would welcome Paul himself. According to Aristotle, the substitution of one's self was a common rhetorical technique intended to create goodwill among those who must decide a case. Emotional appeal (pathos) was a significant element of rhetorical conclusions. Paul employs two commercial terms—to owe and to charge—which were very familiar to the Hellenistic culture in which Philemon lived. Paul is willing that Philemon charges to his account all bills which Onesimus might owe. His signature, writing in his own hand, guarantees the payment. This is a powerful example of an "appeal to pity" spoken about by Aristotle, Quintilian, and Cicero as an essential part of a rhetorical conclusion.[11]

The capstone of Paul's emotional plea comes when he calls in Philemon's indebtedness as a motive for fulfilling Paul's request. Paul writes, "not that I say to you that you even owe yourself to me" (19). Philemon is a debtor to Paul, and Paul is calling in his debt with this request. The most likely understanding is Paul was instrumental in Philemon's conversion.[12] He owes Paul his life, the least he can do is give Onesimus his life back. We make deposits in the lives of people as pastors. Our influence depends on those deposits. Every time we make an appeal, we are calling in our marker with that person. Like Paul, we sometimes say to a church member, "you owe me." Perhaps we don't say it as baldly as Paul does here, but all

---

11. Martin, "Rhetorical Function of Commercial Language," 321–35; Church, "Rhetorical Structure and Design," 28–30.

12. O'Brien, *Colossians, Philemon*, 301. Moule, *Studies in Colossians and Philemon*, 176.

persuasion seeks to withdraw from the goodwill we have built up with the person being persuaded. We must use the goodwill wisely because if we are always withdrawing we will lose our persuasive ability. We only have so many markers to call. Eventually, we bankrupt our influence.

Paul plays the reciprocity card with great power. The reciprocity principle is embedded in human nature and reinforced by human culture. The rule says we should try to repay what another does for us. The reciprocity principle is so powerful and so universal that every society down through human history has employed it in some form.[13] Paul appeals to the powerful stimulus of reciprocity to move Philemon to do what Paul asks. He follows that plea with an expression of confidence that Philemon will do what Paul wants and accept Onesimus back (21). Such expressions of confidence in the audience were common rhetorical devices, according to Quintilian.[14] Paul has masterfully struck all the right chords in his pastoral influence of Philemon.

## Ethical Model

According to ELM (Elaboration Likelihood Model), when elaboration likelihood is high, the recipient will focus significant resources on the central issues to be decided. The pastor seeks to develop elaboration on the central issues by helping the recipient "over learn" the ideas and internalize the message. Paul develops his main request to Philemon first through implication and issue-relevant information. He eventually makes his request explicit and then anticipates the possible objections to the decision he advocates. Paul makes sure Philemon knows he, Paul, will make good on whatever financial debt remains. This promise removes the objection Paul anticipates from Philemon.

The central and peripheral routes to persuasion exist on a continuum, so they occur coextensively. They are not mutually exclusive concepts, as we can see from Paul's letter. When elaboration likelihood is low, the pastor seeks to use peripheral triggers or cues to secure further elaboration of the issue. These shortcut methods are legitimate within certain ethical boundaries, especially if they lead back to the elaboration of the central issue. Common peripheral routes include liking or similarity, cognitive consistency, reciprocity, scarcity, authority, fear, guilt, minimax, and conformity.

13. Cialdini, *Influence*, 29–31.
14. Church, "Rhetorical Structure and Design," 30.

Paul does not assume Philemon is highly motivated to elaborate on his request. He employs a wide variety of peripheral triggers designed to stimulate Philemon to take this issue seriously. Paul uses the liking or similarity principle when he bases his appeal on their partnership (17) and the personal relationship they have enjoyed (7) and hope to enjoy in the future (22). Paul employs the reciprocity principle (19) as well as minimax—a method of minimizing the cost to Philemon (18) and maximizing the benefit (11, 16). He appeals to cognitive consistency when he cites God's providence (16) as the reason for the situation. Philemon already believes God is providentially at work in human lives, so this fits within a consistent theological framework. Philemon will feel cognitive dissonance as he tries to reconcile his "love for all the saints" (5, 7) with his rejection of Onesimus if he should refuse Paul's request. Paul uses an ancient form of attribution theory when he expresses his confidence in Philemon (21) and commends his Christian character (4–7). He is attributing to Philemon what he expects of Philemon, a powerful tool for influence pastors frequently use.

Yet Paul stops short of many peripheral triggers less ethical persuaders might use in these circumstances. He avoids the use of authority to command Philemon's obedience (8–9). He does not appeal to guilt or fear as a motive. Paul makes no threats and implies no recriminations. He avoids the use of any compliance-conditioning techniques. There are no signs of unethical sequential influence. He does not introduce a lesser decision to ratchet up to a bigger decision, often known as the foot in the door technique.

Truth is Paul's primary concern. He does not withhold information from Philemon. He avoids deceptive or ambiguous words, nor does Paul insult or intimidate Philemon. He is open and honest about his intentions, not hiding his feelings. Paul exercises his influence in the context of love. The letter exudes love. Furthermore, Paul gains no personal advantage in this situation. He can powerfully influence precisely because self-interest does not motivate him. Selfishness does not taint his persuasion. Paul is advocating for someone who has no legal right to advocate for himself, much like a public defender in a modern court. The result is healthy persuasion, for Paul gains no benefit from Philemon's decision. In fact, his offer to pay the debt of Onesimus could cost him dearly, demonstrating the love motive behind the influence.

Relationships are openly acknowledged. There are no secret agendas or connections. Paul does not deny the existing framework of relationships, both legal and personal. Onesimus is a slave. Philemon is an owner. Wrongs have been committed. Paul has no judicial power and, indeed, does not even ask for pardon anywhere in the letter. There is a striking difference between Paul and Pliny, an ancient writer in a similar circumstance, regarding pardon. Pliny wrote a letter to Sabinianus on behalf of one of his servants who had run away from him. Pliny makes a plea for a pardon based on repentance while Paul avoids any discussion of repentance and forgiveness.[15]

Paul advocates a welcoming embrace of love (17) rather than the merciful act of forgiveness. We would expect a Christian to stress repentance and forgiveness and a pagan to stress love, but the exact opposite takes place in this letter. A possible rhetorical reason for this difference might be that a plea for pardon activates a different motive than a plea for love. The clue is found in Pliny's letter after he has made his case for a pardon. Pliny writes, "I'm afraid you will think I am using *pressure, not persuasion*,"[16] which indicates his discomfort with the argument he has just made for pardon. The motive for pardon is often guilt because of anger, as Pliny's letter makes clear. Issues of justice and appeasement, guilt and forgiveness, are central to Pliny's letter, using forgiveness as a pressure point in the relationship.

We pastors are quick to play the forgiveness card in our influence, but Paul avoids such motives in his letter. There are certainly repentance and forgiveness issues in the matter of Onesimus and Philemon, but Paul does not come at the matter from that side. He illustrates an ethical boundary for the Christian by avoiding such motives. The Christian persuader should be careful not to pressure others based upon a guilt response which leads to an obligatory pardon. Forgiveness can be used as a pressure point because Christians know they must forgive. They feel coerced to forgive much like a child is forced to hug another after the other child has said, "I'm sorry." The whole process feels contrived as the forgiver feels pressured. Paul avoids these kinds of guilt-based pressure points in his persuasion.

Paul has a relationship of authority over Philemon, which he implies but refuses to invoke (8). Paul, as an apostle, has power that he does not use. As a pastor, Paul could exercise his spiritual authority over a man he discipled in Christ, but he chooses to appeal to Philemon as an equal partner rather than one who is over another (17). The very fact Paul could invoke his authority and chooses not to do so demonstrates an ethical limitation which pastors

---

15. Pliny, cited by Church, "Rhetorical Structure and Design," 31.
16. Pliny, cited by Church, "Rhetorical Structure and Design," 31 (emphasis added).

would do well to emulate. Authority makes a poor basis for real elaboration. Power plays in the church do not bring lasting change.

Paul backs off from any direct pressure on the decision. He leaves Philemon with the choice (14). Paul wanted him to make his decision voluntarily. Coercion is outside the boundaries of Christian persuasion. He could have manipulated the situation by keeping Onesimus for himself (13), which he would have dearly loved to do (12). He could have coerced Philemon by sending a messenger instead of Onesimus. Philemon would have been in the awkward although legally correct situation of using legal resources to take Onesimus back from Paul. Paul does not want to place his friend in such a situation, so he sends Onesimus back to him, thus placing the choice freely in Philemon's hands. Paul might never see either of them again. Philemon could easily have disregarded the letter and done as he pleased. Paul chose to place the entire decision in Philemon's hands. One wonders how much influence Paul used on Onesimus to get him to go back to his master!

We often seek to retain control in persuasive situations so we can achieve the results we want. How can Paul let go of his control and leave the decision in Philemon's power? Paul places his trust in the providence of God and the power of the Holy Spirit to change minds. The Holy Spirit is the unseen force behind the ethical persuader, which frees him to hand the decision to the other person. It is the Holy Spirit who gives the pastor the confidence to lose control of the situation without fear. The ethical persuader does not need to coerce and control the other party because he is confident he can leave the ultimate decision in the hands of the Holy Spirit. The letter to Philemon breathes that confidence, particularly at the end (21–25). Paul does not fear refusal because he can trust God to accomplish his will.

## Back to Pastor Joe

The seeds of unbelief were sprouting in Pastor Joe. He was tempted to make it happen despite Bob's reluctance. Pastor Joe knew he could bypass Bob and push Ken's nomination through the church. He believed he had the power to get it done. Furthermore, Pastor Joe was confident he could take the dispute public with the other leaders of the church and put Bob in a difficult position. He knew Bob well and thought Bob would give in rather than fight it out with the other leaders. Pastor Joe felt waiting for the process to work out was wasting the church's time and might lead Ken to leave. If Ken left, it would reflect badly on Pastor Joe and his lack of leadership. The truth is Pastor Joe trusted his power more than God's plan. He lacked faith in God the Holy Spirit to work it out in God's time. Pastor Joe was tempted to manipulate the situation to get his way, but he sensed when we manipulate others, we prove our unbelief in God.

Pastor Joe has good options to use his influence with Bob. It will take some time and care. An open and honest conversation is the best approach. He will need to invest wisdom and effort into his relationship with Bob. Pastor Joe can follow the model of Paul with Philemon. He can talk with Bob. He can lay out carefully the reasons why Ken should be in leadership so Bob can focus on the central issue. If Pastor Joe has built up a good account in his relationship with Bob, he can use that goodwill to influence him. If Pastor Joe has helped Bob in the past, he can even remind Bob of that help. He can acknowledge the value of Bob's contributions to the church. He can express his love and respect for Bob if he is genuine in his remarks. Pastor Joe can put his own faith in Ken on the line with Bob. He knows Ken has wronged Bob, but he believes Ken is a changed man. He can ask Bob to trust him on this one, and he will see the difference in time. He can offer to make any wrongs right with Bob. Pastor Joe can present his best case to Bob and ask Bob to seriously consider his request for the good of both Ken and the church. He should use all these methods of influence and then back off. He must leave it with Bob to make his choice without recriminations from Pastor Joe. He must love Bob enough to let it go. He must trust God enough to lose control.

# Appendix

## Pastoral Influence Health Index (PIHI)

*A Testing Tool for Pastors and Church Leaders*

### Definition:

HEALTHY PASTORAL PERSUASION IS influence which is both effective and ethical. Influence is effective when the pastor motivates permanent and measurable changes in beliefs, attitudes, or behaviors. Influence is ethical when a pastor is honest and loving, motivating a change via elaboration of the central issues while respecting the person's responsibility for the decision.

### Instructions:

The following forty statements have been designed to help the pastor and church leadership evaluate pastoral influence. Please answer all the statements as carefully and fairly as possible. The testing tool utilizes two different formats, and each answer has a numerical weight for computation. Scores are tabulated by adding up the numerical values. A composite score adds the two columns together. The testing tool follows the Likert Scale for measuring attitudes. Multiple statements provide a modest correlation between various answers to arrive at the actual numerical index. The test can also calculate separate numerical indices for ethics and effectiveness.

The best way to use the test is for the pastor to complete it for himself. Then the pastor should ask his leadership team to take the test evaluating the pastor. The pastor and leadership team should then compare results leading to a discussion of their respective perspectives.

APPENDIX: PASTORAL INFLUENCE HEALTH INDEX (PIHI)

## Section A

Please indicate whether you Strongly Agree (SA), Agree (A), are Neutral (N), Disagree (D), or Strongly Disagree (SD) with each of these statements regarding the pastor.

1. The pastor waits for the leadership to arrive at a decision until the entire group feels comfortable, even if it takes a long time.
   1. SA  A  N  D  SD

2. The pastor avoids using his authority to make unilateral decisions.
   2. SA  A  N  D  SD

3. The pastor will make sure a group decision is implemented even if it means there are some individual casualties as a result.
   3. SA  A  N  D  SD

4. The pastor avoids using his position for personal gain or advantage.
   4. SA  A  N  D  SD

5. The pastor motivates others to change their attitudes, beliefs, and behaviors.
   5. SA  A  N  D  SD

6. The pastor holds people accountable for follow-through on decisions that have been made.
   6. SA  A  N  D  SD

7. The pastor insists leadership has all the information they need before making a decision.
   7. SA  A  N  D  SD

8. The pastor pushes the leadership to arrive at decisions quickly and efficiently.
   8. SA  A  N  D  SD

9. The pastor admits his mistakes and accepts responsibility for plans that fail.
   9. SA  A  N  D  SD

10. The pastor breaks down large objectives into smaller goals and shows people how those objectives can be reasonably accomplished.
    10. SA  A  N  D  SD

11. The pastor acknowledges when he does not know the answer to a question.
    11. SA  A  N  D  SD

12. The pastor mobilizes volunteers to invest significant amounts of time, energy, and money in the ministry of the church.
    12. SA  A  N  D  SD

## APPENDIX: PASTORAL INFLUENCE HEALTH INDEX (PIHI)

13. The pastor avoids using guilt or humiliation to intimidate others in group discussions.    13.   SA   A   N   D   SD

14. The pastor establishes clear goals for the church and leads the church to achieve those goals.    14.   SA   A   N   D   SD

15. The pastor has demonstrated the ability to move the church through significant changes in structure, programs, or ministries within the last five years.    15.   SA   A   N   D   SD

16. The pastor encourages questions or alternatives when the leadership is considering a plan he proposed.    16.   SA   A   N   D   SD

17. The pastor will make sure a decision is made within the specified time frame, even if all the information is not available.    17.   SA   A   N   D   SD

18. The pastor often shows people how a decision will benefit them.    18.   SA   A   N   D   SD

19. The pastor avoids theological jargon or technical language as a way to emphasize his expertise.    19.   SA   A   N   D   SD

20. The pastor shares decision-making power with other leaders.    20.   SA   A   N   D   SD

## Section B:

Please indicate whether you believe these statements Never (N), Rarely (R), Sometimes (S), Often (O), or Always (A) accurately characterize how the pastor functions in this ministry.

21. The pastor cares more about the feelings of the people involved than getting the job done.    21.   N   R   S   O   A

## APPENDIX: PASTORAL INFLUENCE HEALTH INDEX (PIHI)

22. When the group is debating a decision, the pastor will mention specific ministries he has performed for the benefit of key leaders in the church.  22.  N  R  S  O  A

23. The pastor avoids facing unpleasant problems rather than making sure changes are implemented to correct those problems.  23.  N  R  S  O  A

24. The pastor allows group conflict to stop the progress toward the goals which have been established.  24.  N  R  S  O  A

25. The pastor makes people feel ashamed or inadequate if they disagree with him.  25.  N  R  S  O  A

26. Short-term results are more important to the pastor than achieving long-term goals.  26  N  R  S  O  A

27. The pastor uses the fact that people like and respect him to accomplish his goals for the church.  27.  N  R  S  O  A

28. The pastor emphasizes how much he has prayed about a specific matter as a reason why the leadership should agree with his proposal.  28.  N  R  S  O  A

29. The pastor fears taking a strong stand or using his position decisively on controversial issues.  29.  N  R  S  O  A

30. The pastor makes strong emotional appeals to the leadership when he is advocating a particular position.  30.  N  R  S  O  A

31. The pastor allows the leadership to get distracted by peripheral issues instead of focusing on the central matter to be decided.  31.  N  R  S  O  A

32. The pastor makes others feel guilty so they will do what he is asking them to do.  32.  N  R  S  O  A

33. The pastor uses the pulpit to advance his agenda for the church.  33.  N  R  S  O  A

34. The pastor acts like he is an authority on a subject even if he does not know what he is talking about.  34.  N  R  S  O  A

## APPENDIX: PASTORAL INFLUENCE HEALTH INDEX (PIHI)

35. Sloppy, mediocre programs and inefficient decision-making are accepted by the pastor since everyone is doing the best they can do.    35.   N   R   S   O   A

36. The pastor hides his intentions from other leaders, making them guess how he feels about a subject.    36.   N   R   S   O   A

37. The pastor is satisfied to work with the people where they are rather than inspire them to accept new challenges.    37.   N   R   S   O   A

38. The pastor is more interested in significant personal sharing by the leadership rather than running a tight meeting focused on the agenda.    38.   N   R   S   O   A

39. The pastor uses ambiguous or vague language, which allows people to interpret his position in multiple ways.    39.   N   R   S   O   A

40. The pastor considers the pulpit unavailable for addressing major church decisions.    40.   N   R   S   O   A

APPENDIX: PASTORAL INFLUENCE HEALTH INDEX (PIHI)

## PIHI Rating Sheet

Rating Key:

SA = 5; A = 4; N = 3; D = 2; SD = 1

N = 5; R = 4; S = 3; O = 2; A = 1

| Ethics Score | Composite Score | Effectiveness Score |
|---|---|---|
| 1– | | 3– |
| 2– | | 5– |
| 4– | | 6– |
| 7– | | 8– |
| 9– | | 10– |
| 11– | | 12– |
| 13– | | 14– |
| 16– | | 15– |
| 19– | | 17– |
| 20– | | 18– |
| 22– | | 21– |
| 25– | | 23– |
| 27– | | 24– |
| 28– | | 26– |
| 30– | | 29– |
| 32– | | 31– |
| 33– | | 35– |
| 34– | | 37– |
| 36– | | 38– |
| 39– | | 40– |

# Bibliography

Ahlstrom, Sydney. *A Religious History of the American People*. 2 vols. New York: Image, 1975.
Anderson, Leith. *Dying for Change*. Minneapolis: Bethany House, 1990.
Anthony, Michael. *The Effective Church Board: A Handbook for Mentoring and Training Servant Leaders*. Grand Rapids: Baker, 1993.
Aristotle. *The Art of Rhetoric*. Translated by John Henry Freese. *The Loeb Classical Library*. New York: G.P. Putnam's Sons, 1926.
Arndt, William F., and F. Wilbur Gingrich. *A Greek-English Lexicon of the New Testament and Other Early Christian Literature*. 2nd ed. Chicago: University of Chicago Press, 1979.
Aubuchon, Norbert. *The Anatomy of Persuasion*. New York: AMACOM, 1997.
Backus, William. *Telling Each Other the Truth*. Minneapolis: Bethany House, 1985.
"Baptist Pastor's Therapy Controversial: Female Congregants Describe Purported Repressed Memories of Sexual Abuse." *Bangor Daily News*, May 14, 2002. https://www.archive.bangordailynews.com/2002/05/14/baptist-pastors-therapy-controversial-female-congregants-describe-purported-repressed-memories-of-sexual-abuse/.
Barna, George. *Marketing the Church: What They Never Taught You about Church Growth*. Carol Stream, IL: Navpress, 1988.
———. *A Step-by-Step Guide to Church Marketing: Breaking Ground for the Harvest*. Ventura, CA: Regal, 1992.
Bernard, J. H. *A Critical and Exegetical Commentary on the Gospel According to St. John*. 2 vols. Edinburgh: T. & T. Clark, 1976.
Betz, Hans Dieter. *Galatians: A Commentary on Paul's Letter to the Churches in Galatia*. Philadelphia: Fortress, 1979.
———. *2 Corinthians 8 and 9: A Commentary on Two Administrative Letters of the Apostle Paul*. Philadelphia: Fortress, 1985.
Blackaby, Henry, and Richard Blackaby. *Spiritual Leadership: Moving People on to God's Agenda*. Revised and expanded edition. Nashville: B&H, 2011.
Bolt, Martin, and David Myers. *The Human Connection: How People Change People*. Downers Grove: InterVarsity, 1984.
Brembeck, Winston L. and William S. Howell. *Persuasion: A Means of Social Control*. New York: Prentice-Hall, 1952.

Brown, Colin. "Proclamation." In *The New International Dictionary of New Testament Theology*, edited by Colin Brown, 3:44–68. 3 vols. Grand Rapids: Zondervan, 1971.

Brown, Peter. *Power and Persuasion in Late Antiquity: Towards a Christian Empire*. Madison: University of Wisconsin Press, 1992.

Bruce, F. F. *The Epistle to the Galatians: A Commentary on the Greek Text*. NIGTC. Grand Rapids: Eerdmans, 1982.

———. *Paul: Apostle of the Heart Set Free*. Grand Rapids: Eerdmans, 1977.

Bultmann, Rudolph. "Peithō." In *Theological Dictionary of the New Testament*, 10th ed., edited by Gerhard Kittel and Gerhard Friedrich, 6:1–11. 10 vols. Grand Rapids: Eerdmans, 1968.

Burke, Kenneth *A Rhetoric of Motives*. Berkeley: University of California Press, 1999.

Calvin, John. *Calvin: Institutes of the Christian Religion*. Edited by John T. McNeil. Translated and indexed by Ford Lewis Battles. Philadelphia: Westminster, 1960.

Campbell, Barth. "Rhetorical Design in 1 Timothy 4." *Bibliotheca Sacra*, 154.614 (April 1997) 189–204.

Carey, William. *An Enquiry into the Obligations of Christians, to use Means for the Conversion of the Heathens. In which the Religious State of the Different Nations of the World, the Success of Former Undertakings, and the Practicability of Further Undertakings, are Considered.* Leicester: Printed by Ann Ireland, 1791. https://www.wmcarey.edu/carey/enquiry/anenquiry.pdf.

Chase, Richard. "The Classical Conception of Epidiectic." *Quarterly Journal of Speech* 47 (1961) 293–300.

Christensen, David. *Friends with Jesus: Experiencing the Depths of Spiritual Intimacy*. Gorham, ME: The Rephidim Project, 2017.

———. "Healthy Pastoral Persuasion: A Study of the Tension between Ethical and Effective Pastoral Influence Within the Leadership Community of the Local Church." DMin diss., Grace Theological Seminary, 2000.

Church, F. Forrester. "Rhetorical Structure and Design in Paul's Letter to Philemon." *Harvard Theological Review* 71 (1978) 17–33.

Cialdini, Robert. *Influence: The New Psychology of Modern Persuasion*. New York: Morrow, 1984.

———. *Pre-suasion: A Revolutionary Way to Influence and Persuade*. New York: Simon & Schuster, 2016.

Clapp, Philip, et al., eds. *Analytical Concordance of the Greek New Testament*. 2 vols. Grand Rapids: Baker, 1991.

Clark, Gordon. "Wisdom in First Corinthians." *The Journal of the Evangelical Theological Society* 15.4 (Fall 1972) 197–206.

Colson, Charles. "The Power of Illusion." In *Power Religion: The Selling Out of the Evangelical Church?*, edited by Michael Scott Horton, 25–38. Chicago: Moody, 1992.

Cosby, Michael. "Paul's Persuasive Language in Romans 5." In *Persuasive Artistry: Studies in New Testament Rhetoric in Honor of George A. Kennedy*, edited by Duane F. Watson, 209–25. Sheffield: Sheffield Academic Press, 1991.

Cundiff, Merlyn. *Kinesics: The Power of Silent Command*. West Nyack, NY: Parker, 1972.

Cunningham, David S. *Faithful Persuasion: In Aid of a Rhetoric of Christian Theology*. Notre Dame: University of Notre Dame, 1991.

Danker, Frederick W. "Paul's Debt to the 'De Corona' of Demosthenes: A Study of Rhetorical Techniques in Second Corinthians." In *Persuasive Artistry: Studies in New Testament Rhetoric in Honor of George A. Kennedy*, edited by Duane F. Watson, 262–280. Sheffield: Sheffield Academic Press, 1991.

Davis, John Jefferson. *Evangelical Ethics*. Phillipsburg, NJ: Presbyterian and Reformed, 1985.

Dawson, Roger. *Secrets of Power Persuasion*. Englewood Cliffs, NJ: Prentice Hall, 1992.

Deuel, David. "Disability and Biblical Weakness." In *Disability in Mission: The Church's Hidden Treasure*, edited by David Deuel and Nathan John, 9–17. Peabody, MA: Hendrickson, 2019.

Dobson, Edward G., et al. *Mastering Conflict and Controversy*. Portland: Multnomah, 1992.

Donoghue, Denis. *On Eloquence*. New Haven: Yale University Press, 2008.

Edwards, Jonathan. *Freedom of the Will*. Edited by Paul Ramsay. New Haven: Yale University Press, 1957.

Ehninger, Douglas. *Influence, Belief, and Argument: An Introduction to Responsible Persuasion*. Glenview, IL: Scott, Foresman, 1974.

Elliott, Neal "Romans 13:1–7 in the Context of Imperial Propaganda." In *Paul and Empire: Religion and Power in Roman Imperial Society*, edited by Richard A. Horseley, 184–204. Harrisburg, PA: Trinity, 1997.

Enroth, Ronald M. *Churches that Abuse*. Grand Rapids: Zondervan, 1992.

Erickson, Millard. *Christian Theology*. 3rd ed. Grand Rapids: Baker Academic, 2013.

Federer, Bill. "The Fighting Parson of the American Revolution." http://www.selfeducatedamerican.com/2017/10/01/fighting-parson-american-revolution.

Fee, Gordon. *The First Epistle to the Corinthians*. Grand Rapids: Eerdmans, 1987.

Finzel, Hans. *The Top Ten Mistakes Leaders Make*. Wheaton, IL: Victor, 1994.

Friedrich, Gerhard. "kēryx." In *Theological Dictionary of the New Testament*, 10th ed., edited by Gerhard Kittel and Gerhard Friedrich, 3:683–718. 10 vols. Eerdmans, 1984.

Furst, Dieter. "Think, Mean, Consider, Reckon." In *The New International Dictionary of New Testament Theology*, Colin Brown, ed. 3:820–21. 3 vols. Grand Rapids: Zondervan, 1971.

Gangel, Kenneth. *Team Leadership in Christian Ministry: Using Multiple Gifts to Build a Unified Vision*. Revised edition. Chicago: Moody, 1997.

Gangel, Kenneth, and Samuel Canine. *Communication and Conflict Management in Churches and Christian Organizations*. Nashville: Broadman & Holman, 1992.

Geisler, Norman L. *The Christian Ethic of Love*. Grand Rapids: Zondervan, 1973.

———. *Ethics: Alternatives and Issues*. Grand Rapids: Zondervan, 1971.

Gordon, George. *The Theory and Practice of Manipulative Communication*. New York: Hastings, 1971.

Griffin, Emory. *Getting Together: A Guide for Good Groups*. Downers Grove: InterVarsity, 1982.

———. *The Mind Changers: The Art of Christian Persuasion*. Wheaton, IL: Tyndale House, 1976.

Grosheide, F. W. *Commentary on the First Epistle to the Corinthians*. NICNT. Grand Rapids: Eerdmans, 1953.

Grossman, Cathy Lynn. "Billy Graham Reached Millions through His Crusades. Here's How He Did it." *WCNC*, February 22, 2018. https://www.wcnc.com/article/news/nation-now/billy-graham-reached-millions-through-his-crusades-heres-how-he-did-it/465-b7b3ce15-fb06-461a-9eef-1305a6d3df1c.

Guinness, Os. *Sounding Out the Idols of Church Growth*. https://christianreformedink.wordpress.com/reformed-theology-2/ecclesiology/church-growth/sounding-out-the-idols-of-church-growth/.

Haass, Richard. *The Power to Persuade*. Boston: Houghton Mifflin, 1994.
Harrison, R.K. *Encyclopedia of Biblical and Christian Ethics*. Nashville: Thomas Nelson, 1987.
Henry, Carl F. H., ed. *Baker's Dictionary of Christian Ethics*. Grand Rapids: Baker, 1973.
Hester, James. "Placing the Blame: The Presence of Epideictic in Galatians 1 and 2." In *Persuasive Artistry: Studies in New Testament Rhetoric in Honor of George A. Kennedy*. edited by Duane F. Watson, 281–307. Sheffield: Sheffield Academic Press, 1991.
Hodge, Charles. *An Exposition of the First Epistle to the Corinthians*. Grand Rapids: Eerdmans, 1982.
Horsley, Richard A. "Building an Alternative Society." In *Paul and Empire: Religion and Power in Roman Imperial Society*, edited by Richard A. Horsley, 206–52. Harrisburg, PA: Trinity, 1997.
Horton, Michael S. "The Subject of Contemporary Relevance." In *Power Religion: The Selling Out of the Evangelical Church?*, edited by Michael S. Horton, 327–53. Chicago: Moody, 1992.
Hudson, Neil. *Imagine Church: Releasing Whole-Life Disciples*. Nottingham, UK: Inter-Varsity, 2012.
Hughes, Philip Edgecumbe. *Christian Ethics in a Secular Society*. Grand Rapids: Baker, 1983.
Hull, Bill. "Is the Church Growth Movement Really Working?" In *Power Religion: The Selling Out of the Evangelical Church?*, edited by Michael S. Horton, 141–59. Chicago: Moody, 1992.
Hunter III, George. *How to Reach Secular People*. Nashville: Abingdon, 1992.
Hybels, Bill, and Mark Mittelburg. *Becoming a Contagious Christian*. Grand Rapids: Zondervan, 1994.
Jensen, Phillip, and Paul Grimmond. *The Archer and the Arrow: Preaching the Very Words of God*. Kingsford, SA: Matthias Media, 2010.
Johannesen, Richard L. *Ethics and Persuasion: Selected Readings*. New York: Random House, 1967.
Jowett, Garth, and Victoria O'Donnell. *Propaganda and Persuasion*. Newbury Park, CA: Sage, 1986.
Judge, E. A. "Paul's Boasting in Relation to Contemporary Professional Practice." *Australian Biblical Review* 16 (1968) 37–50.
J.v. "Preaching the Brand Gospel." *Adweek*, July 18, 2005. https://www.adweek.com/brand-marketing/preaching-brand-gospel-80630/.
Kelley, Charles M. *The Destructive Achiever: Power and Ethics in the American Corporation*. New York: Addison-Wesley, 1988.
Kennedy, George. *The Art of Persuasion in Greece*. Princeton: Princeton University Press, 1963.
———. *The Art of Rhetoric in the Roman World, 300 B.C. – A.D. 300*. Princeton: Princeton University Press, 1972.
———. *New Testament Interpretation through Rhetorical Criticism*. Chapel Hill: University of North Carolina Press, 1984.
Kinneavy, James L. *Greek Rhetorical Origins of Christian Faith: An Inquiry*. Oxford: Oxford University Press, 1987.
Koepke, Calvin. "Branding the Gospel." *ChurchMag*, June 2, 2014. https://www.churchm.ag/branding-the-gospel/.

## BIBLIOGRAPHY

Kouzes, James M., and Barry Z. Posner. *The Leadership Challenge: How to Keep Getting Extraordinary Things Done in Organizations*. San Francisco: Jossey-Bass, 1995.

Kuo, Stephanie. "MegaFest: A Giant Faith and Family Festival Promises to Bring People Out and Lift Them Up." *Kera News*, June 28, 2017. https://www.keranews.org/post/megafest-giant-faith-and-family-promises/bring/people/out/and/lift-them.

Lazzeri, Antonella. "If I Hadn't Spotted that the Sea was Fizzing Then My Parents, Sister and Me Would All Be Dead." *The Sun*, 26th December 2014. Updated 5th April 2016. http://www.thesun.co.uk/archives/news/635504/if-i-hadnt-spotted-that-the-sea-was-fizzing-then-my-parents-sister-and-me-would-all-be-dead/.

Leblanc, Douglas. "Thou Shalt Not Be Negative." *Christianity Today*, April 14, 2005. https://www.christianitytoday.com/ct/2005/april/33.103.html

Levison, John R. "Did the Spirit Inspire Rhetoric? An Exploration of George Kennedy's Definition of Early Christian Rhetoric." In *Persuasive Artistry: Studies in New Testament Rhetoric in Honor of George A. Kennedy*, edited by Duane F. Watson, 25–40. Sheffield: Sheffield Academic Press, 1991.

Liddell, Henry George, and Robert Scott. *A Greek-English Lexicon, Based on the German Work of Francis Passow*. New York: Harper and Brothers, 1860.

Lifton, Robert. *Thought Reform and the Psychology of Totalism*. Chapel Hill: University of North Carolina Press, 1989.

Litfin, Duane. *Paul's Theology of Preaching: The Apostle's Challenge to the Art of Persuasion in Ancient Corinth*. Downers Grove, IL: InterVarsity, 2015.

———. "The Perils of Persuasive Preaching." *Christianity Today* 21.9 (February 4, 1977), 14–17.

———. *Public Speaking: A Handbook for Christians*. Grand Rapids: Baker, 1981.

———. *St. Paul's Theology of Proclamation: 1 Corinthians 1-4 and Greco-Roman Rhetoric*. Cambridge: Cambridge University Press, 1994.

Lloyd-Jones, D. Martyn. *Preaching and Preachers*. Grand Rapids: Zondervan, 1971.

Lohse, Eduard. *A Commentary on the Epistles to the Colossians and Philemon*. Translated by William R. Poehlmann and Robert J. Karris. Edited by Helmet Koester. Philadelphia: Fortress, 1971.

London, H.B., Jr., and Neil B. Wiseman. *Pastors at Risk: Help for Pastors and Hope for the Church*. Wheaton, IL: Victor, 1993.

Luther, Martin. *The Bondage of the Will: A New Translation of DE SERVO ARBITRIO (1525), Martin Luther's Reply to Erasmus of Rotterdam*. Translated by J. I. Packer and O. R. Johnson. New York: Revell, 1957.

MacArthur, John, Jr. *The MacArthur New Testament Commentary: 1 Corinthians*. Chicago: Moody, 1984.

———. *Our Sufficiency in Christ: Three Deadly Influences that Undermine Your Spiritual Life*. Dallas: Word, 1991.

Macquarrie, John. *Dictionary of Christian Ethics*. Philadelphia: Westminster, 1967.

Martin, Clarice J. "The Rhetorical Function of Commercial Language in Paul's Letter to Philemon." In *Persuasive Artistry: Studies in New Testament Rhetoric in Honor of George A. Kennedy*, edited by Duane F. Watson, 321–37. Sheffield: Sheffield Academic Press, 1991.

Maxwell, John, and Jim Dornan. *Becoming a Person of Influence: How to Positively Impact the Lives of Others*. Nashville: Thomas Nelson, 1997.

## BIBLIOGRAPHY

McGrath, Alistair. "A Better Way: The Priesthood of All Believers." In *Power Religion: The Selling Out of the Evangelical Church?*, edited by Michael Scott Horton, 301–13. Chicago: Moody. 1992.

McLaughlin, Raymond. *Communication for the Church*. Grand Rapids: Zondervan, 1968.

———. "The Ethics of Persuasive Preaching." *The Journal of the Evangelical Theology Society* 15.2 (Spring 1972) 93–106.

———. *The Ethics of Persuasive Preaching*. Grand Rapids: Baker, 1979.

Merrill, Eugene. "Isaiah 40–55 as an Anti-Babylonian Polemic." *Grace Theological Journal* 8.1 (Spring 1987) 3–18.

Meyer, Heinrich A. W. *Critical and Exegetical Hand-book to the Epistles to the Corinthians*. Peabody, MA: Hendrickson, 1983.

Michel, Otto. "Faith, Persuade, Belief, Unbelief." In *The New International Dictionary of New Testament Theology*. edited by Colin Brown, 1:587–606. 3 vols. Grand Rapids: Zondervan. 1975.

Millard, Catherine, "Preachers and Pulpits of the American Revolution." http://www.christianheritagemins.org/articles/Preachers/%20Pulpits%20of/%20American%20Revolution.pdf.

Miller, Calvin. *Marketplace Preaching: How to Return the Sermon to Where it Belongs*. Grand Rapids: Baker, 1995.

Moon, Ruth. "Acts 29 Removes Mars Hill, Asks Mark Driscoll to Step Down and Seek Help." *Christianity Today*, August 8, 2014. https://www.christianitytoday.com/news/2014/august/acts-29-removes-mars-hill-asks-mark-driscoll-matt-chandler.html.

Morris, Leon. *The First Epistle of Paul to the Corinthians: An Introduction and Commentary*. TNTC. Grand Rapids: Eerdmans, 1983.

———. *The Gospel According to John*. Grand Rapids: Eerdmans, 1971.

Moule, H.C.G. *Studies in Colossians and Philemon*. Grand Rapids: Kregel, 1977.

Moulton, James Hope. *A Grammar of New Testament Greek*. Vol. III: *Syntax* by Nigel Turner. 4 vols. Edinburgh: T. & T. Clark, 1963.

Myers, Kenneth. "A Better Way: Proclamation Instead of Protest." In *Power Religion: The Selling out of the Evangelical Church?*, edited by Michael Scott Horton, 39-57. Chicago: Moody, 1992.

Nielsen, Richard. *The Politics of Ethics: Methods for Acting, Learning, and Sometimes Fighting with Others in Addressing Ethics Problems in Organizational Life*. New York: Oxford University Press, 1996.

Nirenberg, Jesse. *Breaking through to Each Other: Creative Persuasion on the Job and in the Home*. New York: Harper and Row, 1976.

O'Brien, Peter T. *Colossians, Philemon*. WBC. Waco: Word, 1990.

O'Keefe, Daniel J. *Persuasion: Theory and Practice*. Newbury Park, CA: Sage, 1990.

Oravec, Christine. "Observation in Aristotle's Theory of Rhetoric" *Philosophy and Rhetoric* 9 (1976) 162–74.

Overstreet, R. Larry. *Persuasive Preaching: A Biblical and Practical Guide to the Effective Use of Persuasion*. Wooster, OH: Weaver, 2014.

Packard, Vance. *The Hidden Persuaders*. London: Longmans, Green, 1957.

Patterson, Ben. "The Preacher as Pitchman." *Leadership* 6 (1985) 72–75.

Perloff, Richard. *The Dynamics of Persuasion*. Hillsdale, NJ: Erlbaum, 1993.

## BIBLIOGRAPHY

Perry, Abby. "Willow Creek and Harvest Struggle to Move On." *Christianity Today*, February 13, 2020. https://www.christianitytoday.com/ct/2020/february-web-only/willow-creek-harvest-after-hybels-macdonald-moving-on.html.

Petty, Richard, and John Cacioppo. *Communication and Persuasion: Central and Peripheral Routes to Attitude Change*. New York: Springer-Verlag, 1986.

Piper, John. *Desiring God: Meditations of a Christian Hedonist*. Portland: Multnomah, 1986.

———. *Expository Exultation: Christian Preaching as Worship*. Wheaton, IL: Crossway, 2018.

Pogoloff, Stephen. "Isocrates and Contemporary Hermeneutics." In *Persuasive Artistry: Studies in New Testament Rhetoric in Honor of George A. Kennedy*, edited by Duane F. Watson, 338–62. Sheffield: Sheffield Academic Press, 1991.

Quebedeaux, Richard. *By What Authority: The Rise of Personality Cults in American Christianity*. San Francisco: Harper & Row, 1982.

Rainer, Thom. *Eating the Elephant: Bite-Sized Steps to Achieve Long-Term Growth in Your Church*. Nashville: Broadman and Holman, 1994.

Rapp, Christof. "Aristotle's Rhetoric." In *Stanford Encyclopedia of Philosophy*. Edited by Edward N. Zalta. 2010. https://plato.stanford.edu/entries/aristotle-rhetoric/

Reid, Marty. "A Consideration of the Function of Romans 1:8–15 in Light of Greco-Roman Rhetoric." *Journal of the Evangelical Theological Society* 38.2 (June 1995) 182–201.

Reising, Richard. *Church Marketing 101: Preparing Your Church for Greater Growth*. Grand Rapids: Baker, 2006.

Rienecker, Fritz. *A Linguistic Key to the Greek New Testament*. Edited by Cleon Rogers. Grand Rapids: Regency Reference Library, 1980.

Robertson, A.T. *A Grammar of the Greek New Testament in the Light of Historical Research*. Nashville: Broadman, 1934.

Ross, Bobby, Jr. "Sex, Money . . . Pride? Why Pastors are Stepping Down." *Christianity Today*, July 14, 2011. https://www.christianitytoday.com/ct/2011/julyweb-only/sexmoneypride.html.

Roys, Julie. "RESTORE Chicago Video: Lina Abujamra's Powerful Letter of Forgiveness Over Church Hurt." https://julieroys.com/restore-chicago-video-lina-abujamras-powerful-letter-of-forgiveness-over-church-hurt/.

Rusk, Tom. *The Power of Ethical Persuasion: From Conflict to Partnership at Work and in Private Life*. New York: Viking, 1993.

Russell, Walter B. "Rhetorical Analysis of the Book of Galatians, Part I." *Bibliotheca Sacra* 150.599 (July 1993) 342–59.

Sanders, Oswald. *Spiritual Leadership*. Chicago: Moody, 1967.

Schmidt, Anna. "Groupthink." *Encyclopedia Britannica*. http://www.britannica.com/science/groupthink

Schurer, Emil. *The History of the Jewish People in the Age of Jesus Christ*. 2 vols. Edited by Geza Vermes, et al. Edinburgh: T. & T. Clark, 1979.

Seamands, David. *Healing for Damaged Emotions*. Colorado Springs, Colorado: Victor, 2002.

Shelley, Marshall. "Surviving the Power Play." In *Mastering Conflict and Controversy*, by Edward G. Dobson et al., 67–80. Portland: Multnomah, 1992.

Shellnutt, Kate. "Acts 29 CEO Removed Amid Accusations of Abusive Leadership." *Christianity Today*, February 7, 2020. https://www.christianitytoday.com/news/2020/february/acts-29-ceo-steve-timmis-removed-spiritual-abuse-tch.html.

———. "Darrin Patrick Removed from Acts 29 Megachurch for Historical Pattern of Sin." *Christianity Today*, April 13, 2016. https://www.christianitytoday.com/news/2016/april/darrin-patrick-removed-acts-29-megachurch-journey.html.

———. "Willow Creek Investigation: Allegations against Bill Hybels are Credible." *Christianity Today*, February 28, 2019. https://www.christianitytoday.com/news/2019/february/willow-creek-bill-hybels-investigation-iag-report.html.

Shellnutt, Kate, and Morgan Lee. "Mark Driscoll Resigns from Mars Hill." *Christianity Today*, October 15, 2014. https://www.christianitytoday.com/ct/2014/october-web-only/mark-driscoll-resigns-from-mars-hill.html.

Shostrum, Everett. *Man the Manipulator: The Inner Journey from Manipulation to Actualization*. Nashville: Abingdon, 1975.

Singer, Margaret. *Cults in Our Midst*. San Francisco: Jossey-Bass, 1995.

Smillie, Gene R. "Ephesians 6:19–20: A Mystery for the Sake of Which the Apostle is an Ambassador in Chains." *Trinity Journal* 18.2 (Fall 1997) 200–23.

Smith, Fred. "The Manipulation Game." *Leadership* 6 (Fall 1985) 110–16.

———. "Motivation Versus Manipulation." In *Leadership Handbooks of Practical Theology*, vol. 3 *Leadership and Administration*, edited by James D. Berkeley, 280–81. 3 vols. Grand Rapids: Baker, 1994.

Smith, Warren Cole. "Buying A Bestseller." *World Magazine*, February 21, 2015. https://world.wng.org/2015/02/buying_a_bestseller.

Spader, Dann, and Gary Mayes. *Growing a Healthy Church*. Chicago: Moody, 1991.

Spence, Gerry. *How to Argue and Win Every Time: At Home, at Work, in Court, Everywhere, Every Day*. New York: St. Martin's, 1995.

Sproul, R. C. *Willing to Believe: The Controversy over Free Will*. Grand Rapids: Baker, 1997.

Spurgeon, C. H. "Compel Them to Come in." In *The New Park Street Pulpit Sermons*, edited by James Paul et al., 5:17–24. 6 vols. London: Passmore & Alabaster, 1859.

Stetzer, Ed. "Power and Pastors: Part 2." *Christianity Today*, March 14, 2019. https://www.christianitytoday.com/edstetzer/2019/march/power-and-pastors-part-2.html.

Stetzer, Ed, and Thom Rainer. *Transformational Church: Creating a New Scorecard for Congregations*. Nashville: Broadman and Holman, 2010.

Stitzinger, James. "The History of Expository Preaching." *The Master's Seminary Journal* 3.1 (Spring 1992) 5–32.

Stout, Harry. *The New England Soul: Preaching and Religious Culture in Colonial New England*. New York: Oxford University Press, 1986.

Stowell, Joseph. *Shepherding the Church: Effective Spiritual Leadership in a Changing Culture*. Chicago: Moody, 1997.

Tracy, Kate. "Mars Hill Defends How Mark Driscoll's 'Real Marriage' Became a Bestseller." *Christianity Today*, March 7, 2014. https://www.christianitytoday.com/news/2014/march/did-mark-driscoll-real-marriage-earn-nyt-bestseller-status-html.

Vines, Jerry, and Jim Shaddix. *Progress in the Pulpit: How to Grow in Your Preaching*. Chicago: Moody, 2017.

Viola, Frank, and George Barna. *Pagan Christianity? Exploring the Roots of Our Christian Practices*. Carol Stream, IL: Tyndale, 2008.

Wagenmaker, Sally. "Harvest Bible Chapel—Legal Evaluation Report." *Wagenmaker & Oberly*, November 21, 2019. Report.HBC.Legal–Eval.with–Forensic–Accounting.2019–11–19.pdf.

Watson, Duane F. "1 Corinthians 10:23—11:1 in the Light of Greco-Roman Rhetoric: The Role of Rhetorical Questions." *Journal of Biblical Literature* 108.2 (1989) 301–18.

———. "Paul's Speech to the Ephesian Elders (Acts 20:17–38): Epideictic Rhetoric of Farewell." In *Persuasive Artistry: Studies in New Testament Rhetoric in Honor of George A. Kennedy,* edited by Duane Watson, 184–208. Sheffield: Sheffield Academic Press, 1991.

———. "A Rhetorical Analysis of 3 John: A Study in Epistolary Rhetoric." *The Catholic Biblical Quarterly* 51 (1989) 479–501.

Weber, Jeremy. "Mark Driscoll Retracts Bestseller Book Status, Resets Life." *Christianity Today,* March 17, 2014. https://www.christianitytoday.com/news/2014/march/mark-driscoll-retracts-bestseller-status-resets-life.html.

Webster, Douglas. *Selling Jesus. What's Wrong with Marketing the Church?* Westmont, IL: InterVarsity, 1992.

*Webster's New World College Dictionary.* 3rd ed. Edited by Victoria Neufeldt. New York: Simon & Schuster, 1997.

Willhite, Keith. "Audience Relevance in Expository Preaching." *Bibliotheca Sacra* 149.595 (July 1992) 356–70.

"William Carey: Father of Modern Missions." https://www.christianitytoday.com/history/people/missionaries/william-carey.html

Windisch, Hans. "kapēleuō." In *Theological Dictionary of the New Testament,* edited by Gerhard Kittel, 3:603–5. 10 vols. Grand Rapids: Eerdmans, 1965.

Winter, Bruce. *Philo and Paul among the Sophists: Alexandrian and Corinthian Responses to a Julio-Claudian Movement.* Grand Rapids: Eerdmans, 2002.

Witherington III, Ben. *Conflict and Community in Corinth: A Socio-Rhetorical Commentary on 1 and 2 Corinthians.* Grand Rapids: Eerdmans, 1995.

———. *The Paul Quest: The Renewed Search for the Jew of Tarsus.* Downers Grove, IL: InterVarsity, 1998.

Woodward, Gary. *Persuasion and Influence in American Life.* Prospect Heights, IL: Waveland, 1988.

Wuellner, Wilhelm. "Paul's Rhetoric of Argumentation in Romans." *Catholic Biblical Quarterly* 38 (1976) 330–51.

Zuker, Elaina. *The Seven Secrets of Influence.* New York: McGraw-Hill, 1991.

www.ingramcontent.com/pod-product-compliance
Lightning Source LLC
Chambersburg PA
CBHW071450150426
43191CB00008B/1303